SECOND EDITION

PROCESS AND PRACTICE
A Guide to Basic Writing

SECOND EDITION

PROCESS AND PRACTICE
A Guide to Basic Writing

Philip Eggers

Borough of Manhattan Community College
The City University of New York

SCOTT, FORESMAN/LITTLE, BROWN HIGHER EDUCATION

A Division of Scott, Foresman and Company

Glenview, Illinois   London, England

A separate Instructor's Edition is available for this text. It may be obtained through your local Scott, Foresman/Little, Brown representative or by writing to Skills Editor, Higher Education Division, Scott, Foresman/Little, Brown, 1900 East Lake Avenue, Glenview, Illinois, 60025.

ACKNOWLEDGMENTS

Cover © Jim Salvati/The Image Bank   51 Museum of the City of New York   60 "Evening" by John Koch, Courtesy Kraushaar Galleries, NY; Photo: © G. Clements 61 (top) © Jean-Claude Lejeune   61 (bottom) UPI/Bettmann Newsphotos 105 Scott, Foresman   106 Thomas Hart Benton mural (detail). Courtesy The Harry S. Truman Library

Library of Congress Cataloging-in-Publication Data

Eggers, Philip.
    Process and practice : a guide to basic writing / Philip Eggers. –
– 2nd ed.
      p.   cm.
  ISBN 0-673-38581-7
  1. English language—Rhetoric. 2. English language–
– Grammar—1950–   I. Title.
PE1408.E358 1989
808'.042—dc 20   89-10631
                                  CIP

ISBN 0-673-47379-1 (Instructor's Edition)

PREFACE

TO THE INSTRUCTOR

In this second edition, *Process and Practice* retains its original purpose: to help instructors help students improve their writing in the two areas where they are most likely to need instruction: mastering the stages of the writing cycle and controlling the elements of grammar, particularly verb forms and sentence divisions. The book is built around the easily recognizable stages of the writing process, placing each activity or drill in its proper context as part of an organic whole. With this larger framework made visible to them, students can practice separate elements with the sense that they are aiming at a goal, not doing isolated exercises in verbal gymnastics.

The writing process, of course, is recursive and irregular, more nearly a spiral than a straight line. Much retracing and foreshadowing is necessary, since every element bears some relation to other elements. Grammar in particular, although most crucial in the final proofreading stage, is an aspect of all verbal communication at any stage. Therefore, Unit 5 is designed to be as mobile as a free modifier in a sentence. It can serve as a workbook for systematic drill throughout the course or as a handbook for targeted individual work on errors as they occur. Through cross-referenced footnotes in other units, Unit 5 can also be used to supplement writing activities with lessons in grammatical problems most likely to arise in particular rhetorical modes.

Because students develop better fluency when they do not have to struggle with unfamiliar subject matters, many of the writing assignments, model paragraphs, and model essays in *Process and Practice* contain material close to students' personal experiences. However, because the purpose of developmental writing is to enable students to enter discourse communities where higher levels of articulateness and critical thinking are expected, the activities and drills also contain varied topics of general interest and educational value. Such content will stimulate students' imaginations and intellectual curiosity.

The purpose of this second edition of *Process and Practice* remains essentially the same as that of the first: to be as useful, convenient, and comprehensive as possible while remaining modest in size and price. It is difficult to navigate the course between the demands of an encyclopedic but intimidating and costly textbook on the one hand and the constraints of a scaled-down, only-what-you-need-to-know workbook on the other. Without being exhaustive or exhausting, *Process and Practice* omits nothing important in its coverage of the stages of the writing process or the features of grammar that cause serious problems for basic writing students.

The response from student and faculty users of the first edition indicates that its general intention was sound. It seems to have struck a successful balance, simultaneously offering compactness and substantial coverage. Because of the input of colleagues and students, however, certain topics omitted from the first edition are included in this new edition; expanding the book to include them has not detracted from its convenience and compactness. There is an expanded section on types of fragments in Unit 5, along with treatment of capitalization and apostrophes. A diagnostic test is presented early in Unit 5, not to imply that short answer tests are the way to teach grammar but to give teachers a quick way to spot individual problem areas. In Unit 4, there are added sections on diction that include precision, idiom, connotation, specificity, and wordiness. In the interest of brevity, the first edition did not include these topics. However, the second edition reflects the opinion that most basic writers have serious and frequent enough trouble in some of these areas to warrant their inclusion, even in a book that strives for compactness. Unit 4 also includes a discussion of revising on word processors, since revision is the crucial stage at which computers offer unique advantages even to beginning writers.

The second edition also contains updated material where it seemed that current events and social changes may have shifted students' interests slightly. These alterations will be evident not only in the content of some grammatical exercises and writing assignments but also in the sample paragraphs and essays in Units 2 and 3 (for example, the model essay on helping the homeless in Unit 3). Such changes, along with the added writing assignments and the reorganization of Unit 2 for clearer subdivision into homework assignments, should make the second edition even more "user friendly" than the first.

Although the most important effort has to come from the students themselves, this is not a self-help book. You, the instructor, must provide the human link, the emotional stimulus, that makes writing genuinely part of the students' lives. Only by receiving attentive and authentic responses from you and from one another will they experience their writing as true communication. How you achieve this is up to you; a book is only a tool in the hands of the ultimate craftsperson. The quality of your students' writing depends finally on your efforts and theirs.

I want to thank the reviewers of this second edition for their critical remarks and recommendations. They include Lois Friesen, Butler County Community College; Rosemary Hunkeler, University of Wisconsin/Parkside; Linda Lane, Foothill College; and Dale Purvis, Georgia Southern College. I appreciate also the guidance of Colleen McCauley, project editor at Scott, Foresman, and I am grateful to Anne Smith and Patricia Rossi of Scott, Foresman, who provided irreplaceable help with both this edition and the first.

My colleagues and students at Borough of Manhattan Community College continue to be the main source of what I know and learn about the writing process. Finally, to Jane and Tori I am boundlessly grateful for giving special meaning to the process and practice of living.

TO THE STUDENT

Perhaps you are one of the lucky students who can devour whole books in a few hours or who love to write poems, diaries, and term papers. Or you may be one of those who "hate English," or believe they do, and who would rather suffer through root canal therapy without anesthesia than write another 500-word theme. More likely, you are somewhere in the middle. Most people enjoy reading and writing at least once in a while, but even the best writers report a certain amount of struggle in their attempts to make the words come out right. Every writer is different, but whatever your writing habits are, you will be able to benefit from using this book.

Process and Practice is not intended to make your writing like a product on an assembly line, the same as everyone else's and following the same formulas. Rather, this book will draw you into the *process* of mental discovery that writing almost magically entails. As you become a better writer, you will gain a keener sense of yourself as an individual. Nothing is more human and more individualistic than writing, yet writing flourishes best as a social activity. By writing as part of a group, you will discover your powers as well as your weaknesses, and your talents as well as the areas where you repeatedly make mistakes. As you share your writing with others, you will develop a distinctive style and voice. Your writing will become as individual as your personal experiences because it is from these experiences that most of your ideas will come. The activities in Unit 1 will help you concentrate on these experiences without becoming distracted by anxieties over errors. In Unit 2 and Unit 3 you will explore paragraph writing and essay writing. The exercises and writing assignments in these units will teach you to develop and organize material, to connect specific experiences to general ideas, and to support topic sentences and thesis statments with interesting, convincing examples. Unit 4 will give you practice in sharpening your sense of style, helping you to notice *how* you write as well as *what* you write.

Although the *process* of discovery and expression is the goal, frequent *practice* is also important. Gaining control over the basics of grammar, spelling, and punctuation by means of the exercises in Unit 5 will free you to achieve the larger goals of the writing process. Mastering the basics will not turn you into a conformist, even though the rules of grammar and spelling are the same for everybody. In fact, nothing is more conformist than making mistakes; writing teachers see the same boring errors again and again. Only by freeing yourself from such errors can you fully reach your potential as a writer. Use

Unit 5 as you need it. Find out through the diagnostic test and your teacher's advice how much intensive work you need and in what areas. If you need intensive work in several areas, adopt the no-pain/no-gain attitude of physical fitness trainers. The results are worth it. Mastering the basics is satisfying in itself, and even more important is the pleasure of writing with feeling, precision, insight, and originality.

CONTENTS

SECOND EDITION

PROCESS AND PRACTICE
A Guide to Basic Writing

PREWRITING

The first stage in the writing process includes prewriting activities. Some of these will limber up your mental muscles and get the ink flowing. Others will allow you to explore topics without pausing to worry about organization or corrections. Remember that your prewriting activities are for practice and exploration; in doing them you should concentrate on facts, ideas, and feelings more than on the language itself. You should be trying to discover as much as you can, not trying to avoid red marks on your paper. In prewriting activities, unlike the later stages of the writing process, more is always better, so keep your pen moving.

FREEWRITING

First of all, write. Write about anything on your mind, and let your mind wander. Write for five or ten minutes without letting your pen stop. If you can't think of anything, write the same word several times until you get moving again. There is no such thing as right or wrong in this activity, except for stopping before the time is up.

This kind of writing is called **freewriting** or automatic writing. Freewriting means writing without pausing for a given length of time or until you have written a certain amount, such as a full page. You can develop fluency in freewriting by doing it regularly. If you sometimes find yourself saying, "I can't get started," freewriting will make it easier for you to become unstuck. Some teachers have students do freewriting for five or ten minutes every day, whereas others assign it only at the beginning of the semester. If your teacher does not require you to do it, practice freewriting on your own, especially in the first weeks of your writing course.

If you become anxious about being timed when you write, you may want to aim for filling up a page when you freewrite. Writing at least a page at a time makes you better able to reach for the full paragraph and complete essay later, even though your freewriting sample may be very different from actual paragraphs and essays. For one thing, your sample may contain repetitions and mistakes, and may wander from one topic to another. Some of what you say may be nonsense; some of it may seem to come from left field. The main purpose of freewriting is to let your writing flow rhythmically and endlessly, like the current of a river. Sometimes it won't: there may be a few rocks in the river, and you may get stuck. With practice, however, your pauses will become brief, and the river will flow again.

Here are two examples of freewriting done by students:

Here we go again, writing about what ever came into my head. Last time I wrote it was raining outside, now I'm writing and it's raining again. Boy is it hot in here. I hope I finish this page without my hand getting tired. Yesterday I went to the movies with Barbara and Joanne, boy was it fun. I had a nice hamburger and some fries afterward. Sonya just came into the class late. Why is she always late? The teacher ought to do something about her, she's stuck on herself. Stuck. I'm stuck. This afternoon is the nursing quiz and I'm not ready for it. Nursing is easier than last term anyway. I hope I get to meet that guy named Kevin in the class next door. He tells funny stories and seems to like me. He's kind of funky though. I'm tired of going out with Marvin all the time because he thinks he's so cool. He always borrows money from me but forgets about it and never wants to pay me back. Some guys don't have any responsibility but Kevin is grown up. I talked to him last week about his job and he really impress me with his attitude.

Here I am thinking about what to write about. My mind is meandering and I don't have ideas yet—I wonder if I used that word right. I was thinking about my accounting professor. His name is Harrison. He is an amusing middle-age man. I always looks forward to that class and I like English even better everyone is friendly and we all feel relaxed when we write. I went to the movies Saturday night with my younger son. The film was alright but it was a karate movie and the only ones I like are Bruce Lee movies, but my son enjoyed it anyway. I've been up since a quarter to six, but even though I was up that early I got to my first class late. Stuck. I'm stuck. My mind wanders to my baby girl's birthday party. She's going on two this April 17 and we are going to have a few people over.

These students were not trying to write essays on assigned subjects; instead, topics came to them as they wrote. The first girl had a lot to say about a new young man she had met, and the second student was thinking about accounting and karate movies. Try to develop a conversational ease in your freewriting: pick up a topic and stay with it as long as it interests you, the way people do in conversation. The benefits of freewriting usually come by accident. You learn to focus on an idea and develop it and to move from one idea to a related one. By doing freewriting every day in a journal, you may find that you begin to sharpen your statements of ideas. Instead of having vague, muddy impressions of your experiences, you will begin stating clear opinions about them. Don't try to do anything more than keep the words coming. The improvement comes unconsciously.

EXERCISE I: FREEWRITING

Practice freewriting by writing without stopping for five minutes. Don't hurry; just keep the pen moving. Begin with a key word so that your mind is focused, but don't try to compose a formal essay. Here are some possible key words: *college, weekends, teachers, shopping, horror movies, traveling, sports, parents.* After five minutes of writing, stop. How much have you written? You will probably find that when you do not have to worry about grammar, spelling, organization, or your teacher's criticisms, you are able to write a whole page in a very short time.

Do a five-minute exercise like this every day for a week. When this routine becomes easy, try ten-minute writing sessions. Begin with some key word or idea in mind, but don't try to "stay on the topic"; just write naturally the way you talk in conversation. If you discover yourself writing so well that you actually want to read your freewriting sample to someone, go right ahead. But do not write with the intent of satisfying a critic. You may feel more confident and be more fluent writing just for yourself.

EXERCISE II: FREEWRITING

Without timing yourself, write continuously until you have filled an 8 1/2-by-11-inch page. If you feel comfortable doing this activity, try it once noting the time you start and the time you stop, but not worrying about the time as you write. You will probably be surprised at how little time it takes to write a full page. Students who worry about completing timed examinations, which usually have one-hour or two-hour time limits, often find that they can write the required number of words in far less than the time limit once they have become used to freewriting. If you have more success with the page limit than with the time limit, stretch out to two pages until you become comfortable with that length. Keep up the freewriting long enough to notice a real improvement in fluency—at least three to four weeks of daily writing.

EXERCISE III: FREEWRITING

Collect all of your informal writing in one journal or notebook. Don't worry about how unimportant some of the entries may seem. Your informal writing is your best source of ideas for essay topics later because it expresses your opinions and interests. Since all formal essays should begin with prewriting activities, your journal will provide some ready-made prewriting that will get you started on formal assignments.

FOCUSED WRITING

After you have been freewriting for several weeks, you will develop a new attitude toward writing. Writing will become an everyday activity, like walking, conversing, and reading. You will stop regarding writing as a formal, specialized job that you can do only when wearing a suit. You will stop worrying about a teacher looking over your shoulder with a red pencil, poised to find your mistakes. You will write for yourself because you like to write— anywhere it is convenient, any time you feel like it, and about any subject on which you want to state your opinions.

This new positive attitude will make your writing better, but it will not produce finished, organized essays. The next step is **focused writing**, which will bring you a little closer to the process of composing organized paragraphs and essays. Focused writing is a not-quite-so-free exercise in which you write on a single topic during a chosen period of time. As in freewriting, you maintain a steady rhythm, concentrating on letting the words flow without being distracted by problems of grammar, spelling, or organization. In focused writing, however, you steer in one direction. In freewriting there is only one *don't*: Don't stop. In focused writing there are two: Don't stop and don't wander off the subject.

Naturally, you will do this better if you have become comfortable writing continuously for two pages or ten minutes in your freewriting. And of course you should phase in your focused writing by choosing subjects familiar to you. Here is one student's focused writing about subways:

> The subway is a pain in the neck. It smells terrible down there. Bag ladies with infected feet and bums always begging, then the train takes so long to come. Sometimes I lean over the track and I wanna go down the track to meet it. When I get on the train sometimes I have to stand up usually when my feet are hurting and the train is shaking and its all hot and stuffy. You think you're just going to die! On the subway tracks sometimes you can see the rats walking around look-

ing for food and they look real nasty. Some of them are big and fat like cats. During the summer the subway is hot and during the winter it's cold. It is like going down into hell. Boxes crushed from trampling feet, newspapers flying here and there. Coffee cups are placed on any convenient spots and cigarette butts are everywhere. Trains pulling in and out of the station sound like a volcano. If you try to speak to the person next to you, they can't hear a word you are saying.

This student stayed on the topic very well and expressed some strong feeling about her experience with the subway. She did not plan to express a particular emotion; she simply explored the thoughts and feelings she already had. You may find yourself jumping from one thought to another, and making some writing errors. The important thing, however, is to discover how much you can say about the subject.

EXERCISE I: FOCUSED WRITING

Do focused writing for five minutes beginning with the statement, "I have always liked (or disliked) my _____ ." (Fill in some feature of your appearance, such as your hair, weight, height, nose, face, eyes, etc.) Write about how this feature has brought you satisfaction or dissatisfaction.

EXERCISE II: FOCUSED WRITING

Do focused writing for five minutes beginning with the statement, "There are many things I like about being _____ years old." Tell about the advantages of being your age and how you feel about it.

EXERCISE III: FOCUSED WRITING

Write, without stopping, a whole page on the subject of your family. Don't try to organize your thoughts first; just write everything that comes to mind.

EXERCISE IV: FOCUSED WRITING

Do focused writing for ten minutes or two pages (whichever you find easier) on subjects from the following list:

1. The worst purchase you ever made
2. The kind of car you'd like to own
3. What you like to do on dates
4. The kinds of food you like to eat
5. Television programs you love and hate
6. Your friends' different attitudes toward marriage
7. How you like to dress
8. How computers make your life easier or harder

BRAINSTORMING: MAKING LISTS

Like freewriting and focused writing, **brainstorming**—spilling all the facts, ideas, examples, and feelings you have on a particular subject—is another prewriting activity. Brainstorming is much like focused writing except that you do not write continuously. You simply jot down everything you can in the form of a big list. Making lists conditions your mind for writing by improving your ability to explore a subject. The list can be a jumble of words, phrases, and statements. Don't censor anything at first. Selecting and organizing come later.

You have made plenty of lists before in your life—shopping lists, lists of things to do, lists of books to read and people to invite. When you made such lists, did you worry about how you put words together or how you spelled them? No, you just wanted to be sure you didn't miss anything or anyone important. Do that when you make lists as a prewriting activity.

Remember: the biggest problem for beginning writers is not what they do wrong but what they never do at all. A list of specific words, phrases, and statements about a subject serves as a range finder; it allows you to see how much is included in the subject. Lists also enable you to notice the details that bring writing to life. When you make lists, pay special attention to the concrete details that make a subject unique.

Here is a list made by a student about the classroom in which she was sitting:

large trapezoid shape	clock over door, one hour behind
It's too hot in here.	Why do I dislike this room?
venetian blinds, one broken	one wall solid windows
tan carpet, needs cleaning	view of the new student center
coat hangers, no coats	room number M33
I had French here last term.	map of Caribbean on back wall
movie screen	no wastebasket, cups on floor
chalkboard, algebra equations	chairs arranged in irregular rows,
37 chairs, bright colors	four and a half rows
sound proof ceiling	

Making lists on topics of the kind you will write about in college courses will challenge your mind still more: you won't be able to just write down what you see. Instead, you may have to look inside your head for ideas. You may produce lists that seem jumbled; the facts and ideas may not fit together. Don't worry, just explore the subject. Here is a list containing everything one student could think of about jobs:

pay scales	discrimination against senior
jobs in health care	citizens
private industry	changes in future job market
I have had three jobs.	husband and wife both working
computers changing many jobs	jobs in socialist countries

bilingual job opportunities
women in "men's" jobs
unions
commuting to work
health hazards on some jobs
unemployment
pensions
jobs overseas
owning small businesses
blue collar jobs
military, government jobs
college training for jobs
changing jobs and careers
interviewing for jobs
jobs for immigrants

why people choose jobs
temporary jobs
working while going to college
boring jobs
jobs in entertainment
working mothers
forty hour week
vacations
fringe benefits
counseling for jobs at college
jobs for handicapped people
jobs that change locations often
dangerous jobs
minimum wage

EXERCISE I: BRAINSTORMING

Make a list of everything you notice about a room you are in—a classroom, room at home, or office where you work. See how many details you can mention. Compete with another student to see whose list has more entries. Train yourself to be a sharp observer.

EXERCISE II: BRAINSTORMING

Make lists of everything you can think of on the topics that follow. Try to cover every square inch of each subject, remembering that there is always one more idea or fact hidden somewhere. Spend ten minutes on each topic.

1. Television—jot down facts, ideas, personal opinions, and experiences.
2. Yourself—put down as many facts, descriptive details, and thoughts about yourself as you can.
3. An activity you engage in, such as martial arts, playing the guitar, cooking, using a computer.
4. A social issue like drug abuse, child abuse, divorce, poverty, street crime, unemployment, sexism, immigration.

ORGANIZING IDEAS

Before you do any serious composing of paragraphs or essays, practice grouping ideas. Get into the habit of seeing large patterns before you fill in details; make rough sketches of your subjects before your work out the fine points. Learn to break down lists into a few main categories. After you compile lists, look them over to identify the large groups of ideas into which they can be divided. Some items may not fit and will have to be dropped. Look back at the student's list concerning jobs and divide the items into the categories on the next page.

Types of jobs: Problems with jobs:

Rewards of jobs: Preparing for jobs:

Other (items that do not fit the previous categories):

EXERCISE I: GROUPING

All of the items in the following list have to do with college, but they belong in different categories or subgroups. Identify three main categories. Three items in the list do not fit any of the three main categories. List these three separately.

accounting	activities fee	karate club
debating team	college deans	cost of books
tuition	glee club	astronomy
clothing expenses	drama society	cost of equipment
foreign films	American history	insurance cost
student government	grade point average	French club
chess team	sociology	wrestling team
room and board	travel expenses	Spanish
psychology	anthropology	telephone bills
mathematics	chemistry	

Name the three categories: 1. _____

2. _____ 3. _____

Name the three items that do not fit: 1. _____

2. _____ 3. _____

E X E R C I S E I I : G R O U P I N G

Identify the three main categories of items in the following list. The general subject is teenage problems. Two of the items do not belong in any of the three subgroups. List these two separately.

peer group's use of drugs
parents too strict about curfews
absenteeism from school
choosing courses in school
sharing family chores
talking to parents about sex
alcoholism among peers
competition with brothers and
    sisters
changing schools
sharing secrets with brothers and
    sisters
having to share a room at home
fads in clothing and hair styles
    among peers
boredom with classes
dropping out of school
showing respect for parents
teenage gangs
organized crime

school counselors not helpful
parents don't understand
not popular with peer group
jealousy among friends
foreign cars
too much academic pressure
getting respect from parents
danger from sexually transmitted
    diseases
ethnic differences among friends
younger brothers and sisters
    invading one's privacy
girls being interested in older
    boys
snobbishness among friends
too much emphasis on grades
athletes get all the attention in
    school
teenage pregnancy

Name the three categories: 1. _____

2. _____ 3. _____

Name the two items that do not fit: 1. _____

2. _____

E X E R C I S E I I I : G R O U P I N G

Choose one of your lists from the brainstorming exercises. Divide the items into categories as in the exercise above, eliminating any items that do not fit into your three or four main groups.

CLUSTERING

Another prewriting activity that many students and teachers find valuable is **clustering**: a way of making an unsystematic diagram of your thoughts on a subject and showing connections between ideas. Like brainstorming, cluster-ing brings out many half-forgotten bits of information on a subject. Begin clustering by writing your main topic in the middle of the page and circling it:

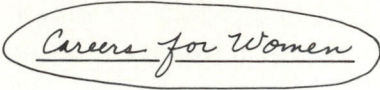

Next, develop a diagram spreading out like a spider in all directions, showing some of the related ideas:

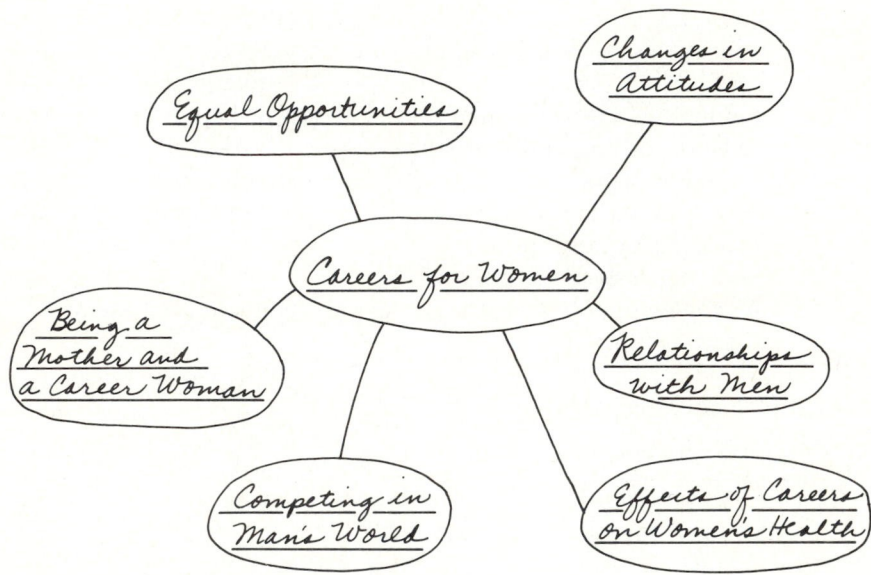

Each of these related ideas has many facts, thoughts, and examples connected to it. Fill in the map as much as you can:

Don't worry if your cluster begins to spread out all over the page. The more ideas the better.

What can you do with a cluster?

1. Discover new ideas on the topic.
2. See links between subtopics.

3. Identify supporting details.
4. Identify specific ideas that might provide a thesis if your main topic is too broad.

"Careers for Women" is obviously too broad for a single essay. Looking at the cluster, you might decide that only one part of it would give you a better thesis. How about "Women Are Beginning to Feel the Effect of Careers on Their Health"? Now make a more detailed cluster on that topic:

EXERCISE: CLUSTERING

The following cluster has been partially filled in. Complete the cluster with items that relate to each of the subtopics in the cluster.

Other Prewriting Techniques

No one prewriting technique is for best for everybody. Each writer has to find the technique that is most helpful in exploring a topic and arranging material. Here are a few other methods often used by writers and teachers:

Ask Yourself Questions. Journalists for years have used the five W's—who, what, when, where, and why—to develop their material. Ask yourself these questions about your subject. Imagine also that you are being interviewed about your topic. What questions would an interviewer ask you?

Use the Five Senses.   Good writing makes imaginative use of all five senses, not just the eyes. Make a list of facts about a familiar object, such as a coin, a hat, a piece of jewelry, or a pear. Underline all facts that are *not* visual. Have you mentioned impressions of taste, hearing, smell, or touch?

Keep a Journal.   Many famous writers have kept daily journals or notebooks; some were even published. If you are good at daily practice and like to spend a few minutes a day alone with your thoughts, keep a journal or notebook. Don't try to make it a diary, in which you monotonously record every event of every day, whether interesting or not. Instead, choose the most interesting thought, memory, dream, or incident of the day and write about that.

READING ALOUD: GETTING FEEDBACK

At all stages of the writing process, you can benefit by reading your writing aloud to other people. Don't cringe! Once you become used to reading your writing aloud, you will enjoy it. Many people are a little self-conscious at first; if you are, try reading to just one person with whom you feel comfortable, and have that person read his or her work to you. The other person does not have to be an expert on grammar or even highly educated. The purpose of reading aloud is not to catch mistakes, it is to help you explore the subject further and discover whether your writing comes across the way you expect it to.

Your instructor may have you read aloud in class, either in a small group or with the whole class listening. This is a big opportunity; take advantage of it as much as you can. Listen to what others say about your writing. They may often say what you expect, and your meaning and feelings may come across exactly as you intended. Sometimes, however, other people will respond differently than you thought they would. They may ask for more information on something that was not clear to them, they may share their excitement over what aroused them, they may suggest related ideas or facts that you should include, and they may disagree with your opinions. Listen to all of it. You don't have to agree with everything said, but you should consider it.

In the prewriting stage, getting feedback will chiefly help you to discover the possibilities of your subject and to clarify your attitude toward it. When other people tell you in their own words exactly what they think you have said and what you meant and felt, they help you form a clear picture of your own purpose. Sometimes what *they* think you meant is not what *you* really meant. In that case, you may have to state your ideas differently. Sometimes, too, other people detect your hidden feelings and intentions, which you should bring out more clearly. You never can predict what others will discover in your writing until you read it to them and hear what they have to say. You may also be surprised at how much they enjoy listening to you!

Types of Feedback to Get from Your Listeners

Here are some guidelines on getting feedback. When you have another person or group of persons listen to you read your writing aloud, have them give you these responses:

What You Said. At first it may seem silly to have them merely repeat your ideas, but by doing this they help you to recognize your own thoughts and feelings and to discover whether you really communicated them.

What You Felt About the Subject. When you do focused writing, you are not thinking much about your feelings—you are just expressing them. A listener can often recognize your feelings better than you can.

What Interested the Listener Most. You may be surprised to find that some of your minor details excited the listener more than what you considered your important ideas. Be ready to open your mind to your listener's reactions; these reactions often give you hints on what to expand and emphasize.

What the Listener Wanted to Hear More or Less About. While doing focused writing, you don't think much about the reader. Feedback from a listener afterward, however, can help you determine what is going to be interesting to readers and what will bore them. One listener may not give you a completely reliable indication, but if you get the same response from many people in a group, you had better consider it carefully!

What the Listener Did not Understand. One lesson all beginning writers need to learn (and advanced writers should never forget) is that there is no guarantee that the reader will know what you mean just because *you* know what you mean. A large part of the craft of writing is stating as clearly and simply as possible exactly what you mean. Only the listener can tell you what he or she does not understand. Of course, some listeners may not be paying attention, so a single person's reaction is not always enough. Again, if a number of people say the same thing, you had better be ready to change your phrasing. Write so that no careful listener can misunderstand you.

INCLUDING YOUR AUDIENCE

Once you have become comfortable reading your writing aloud, especially if you have done it with a group, begin considering your audience as you write. Freewriting and focused writing do not require an audience; you are thinking only about the flow of language and the subject. Finished, organized writing, however, such as college term papers, business reports and letters, magazine articles, and so on, always includes an audience. The writer is communicating to someone or some group of people. The way you express yourself on paper is influenced by the person or group for whom you are writing. Although your style should always be your own, your audience determines in part what facts you choose to communicate, the difficulty of the words you select, the tone you adopt (serious, funny, casual, formal, etc.), and how much explaining you do.

Including your audience should be part of your strategy. Unlike freewriting, organized writing is done for purposes other than practice. These purposes vary widely: writers may want to inform, entertain, persuade, or share emotions. Whatever your purpose—and you may have several purposes at once—you will be more effective if you remember your audience. Getting feedback from reading aloud is the best practice possible for developing a sense of your audience. It encourages you to consider what your readers know about the subject, what their prejudices may be, what their level of education is, and what they may feel about your statements.

Here are some guidelines to follow in writing for your audience:

Find the Right Voice.   Your writing should sound authentic and should be appropriate for the subject, situation, and reader. Since most of your college writing will be read by the teacher and other members of the class, your tone should be natural and direct but not as personal as if you were writing to a close friend or family member. Don't strain to sound "intellectual" or "businesslike" either, or you may adopt a voice that sounds artificial. Here is a sample of writing that shows this kind of straining:

> Accounting has often been considered by myself to provide the required remuneration and advancement potential necessary for me to further my goals in a professional career of my choice. Additionally, such a career possibility will enable me to enhance myself in my pursuit of fulfillment of my personal satisfaction.

What's wrong with this? The writer is so busy trying to sound impressive that he or she winds up not saying much of anything. It's better not to be pompous. Write the way you would talk to other adults in a semiformal situation such as a job interview:

> I have chosen to become an accountant for several reasons. Having above average ability in mathematics and a quick memory, I should be able to do the work well. I also enjoy being efficient and helping others improve the efficiency of their work. The high salaries earned by successful accountants appeal to me as well, and my parents will be pleased if I become the first C.P.A. in the family.

This passage may be less "impressive" because it doesn't use many big words, but it has something to say and sounds like an actual person talking to someone else. Finding the right voice means using a tone somewhere between stilted, artificial language and the casual language of private conversation.

Use the Appropriate Vocabulary.   For most college writing, use adult vocabulary. Explore the range of word choices available, always trying to use the most precise words, not just the biggest ones. If you are studying a technical field like nursing, remember that nonspecialists may not know the technical terms you have learned, so explain these terms if you use them. Slang and street talk, at the other extreme, should be used only for special effects such as humor or surprise. Writers who rely on slang for emphasis become lazy and choose the first slang term that comes to mind instead of considering more precise options. For example, a slang term that has been around for a long time is *knock*—to "knock" something you don't like. Consider all the alternatives many people never think of—*put down, belittle, disparage, minimize, denigrate,* and *ridicule.* Most slang terms, which began as colorful and imaginative inventions, quickly become stale; they are the mark of a careless writer or speaker. Using frequent slang will cause the reader to lose respect for your grasp of the subject and the seriousness of your intentions. Select the best words for your purpose. Use simple language if you write for children, adult language for adults, and technical language for specialists. And don't forget to look for synonyms (words that have similar meanings) in *Roget's Thesaurus.*

Respect Your Reader.   Readers will be annoyed if you talk down to them or leave them no room to disagree. Give them the right to have their own opinions and feelings. Some writers prefer to antagonize their readers in order to provoke an angry exchange of opinion. In most college writing, however, your purpose is to weigh evidence and present ideas, not to propagandize or incite anger. If you wish to explain facts or persuade the reader to agree with your opinion, adopting a prejudiced attitude will weaken your effect. Blatant biases will usually cause the reader to stop reading entirely or to ignore your argument. Recognizing the reader's right to differ with you, on the other hand, may make it possible to win the reader to your side.

Recognize Your Readers' Knowledge of the Subject.   If you are writing informatively for people who know very little about your subject, explain everything they need to know. If you are writing about basketball and your readers are all coaches, however, don't explain what a free throw is.

Write for the Same Audience Throughout.   Sometimes students begin term papers with a general introduction that tells the reader facts any nine-year-old would know; then they suddenly jump into the most specialized, technical discussion imaginable. Decide whom you're writing for.

EXERCISE I: INCLUDING YOUR AUDIENCE

Read the following contrasting samples of writing aloud with a group and discuss the ways in which the two samples have been influenced by the audience for whom they were written. Consider the differences in (a) facts selected, (b) use of language, and (c) attitudes or biases. Read:

1. a passage from a standard local newspaper intended to inform, and a passage from a tabloid such as *The National Enquirer* intended to entertain

2. a passage from a magazine intended mostly for women and a passage from a magazine intended mostly for men

3. a passage from an elementary or junior high school textbook and a passage from a college textbook

EXERCISE II: INCLUDING YOUR AUDIENCE

Write about the same subject for two widely different groups of readers. Do this as focused writing. Choose a subject that both groups would be interested in but would have different attitudes about. Don't *plan* to write differently in the two samples—just write *for* the particular audience, and notice afterward how your audience unconsciously affected what you said. Here are some suggestions:

1. college—for a group of high school students and a group of professors
2. marriage—for a group of divorced people and a group of children
3. jobs—for a group of political leaders and a group of handicapped people
4. crime—for a group of prison inmates and a group of police officers
5. your home town—for people who live there and people who have never been there
6. your area of study—for a group of experts and people who are just beginning to study it

STATING YOUR PURPOSE

While practicing freewriting and focused writing, you thought only about putting plenty of words on the page without stopping. You probably discovered, however, that as you explored some subjects, you had strong opinions and feelings about them. You discovered purposes that you had not planned, such as "I want to complain about the subways" or "I want to tell you how exciting it is to be nineteen years old." Perhaps when you read your work aloud, some of your listeners helped you to identify some of these unstated purposes by saying things like "You certainly are angry about the way they treated you on the job" or "You described your sister so well that I feel I've already met her."

Prewriting is a form of exploring what you think and feel. As you move into actual composing, however, you will begin writing with a *stated purpose*. You will learn to tell the reader what you are going to say—not just what your topic is, but how you are going to write about it: defend it, attack it, describe it, compare it with something else, analyze its parts, define it, or persuade the reader to accept your opinion of it. Knowing your purpose is all-important. Many essays succeed or fail because the writer either did or did not have a strong purpose that was clear throughout the essay. Learn to recognize the difference between merely choosing a topic and knowing how you want to discuss it. "Career Women Face Special Health Problems" is a topic; persuading the reader it is true or attacking the premise as untrue is a purpose.

EXERCISE: MAKING A POINT

Make a point about each of these topics. First write nonstop for a few minutes on each topic. Then find a point you have made about the topic and write it in the blank.

Example:

Topic: Professional basketball

Point: _The three-point rule made basketball more exciting._

1. Topic: Marriage

   Your point: _____

2. Topic: Cocaine

   Your point: _____

3. Topic: Diets

   Your point: _____

4. Topic: Television news

   Your point: _____

5. Topic: Pornography

   Your point: _____

6. Topic: Homelessness

   Your point: _____

7. Topic: Cheating in college

   Your point: _____

EXERCISE: STATING YOUR PURPOSE

Read both of the following passages. One of the passages has a clearly stated purpose; the other does not. Which one seems to you to have a clear purpose? Underline the sentence that states that purpose. Suggest what purpose the other passage might have if it were revised.

I love soap operas because they show me all the things that I would like to do if I were rich. I would live the way the Carringtons do, in a huge mansion with stretch limousines parked in the circular driveway. My clothes would be brought in from the most expensive designers' workshops, having been created just to suit my taste and style. No jewelry would be too extravagant for me to wear, and every season I would vacation in a different luxury resort. My friends would be celebrities in show business, politics, sports, and corporations. Whenever I felt like it, I would sit at the head of my company's board of directors.

Most people watch a lot of soap operas on television. Some people don't, but they like to watch the news instead. I think there is too much violence in the news; it always shows a lot of crime, like shoot-outs over drugs. There is some violence in soap operas too, but I like to watch them because of the suspense. My sister watches them because she doesn't want to do her homework. She is still in high school, so I tell her that if she doesn't stop watching soap operas and start studying, she will never get into college. Even if she does, she won't be able to do the work if she keeps watching the soaps. That's the trouble with television; it's so entertaining that people waste a lot of time watching it. They should watch some of the educational programs once in a while; then they would learn something while they are being entertained. Some soap operas do teach you about society and social issues like adoption, divorce, and teenage pregnancy.

COMPUTERS AND THE PREWRITING PROCESS

More and more students today compose and edit their essays on computers. You probably have access to a word processing program at school or at home, at least for occasional use. If you are lucky enough to have one available frequently, don't wait to use it until you think of yourself as an advanced writer. Many students practice prewriting activities like brainstorming, arranging, and outlining on computers. Grammar and spelling drills are also available on software.

Advantages of Word Processing

As a beginning writer, you can benefit greatly from word processing technology. With a word processor you can create a document that you can change easily in all sorts of ways before you consider it completed. Later units of this book take up the kind of composing, revising, editing, and proofreading that you will do in writing formal compositions. Many of the advantages of word processing involve these later stages of writing. However, word processing also offers advantages for prewriting activities. You will feel much freer to explore your ideas and feelings if you use a word processor, because you will worry less about making mistakes. After all, you can correct your mistakes without erasing or pulling out a fresh sheet of paper. Part of the trouble many beginning writers have with writer's block comes from their fear of messing up the neat page they are producing. With word processing, there is no page to mess up.

If you have not worked on a computer before, you may think of it as a machine to be used only after you have done much scribbling and scratching beforehand. Wrong: don't save the computer for the later stages. The chief advantage of word processing is that you can "scribble" and do as many rough drafts and make as many changes as you like until you are ready to consider your work completed. Only when you print out your document do you have a piece of paper with writing that cannot easily be altered.

Opponents of computers in the writing classroom sometimes object that the spelling checks and style analysis programs may make students lazy—students may depend too much on the machine to do their work for them. You will probably find instead that spelling and style checks will teach you to be more conscious of your areas of weakness. Most students, in fact, improve more rapidly in spelling when they use computer spelling checks. A computer will not do your work for you, but it can make you feel freer to express whatever comes to your mind and thus help you to develop a free flow of language. *You* are still the one in charge of exploring your ideas, putting down and arranging the words, composing, editing, and correcting.

Invisible Writing

You may find that freewriting and focused writing are more fun to do on a computer than on paper. Even if you cannot touch-type, you will be able to write an impressive amount in a short time using a word processor. One kind of prewriting activity that you can do on a computer but not on paper is called **invisible writing**. Some students find this even better than freewriting on paper for developing an uninhibited flow of words. To do invisible writing, turn the screen light down so that you cannot see what you write, then write without stopping for a designated number of minutes. When you have finished, turn up the screen light and read your writing. Students who become blocked by their fear of errors sometimes write more freely this way—they seem to be carrying on a conversation with the machine rather than producing a text for someone to fill with corrections in red ink. You may find that invisible writing loosens you up. Like other prewriting activities, it is a skill-builder that works better for some writers than others.

Software Available

An enormous amount of software exists for writers. If you want to buy your own program, consider the cost as well as the kind of writing you expect to do. Some of the older programs, such as Wordstar (MicroPro International) and Bank Street Writer (Broderbund Software), will serve most writers' needs for their own uses; Q&A Write (Symantec) is highly rated as a program for individual use. Programs with more professional features become more expensive. Highly rated software such as XyWrite III (XyQuest Inc.), Nota Bene (Dragonfly Software), Microsoft Word (Microsoft Corp.) and Word-perfect (Wordperfect Corp.) offer many advanced features that are useful for scholars, professional writers, and corporations, but they can cost up to $500, whereas the simpler programs are about half as much or less. Every year new programs for composing and editing appear, as well as specialized programs for teaching grammar, vocabulary, and spelling. Your college may have one or more of the latter programs available, and you will benefit from asking your instructor about the possibilities. Specialized teaching and editing programs include Writer's Workbench (Bell Labs), EPISTLE (IBM), WANDAH (UCLA), Proofreader (Random House), Grammatik (Aspen Software), and HOMER (UCLA). Certain outlining programs such as Think Tank, Kamas, and Framework may also prove helpful.

Getting Started

Nearly all advanced college students now use word processing. Whether or not you are required to include it in your work as a beginning writer, take advantage of any opportunities you have to phase it into your college work. It may help you now and will certainly prove important later. If you are just beginning to learn about word processing, you may want to read a well-known author's account of his first attempts to use it (William Zinsser, *Writing with a Word Processor*, New York, Harper & Row, 1983).

If you have no experience at all with word processing, don't be afraid to try it when the chance arises. Once someone shows you how to use the keyboard commands with one word processing program, you will find it easier to learn another program. Although there are important differences among programs, getting started is more important than worrying about these differences. Learning to use whatever software is available will not be a mistake or waste of time. You will have taken a big step into the high-tech world.

U N 2 I T

PRACTICING PARAGRAPHS

In the first unit you practiced many kinds of prewriting activities. Usually you wrote a page or more at a time without thinking about organization or grammar. Continue to do prewriting, especially the kind that seems to work best for you—focused writing, brainstorming, clustering, writing journals. Think of prewriting exercises as warm-ups. An athlete, even a top professional, does warm-up exercises both during the off-season and before a game. In the same way, professional authors often write journals and use other prewriting techniques before they compose an article, chapter, or book.

Prewriting activities, however, are only warm-ups. To create a finished essay, you must learn to organize and develop your material so that it supports a main point. To acquire this skill, practice writing paragraphs. It is possible to start right out with whole essays, but most writers do better if they first master the chief building block of the essay: the paragraph. The skills required to create effective paragraphs are the same as those required to create effective essays. Paragraph writing practice will condition you to organize material around topic statements and to group your ideas into related units.

PARAGRAPH BASICS

This section covers the key aspects of paragraphs—recognizing them, signaling where they begin, determining their length, creating topic sentences, and using key words in topic sentences.

Recognizing Paragraphs

A paragraph is a medium-sized block of writing that discusses one idea. It is part of an essay, story, article, chapter, report, or business letter.

Signaling Paragraphs

Show your reader where your paragraphs begin by **indenting**—that is, by starting the first sentence about half an inch from the left margin (or five spaces when you type). (Exception: in some business letters the writer skips a line before every paragraph instead of indenting.) The last sentence in your paragraph may end anywhere on the line from left to right; leave the rest of the line blank, like this one.

In most ordinary writing, you will see about two or three paragraphs on every page:

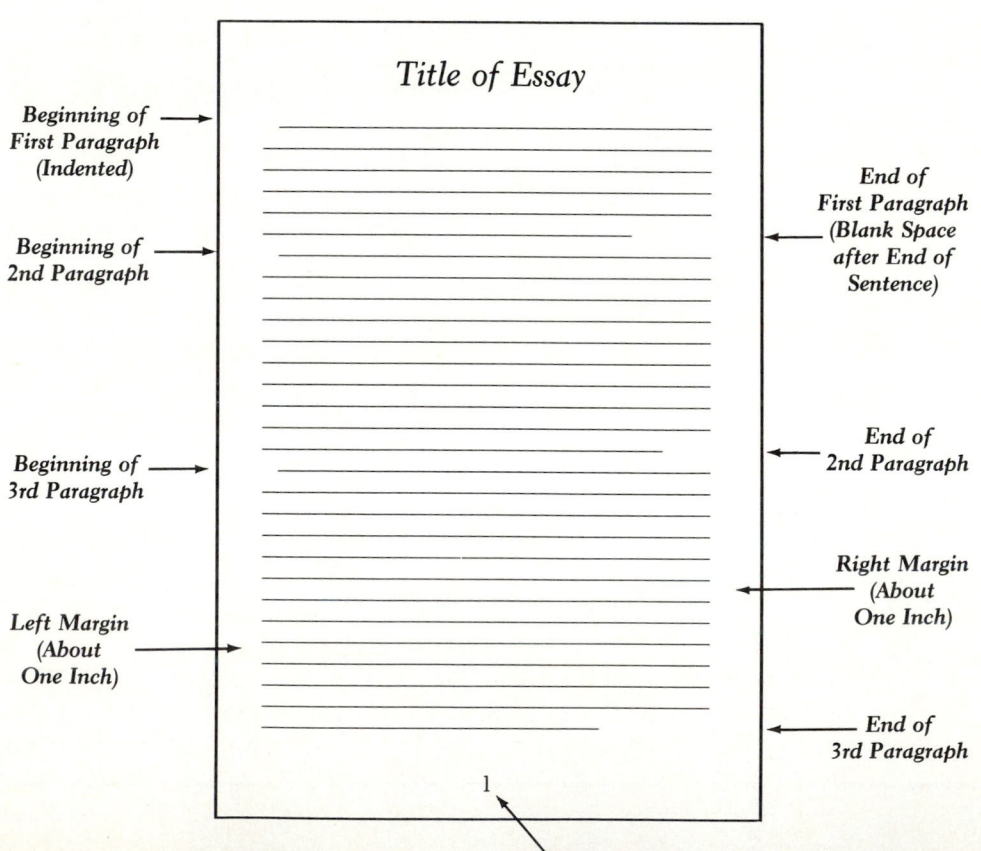

Title of Essay

Beginning of → First Paragraph (Indented)

End of ← First Paragraph (Blank Space after End of Sentence)

Beginning of → 2nd Paragraph

End of ← 2nd Paragraph

Beginning of → 3rd Paragraph

Right Margin ← (About One Inch)

Left Margin → (About One Inch)

End of ← 3rd Paragraph

1

Page Number

Determining Paragraph Length

In this unit you will practice writing full paragraphs, the kind that make up the body of an essay. Such paragraphs usually contain one-hundred to two-hundred words, or about seven to twelve sentences. Introductory and concluding paragraphs are usually shorter, as are paragraphs used for making transitions and paragraphs in dialogue. In published writing, paragraphs may be very short, as in newspaper reports with narrow columns, or very long, as in dense technical articles. What makes a paragraph the right length is not merely the number of words but the way the words fulfill the writer's purpose.

Read the following sample paragraph, noticing its length and overall plan along with the structural details pointed out in the margin. This paragraph was written by a student who was experienced at developing ideas and tying them together.

Sample paragraph:

Topic sentence states opinion

    Raising the legal drinking age is *unfair* to young adults. Legislators who have passed laws raising the minimum drinking age from eighteen to twenty-one are ignoring the rights of young men and women. *Such lawmakers* understandably worry about the many automobile accidents caused by drunken drivers, many of whom are under twenty-one. Although *this problem* demands a rapid solution, *these laws unjustly* penalize all college-age men and women for the wrongdoings of a few. Making *such a change* is *no fairer* than taking away the driver's license of all eighteen- to twenty-one-year-olds. *Furthermore*, it is *unfair* to deny adult privileges to those who shoulder adult responsibilities. *After all*, these young men and women pay taxes, vote, hold down jobs, raise families, and serve their country in war. A *fairer* solution to the problem of drunken driving might be to increase the penalties for drunken drivers of any age and to publicize the dangers of driving while intoxicated.

Key word limits main idea

Body of paragraph discusses main idea

Length of this paragraph: 162 words, 8 sentences

This paragraph begins with a topic sentence that states the main idea: Raising the legal drinking age is unfair to young adults. The rest of the paragraph discusses this idea. To hold the paragraph together, the writer repeats certain key words like *unfair* or uses similar words like *unjustly*. In addition, he includes connecting words and reference words like *such* and *furthermore* to show links between statements. Finally, to avoid boring the reader, he varies his sentences, making some short and simple, others longer and more complicated.

Using Topic Sentences*

Every effective paragraph has a main purpose. Usually this purpose is to express a single idea. In the preceding sample paragraph the idea was that raising the drinking age is unfair. Your topics should be clear and specific like this. One way to be sure they are is to use precise **topic sentences**.

A topic sentence is the sentence, usually the first one in the paragraph, that states the main point of the paragraph. Experienced writers sometimes put topic sentences in the middle or at the end of a paragraph. Occasionally the topic may be so obvious throughout the paragraph that the writer does not need a topic sentence. Despite these exceptions, you should practice beginning your paragraphs with topic sentences. These help you to identify your main points and stick to them.

A topic sentence makes a promise to the reader. It says, "This is what this paragraph is going to discuss." It charts the direction and boundaries of the paragraph. *It should be broader than any other sentence in the paragraph—broad enough to include all the other sentences—but no broader.* If the topic sentence is too general, the topic it presents will not be discussed thoroughly in the paragraph. If the topic sentence is too narrow and factual, it will not cover everything that is in the paragraph.

Can you tell the difference between a broad statement and a limited statement? Which of the following three statements is broadest? Which is most limited?

1. Several of my courses this term require a large amount of homework.
2. My sociology professor assigned a twenty-five-page report and five-hundred pages of reading.
3. College is very difficult.

Only one of these would make an effective topic sentence for a paragraph. Statement 3 is too broad for a single paragraph: discussing all the features of college work and college life that are difficult would take up many pages. Sentence 2 is merely a factual statement; it leads nowhere. Sentence 2 is the kind of statement that is useful to *support* a topic statement. Statement 1 might make a good topic sentence because it is broad enough to include a number of supporting examples (individual courses) but limited enough to be discussed in a paragraph. Furthermore, it serves as a guide, leading the reader to expect a discussion of how much homework each course demands.

EXERCISE I: TOPIC SENTENCES

If the following sentences were in the same paragraph, which one would make a good topic sentence that includes all the others? Which sentence is not on the topic and would not belong in the same paragraph with the others?

---

*Review fragments, run-together sentences, and comma splices in Unit 5.

1. Violinists, singers, and flutists often perform on the sidewalk.
2. Break dancers amaze the public with their coordination.
3. The street life in Manhattan offers visitors a variety of distractions.
4. Dancers on roller skates display uncanny grace and virtuosity.
5. Most of the large stores are not open on Sunday.
6. Vendors hawk scarves, wallets, jewelry, handbags, and toys on many street corners.
7. Con artists lure passersby into card games.
8. Political volunteers stop as many pedestrians as they can to gather signatures on their petitions.
9. Young men and women hand out free passes to live television shows, advertisements for new stores and massage parlors, and free samples of cigarettes and perfume.

Which sentence makes a guiding statment about a whole paragraph

topic? _____

Which sentence is not on the topic at all? _____

How many sentences give factual support for the topic sentence? _____

EXERCISE II: TOPIC SENTENCES

Do a prewriting exercise of your own choosing (focused writing, clustering, brainstorming, and so on) about your own neighborhood. Then look over your material and find a key idea. Write this idea in the form of a topic sentence. List as many supporting details as you can.

WRITING ASSIGNMENT: TOPIC SENTENCES

Write a paragraph of about one-hundred-fifty words beginning with the topic sentence you composed in Exercise II. Be sure to stay on the specific topic!

EXERCISE III: TOPIC SENTENCES

Read the paragraphs below, noticing *all* the supporting points. Then write a topic sentence for each paragraph.

   Paragraph A:

   _____

   _____. Swimming exercises not only the shoulders, arms, and legs but also the large muscles of the back and torso better than other sports do. It is one of the most aerobic sports as well, stimulating both the circulatory and respiratory systems. Few other forms of exercise can equal swimming for producing suppleness through stretching of arm, leg, and torso muscles. Whereas other sports build up separate muscles through short bursts of energy, swimming develops all muscles together in a perfect balance. Furthermore, it enhances the athlete's coordination and rhythm better than most other sports.

Paragraph B:

_____

_____. Despite the claims made for IQ tests, such tests often produce widely different results for the same person. Not only are these tests open to cultural biases, they do not take into account the many kinds of functioning the mind is capable of, from understanding social relationships to identifying musical tones. IQ tests do not account for the way a person reacts to the pressure of a test-taking situation. They do not allow for differences in motivation; is it possible, for instance, that a person who doesn't care about getting a high score will not try as hard as someone who does? IQ tests measure a kind of analytical thinking, but they do not give a picture of the person's learning styles, and they do not say much about the person's learning development over a period of years. Finally, they do not tell how the person applies his or her intelligence in everyday life.

Paragraph C:

_____

_____. Although he had a large wardrobe, Ted always wore ties that clashed with his shirts, socks that didn't match, shirts with cuff buttons missing, and pants that hadn't been pressed for months. His room showed similar signs of carelessness, with clothes and books piled three feet deep on the floor, the bed unmade, and papers heaped in a chaotic mess on his desk and bureau. In his relations with his friends, he remained true to form, often forgetting to pay back money they lent to him, showing up an hour late for films and parties, and neglecting to mention messages or requests that friends told him to pass on to others.

EXERCISE IV: TOPIC SENTENCES

As you could tell from the preceding exercise, it takes concentration to match a good topic sentence with a fully developed paragraph. In the next two paragraphs, something is wrong with the italicized topic sentences. Explain the fault of each one—not on the topic of the paragraph, too broad, too narrow, or not clear. Remember that a good topic sentence should have *one* idea, not two or three.

Paragraph A:

Being the oldest child in the family has both advantages and disadvantages. Whether a boy or girl, the oldest child tends to mature quickly by copying adults' behavior and being called on to be a substitute parent for the younger children. As a result, he or she tends to have strong leadership potential and a firm sense of identity. Unlike younger siblings, the oldest child never has to accept clothes or toys passed down used and half broken from older brothers and sisters. For a few years, too, sometimes for quite a few, the oldest child basks in the undivided attention and love of both parents, developing self-confidence and self-esteem as an only child. Later, by serving as a model held up to the younger children for imitation, the oldest child usually gains the habit of influencing and motivating others.

The problem with the topic sentence in paragraph A is: _____

_____

Paragraph B:

Television commercials are very entertaining. Last year I saw a commercial for a large discount store that sold appliances. The advertisement claimed that the store's prices were the lowest in the state and that the company stood behind the products it sold. Enticed by the commercial, I ordered a washing machine. Although the price seemed reasonable, I learned afterward that a local appliance store sold it at a lower price. Not only that, but the discount outlet demanded a delivery charge, and the delivery men wanted an additional ten dollars to carry the machine into the house and cart the old one away. Then I learned that, unlike other retail stores, the discount outlet would not install the washer. So, after making several telephone calls to the manufacturer and struggling with hoses, fittings, nuts, and bolts, I hooked up the machine myself. I decided not to believe any more commercials without investigating the facts.

The problem with the topic sentence in paragraph B is: _____

_____

A better topic sentence for this paragraph would be: _____

_____

Using Key Words in Topic Sentences

Remember that a topic sentence does more than just name a subject. It expresses an opinion about the subject; it points a direction, opens a discussion, and creates an impression of the subject. A simple statement of fact, such as "It was cold yesterday," does not make a useful topic sentence. Which of these two might make a good topic sentence?

A. I have a friend named Evelyn.

B. My friend Evelyn is very competitive.

Suppose you were going to write a paragraph beginning with sentence A. What would the paragraph say about Evelyn? Almost anything is possible, since the topic sentence gives no specific idea. Sentence B would make a better topic statement because it tells what the paragraph should say about Evelyn. Can you think of examples of behavior that would show how competitive someone is? *Competitive* is the key word in sentence B; it introduces a controlling idea. Most good topic sentences contain such a key word or phrase.

Compare these statements:

Mertz Rent-a-Car offers *rapid advancement* for ambitious employees.
Mertz Rent-a-Car is a *nice place to work*.

Nice is one of those catchall terms that lead nowhere in particular. The first statement makes a sharp, clear point that the paragraph could support with specific facts.

EXERCISE I: KEY WORDS

In the following five sentences, find and underline the key words or phrases that create specific impressions.

Example: For a twelve-year-old, running away from home is a <u>frightening</u> experience.

Frightening tells what impression the whole paragraph should create.

1. My first driving lesson was a hilarious experience.
2. Professional wrestling usually looks faked.
3. An effective job interview requires a manner that is appropriate for the job.
4. Dustin Hoffman has usually played unconventional film roles.
5. Adjusting to a new roommate requires a cooperative approach.

Explain how each key word or phrase gives you ideas about what the paragraph should include. Think of some examples or explanations of each topic statement.

EXERCISE II: KEY WORDS

Underline the key word or phrase in each of the following sentences and decide whether the statement would make an effective topic sentence. If it would, write OK in the blank. If the key word or phrase is too vague, write a more precise one in the blank.

Examples:

The first year of law school is *different*.   *more specialized than college*

Snorkel diving is very *expensive*.   *OK*

1. Hawaii is a good place to visit.   _____

2. My room is arranged efficiently for study.   _____

3. Psychotherapy made Esther more independent.   _____

4. Kung fu is a bad sport for some people.   _____

5. Parochial schools are better than public schools.   _____

6. Stamp collecting teaches you about a lot of things.   _____

7. Arranging a family reunion requires a logical plan.   _____

8. Mexicans are interesting people.   _____

9. Introduction to Abnormal Psychology is a nice course.   _____

10. Professor Hardnose is a demanding teacher.   _____

WRITING ASSIGNMENT I: KEY WORDS

Compose a paragraph using one of the preceding statements as your topic sentence. (Use your version if you improved it.) Include specific details to support the point.

EXERCISE III: KEY WORDS

Read the following two paragraphs, noticing the topic sentences and supporting examples. Then answer the questions.

Paragraph A:

My mother is a wonderful person. She was always there when we needed her, and she taught us many things about life that no one else could teach us. Whenever we wanted something, she was always there to get it for us. She always wanted the best for us. She is a truly beautiful person. She is five feet, four inches tall, has a trim figure, and speaks with a slight Spanish accent. She always emphasized education and wanted us to speak two languages well. Unfortunately, our school did not provide bilingual education, so she had to do the language teaching herself. She worked part-time as a nurse's aide, and her favorite hobbies are sewing and gourmet cooking.

Paragraph B:

My sister is the most systematic organizer I know. She runs her day like clockwork: up at six-thirty, dressed by six-forty-five, finished with breakfast and out of the house by seven. Always at least ten minutes early for work at the bank, she arranges her desk so that she can start off the day's work without a letter or memo out of place. She handles each customer's problem so efficiently that her supervisor is often astonished, and she even knows where to go on her lunch break to avoid waiting in line for a sandwich. When she gets home in the evening, she has already arranged the food and utensils so that dinner never takes her more than thirty minutes to prepare.

1. What is the key word or phrase in the topic sentence of paragraph A?

_____ paragraph B? _____

2. Which of the two key words is more specific? _____

3. Which paragraph is more tightly unified? _____

4. Which statements go off the topic in the paragraph that lacks unity?

_____

_____

5. Which paragraph is better arranged? _____

6. What could be done to improve the faulty paragraph? _____

_____

_____

EXERCISE IV: KEY WORDS

Create a topic sentence based on each of the topics below. Be sure to include a specific key word or phrase and underline it.

    Example: Topic: my hometown

          Topic sentence: _My hometown is very old-fashioned._

1. Topic: my family
  Topic sentence: _____

2. Topic: my job

   Topic sentence: _____
3. Topic: traveling by airplane

   Topic sentence: _____
4. Topic: the President

   Topic sentence: _____
5. Topic: credit cards

   Topic sentence: _____

WRITING ASSIGNMENT II: KEY WORDS

Think about someone you know who has an unusual way of behaving. Brainstorm for ten minutes, listing everything you can think of about how this person behaves. Then look over the list and find one main point that you can make about this person—a point that will include most of the details you have listed. Eliminate the details that do not fit this point. Write a topic sentence using a key word or phrase to describe this person's behavior, and compose an exploratory draft of a paragraph on this subject. Look over your draft to be sure that all sentences belong on the topic and that the whole paragraph reads smoothly. Make revisions; write a final draft.

Sample paragraph:

Read this paragraph after you have brainstormed your topic. Notice how the student who wrote this paragraph succeeded in stating a clear topic sentence and developing it in an interesting way. Try to make your final draft equally unified and interesting.

A Person with an Unusual Way of Behaving

My sister Maggie has a ridiculous way of reading signs. Every sign she sees in a store, on a wall, on a jacket, or even in a car park she reads by singing it out loud. When she went to the hospital last week to visit a friend, she started singing notices like Do Not Trespass, No Smoking, Only for Staff. Nurses looked at her as if she were crazy. Last Saturday we went to the movies, and when she began to read the movie's cast, of course she started singing it. I moved from my seat. She likes singing so much that even when she reads her school books at home, she sings the lessons aloud. Sometimes we're watching television and she begins to sing the little 800 number they put on the bottom of the screen. I really don't like her unique way of reading things.

REVIEW EXERCISE: TOPIC SENTENCES

Choose the topic sentence in each group and mark it *T*. Find one sentence that does not relate to the topic and mark it *X*. The other sentences should all support the topic statement; do not mark them.

_____   1. a. Orange juice costs $1.09.
_____   b. Prices are high in the school cafeteria.
_____   c. Soda costs 60¢.
_____   d. The soup in the cafeteria is usually cold.
_____   e. Hot dogs in the cafeteria cost $2.50.
_____   2. a. Chinese society is trying to control population growth.
_____   b. The Chinese government insists that one child per family is
                 enough.
_____   c. Birth control information is made easily available.
_____   d. Women ask each other every month if they have avoided get-
                 ting pregnant.
_____   e. American tourists are hesitant to visit China since the mas-
                 sacre in Beijing.
_____   3. a. Duane always buys overpriced clothes and records.
_____   b. Duane is a funny mixture of common sense and carelessness.
_____   c. Duane always maintains a good credit rating.
_____   d. Duane is related to a professional basketball star.
_____   e. Duane lost half his income last week in off-track betting.
_____   f. Duane knows where to get the best bargains in sports equip-
                 ment.
_____   4. a. Immigrants often bring new music, art, and food to the
                 United States.
_____   b. Immigrants often take low-paying jobs not sought after by
                 native workers.
_____   c. Immigrants usually enter the country through port cities.
_____   d. Immigrants usually set a good example by their hard work
                 and close family ties.
_____   e. Immigrants provide social and economic benefits to the
                 United States.
_____   5. a. The 1960s was a period when the Democrats were in office.
_____   b. In 1968 there were student protests at many universities
                 against the war in Vietnam.
_____   c. The 1960s was a period of protest and self-expression.
_____   d. Rock music and folk music were popular throughout the
                 1960s.
_____   e. There were many civil rights marches and sit-ins during the
                 1960s.
_____   f. Miniskirts were popular in the 1960s, nudity was common
                 in the theater, and long hair was in fashion.
_____   6. a. Cheryl's stereo set has powerful speakers with a rich bass
                 and clear treble sound.
_____   b. Cheryl is pleased with her new stereo set.
_____   c. Cheryl often attends the ballet and the opera.
_____   d. Cheryl's stereo set contains a superior tape deck and an FM
                 receiver with outstanding reception.
_____   e. Cheryl's stereo is remarkably easy to use.

_____ 7. a. Students who receive A's in mathematics are allowed to register for special honors classes in science.

_____ b. Students with overall grade point averages of B or better have their names placed on the Dean's List.

_____ c. Grade point averages are calculated by the registrar on a computer.

_____ d. High grades give students special honors and privileges.

_____ e. Students with outstanding grades are invited to compete for fellowships in graduate school.

_____ 8. a. A strong dollar makes it inexpensive for Americans to travel abroad.

_____ b. When the American dollar has a high value, many Americans benefit.

_____ c. American consumers can purchase foreign goods more cheaply when the dollar is strong.

_____ d. Some companies are harmed by a strong dollar because they cannot sell their goods abroad.

_____ e. A strong dollar attracts borrowers from abroad and strengthens American savings institutions.

_____ 9. a. Projection is the tendency to blame others for one's own faults.

_____ b. People sometimes hide their true emotions by means of patterns called defense mechanisms.

_____ c. Compensation is a way of making up for one's feeling of poor self-esteem by overdoing some activity.

_____ d. Rationalization is making up false reasons for one's attitudes and actions.

_____ e. Majoring in psychology requires many courses in related social sciences.

_____ 10. a. Chinese food contains a wide variety of ingredients.

_____ b. Most Chinese restaurants have menus in both English and Chinese.

_____ c. Many seafoods are used in Chinese cooking, such as shrimp, squid, and even octopus.

_____ d. Many vegetables appear in Chinese dishes, including broccoli, bean sprouts, snow peas, and mushrooms.

_____ e. Several kinds of meat, including pork and beef, are common in Chinese dishes.

WHAT MAKES A PARAGRAPH GOOD?

In learning to compose good paragraphs, you will also learn most of what it takes to compose good essays. Although you do not have to pay special attention to your paragraphs when you create exploratory drafts, your final drafts will need well-constructed paragraphs to be effective. In this section you will learn the qualities of good paragraphs so that you can create strong paragraphs yourself. The four main elements that combine to make effective, purposeful paragraphs are **unity**, **coherence**, **transitions**, and **development**.

Paragraph Unity

The prefix *uni* means *one*. A unified paragraph has *one* clear purpose. The topic statement, as we have already discussed, is limited enough so that the rest of the paragraph can support it well; no statements should wander off the topic. In your prewriting exercises you first did freewriting, paying no attention to staying on a topic. Then you did focused writing, which meant staying on one topic. A short piece of focused writing is still not a unified paragraph (although it might be the basis for a good paragraph when revised). In your focused writing you may sometimes have had a brilliant new idea and wandered off the topic like a shopper after an unexpected bargain. In your focused writing as well, you did not compose a topic sentence that would fit exactly the amount of writing you were planning to do. Now you will concentrate on the paragraph as a finished product made from the raw materials of your ideas and statements in your focused writing. Above all you must know what your topic is and then stay on the topic. Every sentence in your paragraph should follow logically from the one before, and all sentences should give facts, ideas, or examples that support the topic statement.

EXERCISE I: PARAGRAPH UNITY

This exercise gives you practice in recognizing sentences that support a topic. First read the topic sentence; then read each of the ten sentences that follow. If the sentence supports the topic statement, put a check mark in the blank next to it. If it does not, leave the space blank.

Topic statement: Letter grades (A,B,C,D,F) sometimes harm a college student's learning process.

_____ 1. Students who concentrate too much on grades tend to avoid difficult courses in which they might learn much.

_____ 2. Grades are usually given out twice a semester.

_____ 3. The fear of low grades makes some students hesitant about expressing opinions that disagree with those of the teacher.

_____ 4. Competition for grades gives students a big incentive to learn.

_____ 5. Average students know they cannot earn top grades and they often become discouraged about learning.

_____ 6. Colleges that give grades have a higher percentage of graduates continuing on to graduate school than those that do not give grades.

_____ 7. Grades increase stress, causing some students to lose concentration.

_____ 8. Grades do not reward work done creatively beyond the scope of a course.

_____ 9. Students with high grades are not always "nerds"; some of them are highly popular.

_____ 10. The threat of low grades damages the relationship between teachers and students that is necessary for optimal learning.

EXERCISE II: PARAGRAPH UNITY

The following paragraph is unified except for two sentences that wander off the topic stated in the first sentence. Underline these two irrelevant sentences.

Nutrition has at last become a professional career for well-trained specialists. People who work in nutrition, called nutritionists, have bachelor's degrees in biology and related subjects. Many of them have graduate degrees as well. They can earn the title of Registered Dietitian (R.D.) if they pass a certifying examination. There is intense competition for jobs by people with college degrees. Nutritionists work in a variety of high-level jobs in teaching institutions, government agencies, and private corporations that supply and process food. Some assist in health programs at schools and hospitals, and others provide material for television documentaries on health and fitness. Some people think that exercise is just as important to your health as the food you eat. Nutrition is one of the few careers that offer opportunities in all regions of the country and in both the public and private sectors.

Now read the paragraph aloud with the two irrelevant sentences omitted. It reads more smoothly, doesn't it? Unrelated sentences interrupt the flow of thought and lead the reader off the path, destroying the unity of the paragraph.

EXERCISE III: PARAGRAPH UNITY

The following paragraph also contains two sentences that are not on the topic. Underline the two sentences and read the paragraph aloud with the two sentences omitted.

In the future, workers will have more leisure time and more flexible schedules. Working hours will decrease. Leisure time will be obtained not only through shorter daily hours, but through more three-day weekends, more optional days off, double vacations both summer and winter, and many different kinds of leave without pay. Health foods are likely to become more popular. There will be maternity leave, educational leave, parental leave, and just plain we're-taking-a-year-off-to-go-around-the-world leave. Bilingual employees will be increasingly in demand. All of these and many new devices yet uninvented will be used to package work into jobs of different sizes and shapes to fit the diverse life-styles and changing stages of the people who do it.*

_____

*Caroline Bird, *The Two-Paycheck Marriage*. New York: Rawson, Wade Publishers, Inc., 1979.

Paragraph Coherence

Not only should all sentences in a paragraph support the topic statement, but they should be *arranged in a clear, recognizable order.* **Coherence** means that all the parts of something *cohere*, or hang together. To produce a car engine, you have to have all the right pieces, but you also have to fit the pieces together correctly so the engine can run. The main rule for fitting the pieces of a paragraph together coherently is to *make every sentence follow logically from the one before.* This is one of the important basic principles of good writing. The sentences in a paragraph should read in a natural sequence, like numbers in a row—1, 2, 3, 4, 5—not jump around unpredictably like random numbers—1, 7, 3, 8, 4, 9.

A paragraph with a natural sequence is much easier to read than one without any shape. A coherent paragraph will serve its purpose more effectively than an incoherent one, whether the purpose is to express a feeling, state an opinion, convey an experience or impression, or persuade the reader to agree.

Here is a paragraph that lacks coherence:

My first attempt to register for courses in my freshman year was one of the worst experiences of my life. I'll never go through that again! Most of the courses I planned to take were already closed, so I had to settle for whatever I could get. The first frustration came when I entered the gymnasium and was told that freshmen had to register in the student union. I discovered that I had to stand in not one line but six lines—one for each course I wanted. As I was heading back to my dorm room about ready to explode, I met a friend who told me that I was right in the first place, but now I was late and would have to wait in line because everyone was ahead of me. When I got to the student union, someone told me that freshmen couldn't register until the next day. After I finished five hours later, I found out that I could have done all my registering a week earlier just by seeing my adviser. Nobody had told me it would be difficult, so I was not prepared for five hours of waiting in six long lines, not being able to get the courses I wanted, and constantly receiving false information.

Although the first sentence in the preceding paragraph is a fairly clear and specific topic sentence and all of the following statements support it, the paragraph is still confusing. That is because the order of sentences has been jumbled. Here is the paragraph arranged in a coherent order:

My first attempt to register for courses in my freshman year was one of the worst experiences of my life. Nobody had told me it would be difficult, so I was not prepared for five hours of waiting in six long lines, not being able to get the courses I wanted, and constantly receiving false information. The first frustration came when I entered the gymnasium and was told that freshmen had to register in the student union. When I got to the student union, someone told me that freshmen couldn't register until the next day. As I was heading back to my dorm room about ready to explode, I met a friend who told me that I was right in the first place, but now I was late and would have to wait in line because everyone was ahead of me. I discovered that I had to stand in not one line but six lines—one for each course I wanted. Most of the courses I planned to take were already closed, so I had to settle for whatever I could get. After I finished five hours later, I found out that I could have done all my registering a week earlier just by seeing my adviser. I'll never go through that again!

Coherence can be achieved in paragraphs by arranging the material according to time sequence, spatial sequence, or climactic sequence.

Time Sequence. The sample paragraph you just read is arranged in **time sequence**. It describes a series of actions taking place one after the other: the attempt to register at the gym, the wild-goose chase to the student union, the return to the gym, the five hours of waiting in line, and discovery that all this could have been avoided. Time sequence is the easiest kind of arrangement of material in a paragraph. You have undoubtedly used it in any writing you have done about personal experiences. The main thing to keep in mind is to make the sequence of actions clear; don't leave out any steps that the reader needs to follow the action.

In the next paragraph several gaps occur in the sequence of statements. As a result, the action is difficult to follow. Find the places where something is left out. What belongs in these spaces?

When Sonya gets up in the morning, she is usually still sleepy because her alarm rings at 6 A.M. The first thing she does is head for the kitchen to start coffee and put on an egg to boil. When she is finished in the bathroom, she returns to her bedroom and looks over her wardrobe to choose a dress to wear. Then she gets dressed and goes back to the kitchen to eat her breakfast in a hurry because it is usually about 6:45 by this time. Once she has reached the bus stop, she knows that she will be late if the bus comes later than 7:15. Her subway ride usually takes about half an hour. If everything goes right, she gets to work by 8 A.M.

This student's paragraph came out easier to read when she revised it to include information missing from the first draft:

When Sonya gets up in the morning, she is usually still sleepy because her alarm rings at 6 A.M. The first thing she does is head for the kitchen to start coffee and put on an egg to boil. *Next she goes to the bathroom to shower and fix her hair.* When she is finished in the bathroom, she returns to her bedroom and looks over her wardrobe to choose a dress to wear. Then she gets dressed and goes back to the kitchen to eat her breakfast in a hurry because it is usually about 6:45 by this time. *After breakfast, she rushes to the corner two blocks away to catch a bus.* Once she has reached the bus stop, she knows that she will be late if the bus comes later than 7:15. *The bus takes her to the subway station on the opposite side of the park.* Her subway ride usually takes about half an hour. If everything goes right, she gets to work by 8 A.M.

EXERCISE I: TIME SEQUENCE

Write a paragraph like the one you have just read. First make a list of the things you do when you get up in the morning. Then compose your paragraph, using a smooth time sequence with no necessary information left out.

EXERCISE II: TIME SEQUENCE

Look through your prewriting exercises and find one that includes an experience that took place in time sequence. This can be either something that happened to you or some other event you described. You will need about half a page of writing to make a normal-sized paragraph, an experience whose description covers about this much space. Revise your writing to make a unified paragraph written in time sequence. Since you were not trying to compose neat paragraphs in your prewriting exercises, you may have to add steps that were left out, remove irrelevant sentences, and make other corrections.

Spatial Sequence. Another way of achieving coherence in your paragraphs is by arranging statements in **spatial sequence**. This means that your description follows the placement of items in space, for example, front to back, side to side, up to down, near to far. As with time sequence, be sure not to leave any confusing gaps, and use enough details so that the reader has a clear picture of what you are describing. The paragraph should move like a camera panning (as filmmakers call it) slowly over a scene. If you have ever tried making home videos, you know that if you move the camera too fast, the film will be hard to follow. In filmmaking and writing alike, the viewer or reader has to be given enough time with a few important details to recognize the arrangement, and the focus has to move gradually enough so the picture does not become a confusing blur.

The paragraph that follows is arranged in spatial sequence. What direction of movement does it use to achieve coherence?

As he approached the town, Fred began to feel familiarity. The shopping mall he passed just inside the city limits seemed new to him, because all the buildings were fairly new. Just beyond it, however, he passed a used-car lot that he seemed to know, even though he didn't recognize the name. Soon he crossed some old railroad tracks, and now he knew he had driven this way before. He slowed down as he spotted Dom's service station on his left, and realized he had known it would be there. His memory told him there would be a high school just over the hill on his right as he entered the business section of town. There it was. As he drove past the high school from which he had graduated and nosed his car in anticipation toward the remodeled courthouse in the center of town, he knew he had accidentally returned to his hometown, modernized beyond recognition in the suburbs but still the same at its heart.

In describing a place, such as a building, a neighborhood, or a room, use spatial sequence to give coherence to the picture. Otherwise the details will add up to a jumbled mess. Here is a paragraph that lacks coherence because the descriptive details are not arranged in a recognizable order:

> There was a huge pile of dirty laundry left near the door two weeks ago. One desk was barely visible under a mound of loose term papers, audio cassettes, books and magazines lying open, and camera equipment. One bed was made drum-tight like a marine recruit's bunk. Another desk lined up straight against the wall had every item in place, with pens and pencils positioned in parallel rows, books matched on the shelves above according to height, and papers stacked evenly on one corner. A broken stationary bicycle was lying on its side with a set of free weights scattered under and around it. The other bed looked as if a bar-room fight had taken place on it—the torn and stained wool blanket was littered with cigarettes, crumpled soda cans, socks, and underwear. There was also a computer table with a monitor and printer polished to look like new, and a desk chair carefully placed one foot behind the table.

This paragraph has plenty of descriptive details, but it is hard to follow because the details are not arranged in any pattern. The paragraph reads like a list from brainstorming exercise. Arranged in spatial order, however, the details make a coherent paragraph with the addition of a clear topic sentence and some "spatial orientation" words:

> Michael and Sean's dormitory room looked like an apartment for the odd couple. Everything on the left side showed Sean's incredible sloppiness; everything on the right showed Michael's obsessive tidiness. As you entered the room and looked to the left, you saw first a huge pile of dirty laundry left near the door two weeks ago. Behind it was a broken stationary bicycle lying on its side with a set of free weights scattered under and around it. Behind that was a bed that looked as if a barroom fight had taken place on it—the torn and stained wool blanket was littered with cigarettes, crumpled soda cans, socks, and underwear. The desk in the far corner was barely visible under a mound of loose term papers, audio cassettes, books and magazines lying open, and camera equipment. By contrast, the right side of the room was geometrically perfect. The front was taken up by a bed made drum-tight like a marine recruit's bunk. The desk, lined up straight behind it against the wall, had every item in place, with pens and pencils positioned in parallel rows, books matched on the shelves above according to height, and papers stacked evenly on one corner. Standing in the far right corner was a computer table with a monitor and printer polished to look like new and a desk chair carefully placed one foot behind the table.

EXERCISE I: SPATIAL SEQUENCE

Imagine you are driving in a place that is familiar to you. Compose a paragraph describing your impressions as you draw nearer and nearer to a particular spot. Remember to include enough details to communicate the overall movement from far to near.

EXERCISE II: SPATIAL SEQUENCE

Brainstorm to collect facts about your room. Do not think about composing or arranging. Once you have your list of facts, look it over and try to think of a topic statement that will make your description interesting. Find a key word—*mysterious, boring, messy, casual, neat, colorful*—to describe the overall impression of your room. Then write an exploratory draft in which you describe the room spatially, for example from front to back or left to right. Look over your draft to see if you left anything out or need to add details or make corrections. Write a final draft.

Climactic Sequence.   A third kind of paragraph arrangement is called **climactic sequence**. In this arrangement, sentences build to a climax. They start with less important or less emphatic statements and end with the most important or most emphatic statements. Climactic sequence is effective in paragraphs that discuss ideas rather than tell stories or describe places. A paragraph in climactic sequence may give a series of facts, reasons, or examples to support a point. When you write such paragraphs, be sure to include enough facts and ideas to support your point, and make each sentence follow from the one before and build to a climax.

Here is a paragraph that follows a climactic sequence:

> Crack is the most dangerous drug available. Compared with cocaine and heroin, it is inexpensive and easy to buy in most urban areas. Therefore many teenagers and even children ten or eleven years old are trying it and selling it. Crack is also very easy to use, so people who might hesitate to inject heroine or sniff cocaine may smoke crack. Still more important is its powerful high, which sets in very quickly and leads many people to use it a second and third time. Worst of all, it is powerfully addictive in a short time, it often has devastating effects on the brain, and it can sometimes cause death through its sudden effect on the heart.

This paragraph lists some of the dangers of crack. The writer puts them in a sequence that she believes builds from the somewhat less crucial facts about low cost and ease of use to the more important facts about effects.

Climactic sequence can also be useful in discussing personal topics. In the following paragraph a student discussing the advantages of renting films and watching them on a VCR. Again, the order of sentences moves from the less important to the more important.

> Renting films and watching them on my VCR has quite a few advantages. I don't have to wait until a particular time for a film to begin at a local theater and maybe even wait in line, taking the chance of not getting a ticket. I can also watch the film several times if I want to, or stop it in the middle and rerun part of it if I missed something. Instead of having to pay $7.00 or $8.00 to watch a film at a

theater—twice as much if I take my girlfriend—I can rent a film for $2.71 at the video store where I am a member. The biggest advantage of all is that I can choose a film from hundreds of movies available at the video store instead of having to see one of the four showing at the theater near my home.

EXERCISE I: CLIMACTIC SEQUENCE

Number the following statements in the order you would arrange them in climactic sequence, putting 1 first as the least important and 5 last as the most important.

Topic statement: Owning a car in a large city has several disadvantages. Supporting statements:

_____ 1. Parking in the city is always expensive.
_____ 2. In the city your car is likely to be stolen or broken into.
_____ 3. Insurance rates are highest for urban car owners.
_____ 4. Air pollution in the city tends to damage a car's paint.
_____ 5. Gasoline prices are higher in the city than elsewhere.

EXERCISE II: CLIMACTIC SEQUENCE

Choose one of the topics below for a paragraph to be written in climactic sequence. First brainstorm or do focused writing on the topic. List as many supporting statements as you can, being sure to include only those that specifically support the topic. Using your list of supporting statements, write a first draft beginning with the topic sentence and including your supporting statements in order of increasing importance. You may want to number your statements as in the preceding exercise before writing the rough draft. Write a final draft, being sure that your sentences read smoothly and are correct.

Suggested topic sentences:

1. Waiting until about age 30 to have a baby has several advantages.
2. Current fashions are convenient.
3. State lotteries have a number of benefits for society.
4. Fraternities have several appealing features for college students.
5. Call-in radio talk shows entertain listeners in several ways.
6. I read personal advice columns for a number of reasons.

Paragraph Transitions*

Successful paragraphs move the reader along smoothly from beginning to end. Remember the main rule : *Every sentence should follow logically from the one before.* Having a logical arrangement based on a recognizable order—time sequence, spatial sequence, or climactic sequence—is the most important way to achieve continuity. In addition, you should use **transitional expressions** to

---

*See correcting by subordinating and punctuation (semicolons, commas) in Unit 5.

signal connections to the reader. Your overall plan is like an itinerary you have worked out for a trip. Transitional expressions are like the road signs you will need occasionally to be sure you are going in the right direction.

Tie your sentences together by repeating key words, but don't overdo this: remember that too much repetition makes for boring writing. Use *pronouns* (he, she, it, you, they, we) to refer to persons, places, and things already mentioned. Make sure the person or thing to which any pronoun refers is absolutely clear. Finally, learn to use transitional words and phrases like those listed here to show connections between statements. Each kind of writing has its own kind of transitional expressions. Look over your previous writing to see if you use some of these words occasionally. Which ones have you never used? Practice using these and develop new habits.

Caution: Some writers who discover they have not been using enough transitional expressions to show connections at first use too many. They may put a transitional word or phrase at the beginning of every sentence. As a result, their writing suddenly becomes mechanical and self-conscious. Remember that these transitional expressions are like road signs: you don't need them at every point along the way, but you do need them at key points where the reader might otherwise lose the train of thought.

Transitional Words and Phrases

For Adding Information	also, and, besides, first (second, third), furthermore, in addition, likewise, moreover, too
For Showing Opposites and Contrast	although, but, even though, however, nevertheless, on the other hand, yet
For Showing Time	after, afterward, at last, at that time, before, beforehand, earlier, later, meanwhile, soon, then, while
For Showing Place	above, adjacent to, behind, below, beyond, farther, here, nearby, next to, opposite to, to the left, to the right
For Showing Results or Conclusions	as a result, consequently, finally, hence, in conclusion, so, then, therefore, thus
For Showing Examples	chiefly, especially, first of all, for example, for instance, for one thing, in general, mainly, namely, particularly, specifically

What is missing from the following paragraph?

A term paper in physics submitted at Princeton University in the 1970s brought its author nationwide publicity. There was nothing extraordinary about the methods or sources John Aristotle Phillips used. He startled the public by proving that he could design his own atomic bomb. He had access to some books on physics and nuclear technology. He could not use any secret government material. His project showed that an ordinary undergraduate could design a nuclear bomb by using only information available to the public. He had to spend many hours studying these books. His project did not require special expertise or original discoveries. The extra information he needed was also available to the public. He bought some copies of documents in Washington, D.C. He telephoned the DuPont Company about explosives. He had no secret information. He worked on the project several months. He finished his research. He submitted a workable plan for an atomic bomb. He earned an A for the project. The government kept the paper as a classified document.

The paragraph does not read smoothly because there are no transitional words in it. Sometimes you have to pause and figure out the connection between one sentence and the next. Now read the same paragraph with transitional words included:

A term paper in physics submitted at Princeton University in the 1970s brought its author nationwide publicity. *Although* there was nothing extraordinary about the methods or sources John Aristotle Phillips used, he startled the public by proving that he could design his own atomic bomb. He had access to some books on physics and nuclear technology, *but* he could not use any secret governmental material. *Therefore,* his project showed that an ordinary undergraduate could design a nuclear bomb by using only information available to the public. *Even though* he had to spend many hours studying these books, his project did not require special expertise or original discoveries. *Furthermore,* the extra information he needed was also available to the public. *For instance,* he bought some copies of documents in Washington, D.C., *and* he telephoned the DuPont Company about explosives, *but* he had no secret information. *After* working on the project several months, he finished his research *and* submitted a workable plan for an atomic bomb. He earned an A for the project, *but* the government *later* kept the paper as a classified document.*

EXERCISE I: TRANSITIONAL EXPRESSIONS

Circle the transitional words in the following paragraph. First look back at the list to remind yourself what they are.

Fiction in the media can occasionally be too realistic. For example, a radio drama called *The War of the Worlds* produced by Orson Welles in 1938 scared

*Information from John A. Phillips and David Michaels, MUSHROOM: *The Story of the A Bomb Kid*. Reprinted by permission of William Morrow & Co., Inc. Copyright © 1978 by John Aristotle Phillips.

thousands of listeners into believing the world was coming to an end. In fact, some started to evacuate the cities and even planned suicide. The first thing that made the show realistic was that many people tuned in late and assumed it was a news report. What further added to the effect was that most of the drama was presented in unusually effective broadcast style. In addition, Orson Welles gave it unique realistic touches; for instance, he copied the fumbling and vomiting of the announcer who witnessed the explosion of the Hindenberg blimp. As a result, many listeners believed that the Martians were actually landing in New Jersey. Furthermore, many were carried away by the emotional excitement of the battles and disasters that followed. Although many listeners knew it was just a radio play, so many people across the continent were taken in by its realism that reports of suicides, traffic accidents, and stampeding crowds began occurring everywhere. Consequently, the program brought many threats of lawsuits; in fact, nearly a million dollars in damages was sought in actions against the network. None of the claims, however, could be backed up, so the network did not have to pay anything. Still they did settle one claim: a man who had spent his shoe money trying to escape the disaster received a new pair of shoes from the radio station.*

EXERCISE II: TRANSITIONAL EXPRESSIONS

In the next paragraph, supply missing transitional words from the list below. Be sure that the words you write in the blanks make sense.

although	in addition
also	in fact
but	nevertheless
for instance	soon
however	while

Did Karen Silkwood die in an accident, or was she murdered? Some

incidents make us suspicious of coverups by people in high places. The

Karen Silkwood case, _____, makes an open-minded person

suspect organized foul play. _____ _____, it makes

us worry about companies hiding the truth about nuclear hazards. Karen

Silkwood was an employee at a plutonium factory in Oklahoma. She was

_____ a union leader, a fact that made her unpopular with

---

*Information from John Houseman, *Run-Through*. New York: Simon & Schuster, 1971.

the company's management. What got her into a dangerous situation, _____, was that she began finding serious radiation hazards that endangered the workers' health. _____

_____ she discovered many violations of government regulations and even learned that forty pounds of plutonium was missing from the plant and unaccounted for. She began collecting evidence in secret, intending to present it to the newspapers. Unfortunately, _____ she was on her way to a motel to meet a representative of the *New York Times*, her car ran off the road, hit the wall of a culvert, and was smashed, killing her instantly. Her friends and supporters believed she had been run off the road by another vehicle. _____ no one could prove that she had been murdered, a court case in 1979, five years after her death, ended in the company having to pay a half million dollars in damages to her estate and ten million in penalties.*

EXERCISE III: TRANSITIONAL EXPRESSIONS

Use words from this list to make transitions in the statements below. Be sure to use the logically correct words.

and	moreover
after	nevertheless
although	on the other hand
besides	soon
but	therefore
consequently	then
however	while
meanwhile	

---

*Facts from Howard Kohn, *Who Killed Karen Silkwood?* New York: Summit Books, 1981.

1. The film is supposed to be hilarious. _____ I don't think we will have time to see it this afternoon.

2. In the early stages of the relationship with a client, the social worker should mainly try to discover all the facts. _____ she should begin identifying the sources of the family's problems.

3. _____ many attempts at achieving arms control talks had failed, the President arranged another meeting with the Soviet Premier.

4. Several passersby rushed to help the injured driver of the bus. _____ a stationery store owner called for an ambulance.

5. _____ the computer made funny noises, Yvonne waited impatiently for the record of her transcript to appear on the screen.

6. Joseph waited for two taxis to speed past. _____ a truck and a van had gone by in the other direction, he headed across the busy intersection.

7. The Olympics have always been influenced by politics, _____ only recently have boycotts by major countries occurred.

8. No one in the neighborhood owns a Rolls Royce. _____ it was surprising to see one parked next to the Erwins' driveway.

9. Cigarettes are harmful to your lungs and throat. _____, they are expensive.

10. Silent films developed into a unique art form with special methods and effects. _____, they lasted only a few decades.

EXERCISE IV: TRANSITIONAL EXPRESSIONS

Rewrite the following paragraph, making it read more smoothly by including transitional expressions from the following list:

also	however
although	in fact
and	instead
as well	nevertheless
but	nowadays
even	since
for instance	while

Whales are mysterious communicators. They do not smell and cannot see well. They depend on sound in many ways. They locate prey and determine their location through sound. They communicate with each other by means of songs. These are patterns of sound that change pitch like human music. When speeded up, some of the songs resemble certain familiar melodies. Folksinger Judy Collins did an album in which she sang duets with whales. These songs used to carry for thousands of miles. Whales communicated around the globe through their songs. Their songs are interrupted by the noise of ships' engines. Technology has given human beings instant communication around the earth. It has broken up global exchanges among whales. Whale songs seem to possess meaning like a sort of language. No one has been able to decode these sounds into human meaning. Much research has been done on whale songs. Much mystery remains to be unveiled about them.

WRITING ASSIGNMENT: TRANSITIONAL EXPRESSIONS

Write a paragraph on one of the following topics. Remember to develop your topic, use transitional expressions, and keep your ideas in order.

1. The career of a famous person who interests you. Remember to make the statements follow the sequence of important events in the person's career, and use words referring to time (*first, soon after, next, finally,* etc.) to hold the paragraph together.

2. A favorite possession. Use connecting words to show relationships between your statements; words of time (*when, first, later*) to tell about how you acquired it, words of cause and effect (*because, therefore*) to tell why you value it, and words of position (*on top, inside, on the left, underneath*) to describe what it looks like.

3. A goal you have set for yourself. Use transitional words of cause and effect (*because, therefore*) to tell why you are aiming for that goal, and use words of addition (*and, also, besides, in addition*) to explain the satisfactions this goal will bring you.

4. A place you would like to be right now. Use words of position (*nearby, right, left, on top*) to describe and identify the place, and use cause and effect words (*because, therefore*) to tell why you would like to be there.

Paragraph Development

Although well-developed paragraphs are usually longer than poorly developed ones, **paragraph development** does not depend on length. A long paragraph that wanders off the topic or is repetitious, for instance, is not well developed. Development means supporting the main point with examples, quotations, explanations, facts, statistics, descriptive details, and ideas. There are many kinds of paragraph development, as you will see in the next section of this unit. Some of them may come easily to you; others may require more practice. Some writers, for example, find it easy to write about personal experiences but difficult to write about ideas and social issues. Others are just the opposite: they analyze issues easily but have trouble putting in interesting details when they write about personal experience. Becoming an effective writer means building on your strengths and working on your weaknesses. While you may enjoy one kind of writing because it comes easily to you, you should not neglect the kinds that are more work for you. Most kinds of writing prove interesting once you acquire a little proficiency.

The first step is to develop the habit of supporting all topic sentences adequately and with interesting details and ideas. Some inexperienced writers give the impression of being lazy simply because they do not realize how much supporting material they need to put into their paragraphs. Be ambitious: do not underestimate. Most beginning writers produce paragraphs that are underdeveloped, not overdeveloped. Here, for instance is the rough draft of a paragraph that gives only a sketchy idea of the topic:

> The rock group *Kiss* gained popularity partly through its weird live performances. The people in it had a strange appearance because of their unusual faces and costumes. The total effect was uncanny.

Although this paragraph stays on the topic, it does not say much about it. A reader is likely to feel cheated and to want more details. In this revised draft there is plenty of interesting detail:

> The rock group *Kiss* gained popularity partly through its weird live performances. The members wore long frizzly wigs, jump suits, dragon boots with high heels, and psychedelic face makeup. Towering Gene Simmons would have blood dripping from his Dracula mouth, and fire would shoot out of the mouth of drummer Peter Criss. *Kiss* performed music in an atmosphere of horror and insanity that caused audiences to walk out on its first appearances in 1973, but soon the public became fascinated by the effect. Fans began to pack *Kiss* concerts and buy millions of its albums. Other rock groups were forced to provide more excitement on stage if they wanted to please their fans and compete with *Kiss*.

Often you can tell whether your paragraphs are developed enough by reading your work aloud to other students. Remember that in the prewriting activities in Unit 1 you were advised to get feedback from classmates after they listened to you read your work aloud. One of the main kinds of help they can give you is to tell you what they want to hear more about. Remember that a topic sentence is a sort of promise: it tells the reader what to expect in the paragraph. Your job as a writer is to produce these details that will fulfill the promise made by the topic sentence, and to make these details interesting.

How much development is enough? There are no rules to tell you this. Every paragraph is different, and every paragraph is part of a larger piece of writing with its own purposes. The topic sentence and the curiosity of the reader partly determine how much detail you should put into the paragraph. The purpose of each paragraph within the whole essay sometimes affects paragraph development as well. Keeping these things in mind, remember that in this unit you are trying to master the skill of writing effective paragraphs of a normal length, about seven to twelve sentences. Because that is not a long piece of writing, you need to condense as much vivid detail and fresh thinking into each paragraph as you can.

EXERCISE: PARAGRAPH DEVELOPMENT

The following paragraph stays on the topic but the statements are broad and not supported by examples. Rewrite the paragraph, developing it by adding interesting details from your own experience.

Sample paragraph (undeveloped):

> My clothes reflect my personality. When I am in informal situations, I wear casual clothes that suit my taste. When I dress for action, I wear whatever seems attractive and comfortable for doing my favorite activities. When I want to dress up, I put on clothes that give me the look I want on the job or at social occasions.

WRITING ACTIVITY I: PARAGRAPH DEVELOPMENT

Study the picture on the next page. First list as many items as you can identify. Then group the items into three or four categories. Next write an exploratory draft beginning with the topic sentence, "This shop window contains several kinds of groceries." Once you have completed the draft, look it over to see if you have achieved a smooth flow of language from one sentence to the next. Make any revisions needed, and correct any errors. Write a final draft.

WRITING ACTIVITY II: PARAGRAPH DEVELOPMENT

For additional practice in paragraph development, choose topics from the list that follows. Before composing each paragraph, do whatever kind of prewriting activity works best for you—focused writing, brainstorming, clustering, and so on. Look over your prewriting and find a sentence that states

a significant idea about the topic. Begin the paragraph with this statement as your topic sentence. Be sure to include plenty of supporting details.

1. The worst job you ever had
2. The craziest thing you ever did
3. The worst class you ever attended
4. The best movie you ever saw
5. The biggest challenge you ever faced
6. The most generous thing you ever did
7. Your favorite way to deal with problems
8. A lesson you learned by making a mistake
9. An older person you admire
10. The skill you perform best
11. The accomplishment you are most proud of
12. Where you want to live after college

TYPES OF PARAGRAPHS

Different kinds of writing require different kinds of paragraphs. If the purpose of an essay is to tell about an event, we call it a **narrative**. If its purpose is to create an impression of a person, place, or object, we call it a **descriptive** essay. If it is intended to show similarities or differences between two persons, things, or experiences, we call it **comparative**. If it is meant to help us understand how something happens or how something works, we call it **explanatory** or **expository**. If it is an attempt to convince us of an opinion, we call it **persuasive** or **argumentative**. These classifications of writing are sometimes called **modes**. Most essays fit roughly into one of these modes, but most also contain elements of other modes. When you compose whole essays, and especially when you do exploratory drafts to discover your ideas about a topic, you will often be combining writing modes.

These modes, then, are only convenient classifications that can help in writing practice. They are not like separate species that breed and develop independently of each other. They are more like single skills within a sport, which can be learned and practiced separately but must be combined during actual play. You can practice your forehand, backhand, net game, and serve separately, but when you play tennis you have to use them all. The paragraph practice you will do in this unit is divided for convenience into separate modes, but remember that this is only practice. Creating whole essays, from prewriting exercises to rough draft to revision to final draft, requires many skills. Development of paragraphs is just one of these skills.

Narration: Telling About an Event*

Telling about personal experiences or events that happened to other people is called **narrative writing**. Many short stories, novels, and history books are in this form. In narrative writing, paragraphs tell parts of a larger story and are written in time sequence. A narrative paragraph should (1) have enough details to give the reader a close-up of the events, (2) contain enough transitional expressions to help the reader follow the sequence of actions, and (3) be written in one tense, usually the past tense since the paragraph is usually about actions taking place in the past. Narrative paragraphs may seem the easiest kind to write, but for them to be good you may have to do quite a bit of revision. Try to include well-chosen words and interesting details, and be sure your sentences progress smoothly from beginning to end.

Here is a rough draft of a narrative paragraph written by a student:

> First impressions can sometimes mislead you. Not very long ago I met a guy who impressed me a lot. He seem to be a real cool guy, he asked me out to dinner at a expensive restaurant. Was I angry when he left me with the check after we ate the highest priced dinner on the menu. He said he had to go to the men's room and never came back. Boy, was I furious. I just got my paycheck and had to spend a big chunk of it paying the bill. I'll never go out with a guy like him again!

This student had an interesting story to tell, but she didn't arrange her facts effectively and, as you can see, she made some writing errors. The paragraph needed rearranging, developing, and correcting. Here is her revision:

———————————

*See verb tenses in Unit 5.

First impressions can sometimes mislead you. Last October I met Richard, who impressed me with his sense of humor and warm, caring manner. Although he was very sophisticated, he also showed mature concern for his aging mother and his younger sister. Of course I was excited when he asked me out to an expensive French restaurant for dinner. The date was perfect at first; we carried on wonderful conversation about our favorite films and singers, and he insisted that I order the highest price à la carte items on the menu. I was even beginning to think he was being too generous when he ordered a raspberry tart for my dessert and excused himself to visit the men's room. I waited for ten minutes. My raspberry tart came but my date did not. He disappeared and left me with a check for $87.

In telling about your own experiences, use the **first person** (*I, we*). In telling about an event that happened to someone else, use the **third person** (*she, he, it, they*). When you start a paragraph in the first person, stay in the first person; when you start in the third person, stay in the third person.* Choose one specific event and stick to it; a paragraph that tells about one limited action thoroughly is better than a paragraph that skims over a series of events. The sample paragraph that follows is written in the third person and concentrates on one man's specific goal in 1948:

Sample paragraph: narrative, third person

Preston Tucker tried to manufacture a dream car in the late 1940s but failed because he was ahead of his time. He hoped to see a low, modern-looking automobile with a one-piece windshield, an aluminum air-cooled engine, and safety features such as a collapsing steering column and a third headlight that turned with the wheels. He collected $25 million by selling stock and franchises, and he bought a huge war plant in Chicago to use as his factory. He worked hard to gain support and publicity, but he ran into difficulties with government agencies as well as newspaper columnists who claimed he was a fake. Furthermore, some of his new ideas could not be carried out with the technology of those days. After building only about fifty Tucker cars, he had to close his plant. Today, the Tucker cars still in existence are rare collectors' items.

WRITING ASSIGNMENT I: NARRATIVE PARAGRAPHS

Start with a focused writing exercise in which you write everything that comes to mind about an incident that happened to you in the last week or two—recent enough for you to remember details and specific remarks. Write at least a full page without stopping; you want plenty of material so that you can select the most effective details. Read over your focused writing and think of a topic statement that sums up the meaning of the experience. Now write an exploratory paragraph beginning with the topic sentence and including only the most relevant and interesting material from your focused writing. Read your exploratory draft carefully for errors; if you can, read it aloud to someone else to get feedback on how to improve it. Write a final draft.

---

*See shifts of person in Unit 5.

WRITING ASSIGNMENT II: NARRATIVE PARAGRAPHS

Write a paragraph telling how a person you know (either a friend or a famous person) tried to achieve a specific goal and either succeeded or failed. Include only the facts related to his or her goal. Do not try to tell a whole life story. Notice that in the paragraph about Preston Tucker there are no details about his personal life, training, or experience after 1948. Stay on the specific topic.

Description: Telling About Persons, Places, and Objects*

Three Rules for Writing Good Descriptive Paragraphs
1. Limit your subject.
2. Include concrete details.
3. Arrange your sentences in a spatial sequence.

Rule 1: Limit Your Subject. A descriptive paragraph can be about a large or small subject. If you want to describe the subject thoroughly, you must choose a very small subject. If you want to describe a large subject, you must concentrate on one of its characteristics. Either way, you must limit your topic. Here are some examples of limiting a large subject by choosing a physical characteristic:

Large Subject	*Reduced Subject*
My sister	My sister's face
My favorite city	The business district in my favorite city
My favorite building	The entrance to my favorite building

Another way to limit is to select one characteristic of the subject rather than a physical part of it. The three large subjects could thus be limited in this way:

- My sister's taste in clothes
- The traffic problem in my favorite city
- The efficient use of space in my favorite building

*Review adjectives and adverbs in Unit 5.

EXERCISE: LIMITING DESCRIPTIVE TOPICS

Limit these topics in two ways—first by choosing a physical characteristic of the subject; second by selecting another characteristic.

General Subject	Physical Characteristic	Other Characteristic
Example: San Francisco	*Golden Gate Park*	*San Francisco's climate*
Rolls-Royce		
Miami		
Oprah Winfrey		
Puerto Rico		
Disney World		

Rule 2: Include Concrete Details.   As we have seen, not all description is physical, but descriptive paragraphs almost always include some physical details. Most effective description is rich in details that appeal to the five senses. Don't forget that you can describe not only what you see, but also what you taste, feel, smell, and hear. Read the following paragraph and find words that create sense impressions. Identify the sense that each word appeals to—touch, sight, hearing, taste, or smell.

Sample paragraph:

> Thanksgiving at my grandparents' house was always a delicious, uproarious occasion. When we arrived, the house was filled with the aroma of turkey, mincemeat pies, and home-baked breads wafting from the oven. The shrieks of rowdy children tumbling over one another echoed through the downstairs rooms, and the bellow of a basset hound rang from the back steps. The antique armchairs and sofa were positioned with exquisite care, and the living room sparkled from hours of dusting, sweeping, and scrubbing. A familiar candelabra on the mantel added an extra light and warmth to the crackling fire in the fireplace. The dinner itself was a high point of the year, with bubbling conversation and laughter that never subsided long, with teasing of shy children by good-natured uncles, and the endless family gossip. The Thanksgiving turkey seemed more tender and juicy every year, and a child could wallow in mounds of mashed potatoes with huge dollops of gravy. Homegrown beans and peas, canned since the summer, along with tart cranberry sauce, filled stomachs so full that the hot dessert pies sat cooling on plates while youngsters poked half-heartedly at them.

Think of description as a way of sharing a whole experience with the reader. Don't hold back on the details; remember that the reader doesn't know anything about the experience until you share it with him or her. Choose specific words instead of vague or general ones. Compare the two versions of the following paragraph, noticing how the general words in the first version have been replaced by specific, vivid ones in the second.

Original paragraph:

> After the party the room was a mess. The *furniture* was in *disorder*, and the *walls* and *floor* were *messed up. Party decorations* were lying *all around*. Some people had even left *clothing here and there. In some places* you could still see *food and drink* that hadn't been cleaned up.

Revised paragraph, details added:

> After the party the room was a mess. *Two overturned chairs* huddled in a corner, one with both *back legs* broken off. The *ivory couch*, decorated with *crimson blotches* of spilled punch, protruded at a strange angle into the center of the room. *Hand prints* and *graffiti* in green, red, and yellow crayon had defaced the *elegant wallpaper*, and the *beige carpet* was beautified by three enormous *pink stains. Rainbow-colored streamers* hung limply from the ceiling; and *paper hats* and *horns* covered the *floor, the table, and the television set.* Several *gloves* had been left on the *armchair*, and a *knit cap* and *scarf* lay under the coffee table. Half-emptied *paper cups*, along with plates with remnants of *hors d'oeuvres* and *sandwiches*, had been abandoned on *bookshelves, end tables, and stereo speakers.*

The more detailed paragraph is much longer, of course. As soon as you begin including descriptive details, you will find that your paragraphs will become better developed.

WRITING ASSIGNMENT: DETAILS IN DESCRIPTIVE PARAGRAPHS

Write a paragraph describing a holiday at your home or the home of a relative. Include details that arouse at least three of the five senses. After you have finished, go back and find the words that convey sense impressions, and write which senses they refer to.

EXERCISE: DETAILS IN DESCRIPTIVE PARAGRAPHS

The words in the following list are general and not very descriptive. In the blanks to the right, write specific substitutes for them—words that create sense impressions.

Example:

a large animal   *a rhinoceros*

1. a small building   _____

2. a tall plant   _____

3. things to eat   _____

4. loud sounds   _____

5. a large vehicle   _____

6. bright colors   _____

7. something to wear   _____

8. an interesting profession _____

9. pleasant entertainment   _____

10. an office machine   _____

Rule 3: Arrange Your Sentences in Spatial Sequence.* You have already practiced achieving coherence in your paragraphs using spatial sequence. In most descriptive paragraphs the details should be arranged in an order that follows some physical direction—inside to outside, far to near, top to bottom, and so on. Read the next paragraph and identify what kind of spatial sequence its sentences follow.

> The Duesenberg car of the 1930s was truly elite, both inside and out. Its engine was one of the most powerful of its time, a straight eight-cylinder, 420-cubic inch giant that delivered over three-hundred horsepower. On some models it could accelerate the car from a standstill to 100 miles per hour in seventeen seconds; lighter models could eventually reach 130 miles per hour. Special bearings, springs, and connecting rods enabled the engine to maintain exceptional speeds. The exterior was equally superior, with a wide, low look to its long body. The hood took up nearly half the length, giving it a racing car appearance but with the elegance of the most expensive touring cars. It had fine touches, like wire wheels, and was built on a chassis with a 142.5-inch wheelbase. The chassis alone cost over ten thousand dollars—in the 1930s! It's no wonder that for many years after this, when they saw anything outstanding, people would say, "It's a Doozie!"†

As you probably could tell, this paragraph is arranged on an inside/outside scheme—first a description of what was under the hood, then a description of the car's exterior.

---

*See the discussion of spatial sequence in this unit.
†Facts from Jan P. Norbye, *The 100 Greatest American Cars*. Blue Ridge Summit, Pa.: TAB Books, 1981.

Many other kinds of spatial sequence are possible. Your description could follow the eye's movement in some way—from left to right, bottom to top, and so on. Here is a paragraph describing a circus. In what direction does the eye travel?

In the ring to the right, a troop of clowns were carrying on their hilarious battle with a Volkswagen Beetle that seemed to run by itself. The Beetle chased the clowns around the ring, forward and back, backfiring like a cannon at every turn. In the center ring, four elephants were being led through their balancing act by the trainer while the ringmaster watched from the side. The ring to the left displayed a family of tumblers doing somersaults and leaping onto one another's shoulders from a seesaw. And at a frightening altitude overhead, acrobats were executing heart-stopping turns and twists in midair without the safety of a net.

EXERCISE: SPATIAL SEQUENCE IN DESCRIPTIVE PARAGRAPHS

In the following paragraph, the sentences are not in the right order. Read the paragraph as it is. Then renumber the sentences so that they follow an outside/inside order.

(1) Continuing to the living room, we discovered bare wood benches and chairs separated by piles of dusty pamphlets. (2) On proceeding up the front walk, we saw further homey touches such as the porch swing and the newspaper rack by the screen door. (3) Just as bare was the dining room, which contained neither table nor chairs, but only a large altar and one church pew. (4) From the street, the house where the religious cult lived looked like a normal suburban home. (5) The rest of the downstairs was as empty as if the owners had just moved out. (6) We first noticed the manicured look of the lawn and shrubbery and the fresh, clean appearance of the red bricks and white shutters. (7) Most intruders by this time would want to escape anyway. (8) Only on entering could we tell that the house was inhabited by a group of strange people. (9) Although we thought we could hear chanting voices and footsteps upstairs, it was impossible to see what was happening since the door to the stairway was locked. (10) The entrance hall was painted reddish purple, and a stained glass portrait of Satan stared at the entering visitor.

WRITING ASSIGNMENT: SPATIAL SEQUENCE IN DESCRIPTIVE PARAGRAPHS

Think of a place that is familiar to you, such as a bus or train station, a courtroom, a classroom, a shopping mall, a church or synagogue, a supermarket, or a video arcade. Visualize the scene in your memory as specifically as you can, and brainstorm, making a list of all the descriptive details you can remember. Arrange the items in two or three spatial categories, such as front, middle, back, or left, middle, right. Then write an exploratory draft, remembering to begin with a topic sentence in which a key word or phrase identifies the overall quality of the place. Read over your draft to find gaps that need transitional expressions. Make any improvements in word choice or grammar that are needed. Write a final draft. Remember to include sensory details.

EXTRA WRITING ACTIVITY: DESCRIPTIVE PARAGRAPHS

Choose one of the photographs on this or the next page. Imagine that you are the person in the picture and write a paragraph expressing the thoughts and

feelings that you imagine yourself experiencing as you inhabit that person's body. Use the first person (I think, I feel, and so on) to express these feelings.

Next, give the person an imaginary name, and write a paragraph in the third person (Betty looks, Sam is talking), describing the person from the outside, how he or she looks, how he or she is positioned in the picture, and what he or she is probably thinking. (Remember to watch your *s* endings on verbs with a singular, third person subject: she look*s*.)

Comparative Paragraphs*

Comparing people, objects, places, experiences, or ideas is an important writing exercise. Although few articles or essays do nothing but compare, the ability to make clear, thought-provoking comparisons is a skill every experienced writer needs. Practicing writing comparative paragraphs will develop both your powers of discussing a topic in paragraph form and your ability to think clearly.

Categories of Comparisons	
Parallels:	Pointing out the similarities between two people or things
Contrasts:	Pointing out the differences between two people or things
Comparison/contrast:	Pointing out both similarities and differences between two people or things

When you compare, be sure to discuss both subjects together. Begin your paragraph with a topic sentence that mentions *both* persons or things, not just one. This way you will avoid the trap of discussing one, then the other, and leaving the reader to figure out how the subjects are similar or different. Which of these two sentences makes a better beginning for a comparison?

1. Ballet requires more stamina than basketball.
2. Ballet makes enormous demands on the body.

Either sentence might make a good topic sentence, but only the first sentence starts off with a comparison. We could expect the paragraph to discuss the demands of ballet *and* basketball.

---

*See adjectives and adverbs in comparisons in Unit 5.

EXERCISE I: COMPARATIVE PARAGRAPHS

Choose the three sentences in the group below that would make good topic statements for comparative paragraphs.

1. Some people like snakes as pets.
2. Poodles are easier to train than dalmatians.
3. Last summer was unusually hot.
4. My brother is less reliable than I am.
5. Knowing Spanish is more useful in business than knowing Latin.
6. Students begin algebra in the ninth grade.

Attention to Detail.   One important skill necessary in making good comparisons is the ability to *notice* many detailed similarities and differences. When beginning writers do not succeed in their efforts to compare, they often have not done enough brainstorming. They have found only a few similarities or differences and then given up. For practice, let's consider the similarities and differences between high school and college discovered by an imaginary student named Stanley. If Stanley really brainstormed, he might think of not two or three points of comparison, but many.

Stanley's Experience of High School vs. College

Similarities	*Differences*
many required courses in both	more elective courses in college
extracurricular activities in both, especially athletics	less time for extracurricular activities in college
both are coeducational (boys and girls in both)	lived at home in high school; now live in an apartment near campus
held a job while going to high school and college	worked only on weekends in high school; work two evenings in college
much homework in both	more homework in college; not much time anymore for social life
active social life in both	
liked science and math best in both	more specialized chemistry courses in college
both last four years	lost election in high school; just became vice president of sophomore class in college
both in Colorado	
ran for student government in both	high school was all in one building; college campus has seventeen buildings at two locations
both had modern buildings and good gymnasium	

EXERCISE II: COMPARATIVE PARAGRAPHS

For practice, make a list of the similarities and differences between your own life as a college student and your life as a high school student. Then write a paragraph explaining why you like one of these situations better than the other. Be sure to begin with a comparative statement for your topic sentence.

Three Kinds of Comparison.   The following three paragraphs illustrate the three main kinds of comparison. The first discusses the similarities between two countries, the second contrasts the differences between two sisters, and the third explores both the similarities and the differences between two jobs a student held. Notice that the topic sentences are focused and that they all make comparative statements.

Paragraph 1: Two similar subjects

As island monarchies, Japan and Great Britain have much in common. Both are small in land area but heavily populated, and both rely on the sea for food and imports. Each has a huge capital city that has played a major role in world affairs, and each has been in the forefront of industrial development. Although the surrounding ocean has enabled both to remain culturally isolated during some periods in history, the nearness of the continent has been the source of many wars over the centuries. Both peoples, in fact, derive from their neighboring continents, and their languages have close ties to continental languages—Japanese to Chinese picture writing and English to German and French. Over the centuries both nations have presided over great empires, both of which have disintegrated.

Paragraph 2: Two different or contrasting subjects

My two sisters are so different in their attitude toward work that it is hard to believe they come from the same family. Jill has always been a workaholic, while Joy always wanted to have a good time. When they were little girls, Joy would be skinning her knees in rollerskate races and begging Dad for money to buy candy while Jill was earning Mom's approval for her help with cooking and cleaning. In school Jill studied diligently and brought home stacks of homework. Joy, on the other hand, discovered that school was a social whirl and considered high grades the sign of a boring personality. In high school she was the favorite cheerleader; Jill was president of the honor society. Although Joy dropped out of college after two months, she has joined a country music group and expects to have a career on television without needing any higher education. Jill, with an M.B.A. and piles of honors, is heading up the corporate ladder.

Paragraph 3: Two subjects that are both similar and different

My two jobs as coach of an amateur basketball team and as bartender required some of the same skills but offered different rewards. In both jobs I had to understand people and motivate them. The players needed cheering up when the team was losing, and customers at the bar told me their life stories, expecting me to be their psychoanalyst. Both jobs demanded cool control when tempers flared or fights broke out. Despite these similarities, the satisfactions from the two jobs were different. Besides the high pay, tending bar gave me the feeling that I had helped a few individuals and maybe given them a better outlook. Coaching, on the other hand, was volunteer work, but I received the satisfaction of inspiring teamwork and helping a whole group of kids grow together.

WRITING ASSIGNMENT: COMPARATIVE PARAGRAPHS

Think of two jobs you have had, two members of your family, two places you have lived, or two schools you have attended. Brainstorm to make two lists. On the left write down all the similarities between the two; on the right list the differences. Write an exploratory draft beginning with a comparative topic sentence, such as "My sister and I are alike in our personal habits but very different in our career goals." Look over your work and read it aloud to someone else for feedback. Make revisions and corrections. Write a final draft.

Explanatory Paragraphs*

Explaining how something happens or works is called **process analysis**. Explaining how to do something on the job is called **procedural writing**. Paragraphs of this kind follow a step-by-step plan and are not difficult to organize. However, they do demand great care: you have to be unusually clear and thorough. If you are explaining how to hook up a stereo set, for instance, you cannot make confusing statements or leave anything out; otherwise the set will not work. We are used to giving instructions aloud, with the aid of gestures, tone of voice, and feedback from the listener. A writer can't use these devices. A writer's words have to say it all; he or she has no second chance to discuss what the reader does not understand. All the necessary details have to be included, but unnecessary ones will clutter the explanation and make it harder to follow.

You also have to make sure that the reader can understand all of your terms. If you are writing for experts, you will use specialized terms; if you are writing for general readers, your vocabulary will be no more technical than necessary and you must explain the meaning of all technical terms the first time you use them. Remember your reader. You cannot write the same paragraph for general readers that you would for specialists.

The following paragraph is about how an ordinary gasoline engine works. Is it written for laypersons (nonspecialists) or expert mechanics?

---

*See shifts of person and use of pronouns in Unit 5.

The engine used in most cars is called an internal combustion engine, meaning that it burns fuel inside the cylinders. The gasoline is mixed with air in the carburetor; then the mixture is drawn into the cylinders (most cars now have four or six cylinders). As the piston rises in each cylinder, it compresses the air-fuel mixture, which is ignited by the spark plugs. The small explosion drives the piston down again. On its return, it forces exhaust gases from the cylinder. The piston goes through a four-stroke cycle: first, the intake stroke; next, the compression stroke; third, the power stroke; and last, the exhaust stroke. The up-and-down motion of the piston is converted to circular motion by the crankshaft, from which it is eventually transmitted to the axles and wheels.

Obviously, this paragraph is not written for experts, since it gives only introductory facts. However, the writer does assume that the reader has enough familiarity with engine parts to know what pistons and cylinders look like.

Here is another paragraph explaining a process. This one is about how a particular emotional illness develops. This paragraph covers a few major stages rather than many small steps.

Anorexia nervosa is an emotional illness that leads some people, most often adolescent girls, to starve themselves. It develops in stages, beginning with normal dieting, often by people who are not much overweight in the first place. Social isolation leads to an obsession with food, weight, and exercise. If not treated at the beginning, the condition worsens to a stage in which victims may lose twenty percent of their weight, look like skeletons, have lowered pulse rate and body temperature, lose their menstrual periods, and have thinning hair. Next, in the acute stage, they may develop delusions about their bodies, imagining they are fat when they are terribly underweight, and go through rituals of excessive exercise and limited food intake. They become secretive and sometimes go on huge binges of overeating, after which they vomit the food to keep from gaining weight. Finally, some go into the chronic, or long-lasting stage, in which they can remain socially isolated and unhealthy for years. Some can even starve themselves to death if not given intensive psychiatric help.*

EXERCISE I: ''HOW TO'' PARAGRAPHS

The diagram on the next page is extremely simple, isn't it? Write a paragraph describing it. Give your description to someone who has not seen the figure. See if that person can follow your instructions and produce a perfect copy. No coaching while the other person is drawing! Anything you want to say has to be in the paragraph. Not so easy, is it?

---

*Facts from Steven Levenkron, *Treating and Overcoming Anorexia Nervosa*. New York: Scribner's, 1983.

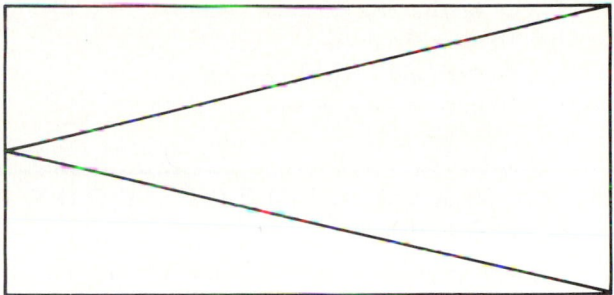

EXERCISE 11: "HOW TO" PARAGRAPHS

"How to" paragraphs should be held together by transitional words that refer to steps in a sequence, such as *first*, *next*, *then*, *after*, and *finally*. Underline the transitional words in this paragraph.

Doing your best on an essay examination requires a systematic approach. Before you do any writing, read the instructions and topics carefully so that you know how many topics you are to discuss and how much time you have for each. Next, choose your topic or topics according to your preparation and knowledge. Then, before actually writing, jot down the main parts of the essay and some of the important facts to support each main point. Only at this point are you ready to write. When you do write, be sure that your introductory paragraph includes a plan or "map" for your whole essay so that you and the grader will know just what you intend to cover. At last it is time to write the main body paragraphs and show how much you know about the subject. Be sure to include plenty of facts. If possible, end with a concluding paragraph that restates your chief ideas without repeating the words of the introduction. Finally, read your paper twice: once for errors in spelling, grammar, and phrasing, and once for revisions in content. If you have done all this, you may not earn an A, but you can feel confident that you have done your best.

WRITING ASSIGNMENT: "HOW TO" PARAGRAPHS

Choose one of the following topics and write a how to paragraph. Remember to begin with a concise, clear topic statement and to develop your discussion step by step, using transitional words.

1. How to meet people at parties
2. How to tune an engine
3. How to behave during a job interview
4. How to choose a college

5. How to feed a dog
6. How to stop smoking
7. How to plan a wedding reception
8. How to earn high grades

WRITING ASSIGNMENT: PROCESS PARAGRAPHS

Write a paragraph explaining how some machine or apparatus works, how some condition like alcoholism or drug addiction develops, how children learn a certain skill, or how students change when they go to college. Remember your reader: write for the general reader, not the specialist.

Persuasive Paragraphs*

Writing that explains why the reader should believe something or why society should do something is called **persuasive writing**. In this kind of writing you are trying to change someone's opinion or give reasons why the opinion is correct. Here are some places you will find persuasive writing and speaking outside the classroom:

• political speeches and debates
• advertisements on television and in magazines
• editorials in newspapers and editorial comments on television
• arguments in private life
• business reports that recommend new policies
• lawyers' speeches in court
• sales pitches in automobile showrooms and stores
• books that recommend changes in laws or public attitudes

These kinds of persuasive writing and talking can range from a few words to a whole book. In practicing persuasive writing, you will develop skills that come into play in other forms of spoken and written communication.

Every attempt at persuasion can be boiled down to one topic sentence. The speaker or writer argues that something *should* or *ought* to be done. Persuasive paragraphs frequently use words like *should, ought, might, must, have to, could, probably, likely, possibly, certainly,* and *undoubtedly.* Such words measure what the writer thinks should be changed in people's attitudes or actions. These words signal *why* relationships—causes, effects, and consequences. They link motives and reasons to actions. Learn to use them correctly in your own paragraphs.

Here are some *why* statements and *should* statements that could serve as topic sentences for persuasive paragraphs.

---

*See mixed sentences and pronouns and antecedents in Unit 5.

1. People who witness a mugging should call the police but should not intervene if the muggers are armed.
2. Students who major in computer programming ought to acquire typing skills.
3. Child abuse must be prevented if we are to have a future generation of healthy parents.
4. It might be better to use the popular vote count than the electoral system in electing a president.
5. Too much emphasis on athletics could damage the academic reputation of a college.
6. Elementary schools should provide activities for children until five o'clock so that working mothers do not have to get afternoon baby-sitters.

Rules for Persuasive Writing

Rule 1. *Be logical and fair.* Don't oversimplify or exaggerate. If you level with your readers, they will respect you and more likely be persuaded.

Rule 2. *Support your opinion.* You won't convince anyone if you just keep restating your opinion. You have to give facts, reasons, examples, testimony (other people's opinions), and personal experience to make a convincing case.

Rule 3. *Remember your readers.* They have the right to disagree and are not necessarily stupid if they do, so don't insult them. Consider the objections they might have to your position and try to answer these objections.

Which of these two statements seems more persuasive?

A. Richard does well in calculus because he comes from Texas.
B. Richard does well in calculus because he had excellent mathematics courses in high school.

Sentence A violates rule 1. It is not a logical statement; the writer imagines a cause-and-effect connection that does not exist. Sentence B is logical. Excellent high school math courses often do prepare students to do well in college math.

Which of these statements is more persuasive?

A. Women can never be good police officers; police work is not women's work.
B. Women can be effective police officers. Commissioners' reports from five major cities state that female officers have performed as well as male officers.

Sentence A violates rule 2. The claim is not supported. The writer states an opinion but does not back it up with evidence. Sentence B makes a claim, then backs it up with a fact. Sentence B is more persuasive. (This does not mean that everyone will *agree* with it without further discussion, only that it goes further than sentence A in discussing the opinion.)

Which of these statements do you find more persuasive?

A. Foreign cars are usually more expensive to repair than American cars, because the imported parts cost a lot.
B. Anyone who buys a foreign car is not only stupid but disloyal to the American way of life.

Sentence B violates rule 3. The writer insults readers who already own foreign cars but does not provide any real support for the opinion. Sentence A makes a more careful claim and backs it up. The writer avoids the impression of knowing everything and giving no one else the right to an opinion.

Which of the following two paragraphs seems to provide more evidence to support the topic statement?

Paragraph A:

The mall on Palm Boulevard is a convenient place to shop. Last weekend my mother and I spent four hours there. We bought a pair of slacks for each of us, a clock radio, and a quartz watch. Then we had a terrific pizza at one of the restaurants. Later we just browsed around, looking at the boutiques and antique shops. There is a lovely indoor fountain with an artificial waterfall, into which we threw pennies for good luck. Mother felt really energetic that day because she had been down with the flu and was excited about getting out and enjoying the crowds for a while. After two hours, though, she began to get tired and so did I, because there was so much to do.

Paragraph B:

The mall on Palm Boulevard is a convenient place to shop. The wide variety of stores allows for one-stop shopping. There are two enormous supermarkets, a half dozen drug stores, fifteen clothing stores of different kinds, three furniture outlets, four sporting goods stores, a high-quality department store, two stationery shops, and fifty-three smaller retail shops of all kinds, from boutiques to coin and stamp shops. Parking is no problem, with a large free parking lot at each end of the mall and a small one with meters near the middle entrance. Benches are located every two-hundred feet for the benefit of weary shoppers, and there is easy access to rest rooms. Customers who want to break for lunch have a choice of restaurants offering six different ethnic cuisines, and there are two fast food restaurants for those in a hurry. Mothers with small children can take advantage of an inexpensive child care service. And if you run short of money, four bank branches with twenty-four-hour cash machines allow you to continue shopping without leaving the mall. Nothing is missing that could make for easy, convenient shopping.

The two preceding paragraphs should show the difference between casually expressing an opinion and really backing it up with evidence. Paragraph A relies on personal experience more than factual evidence and even goes off the topic a little. It reads like a personal letter. A reader who does not know the writer personally wants to know the kinds of information given in paragraph B, not gossip about the writer's personal life. The kind of evidence you include, then, depends on the point you are making and the sort of reader you hope to persuade.

EXERCISE: PERSUASIVE STATEMENTS

Explain whether each of these sentences seems persuasive. If not, explain what is wrong with it.

1. Senator Sly cannot be trusted because he's a politician and all politicians are crooks.
2. You should get another doctor's opinion before having the operation, since it is major surgery and your doctor might be wrong.
3. It is always a mistake to get married young, because young people cannot cope with responsibility.
4. It would not be sensible to invest all of your money in a small business, since over ninety percent of small businesses fail.
5. The strange weather we've been having must be caused by the Russians; they are always trying to play dirty tricks on us with their satellites.
6. Governor Smiley would not make a good president because he looks too much like a television talk show host.
7. The film I saw last night was excellent: the acting was outstanding and the story held my interest.
8. The price you paid for that food processor was too high; it sells for ten dollars less in three other stores.
9. Sally must be smarter than Ellen because Sally went to a more expensive college.
10. I'll probably get a package in the mail tomorrow; it's supposed to rain tomorrow, and the last time I got a package it rained.

WRITING ASSIGNMENT: PERSUASIVE PARAGRAPHS

Read the following two case studies. Then choose one and write a paragraph explaining what you think the person or persons should do in this situation. Giving convincing evidence to show why you recommend a particular course of action.

Case 1:

Oscar is a high school senior with exceptional skill in basketball. He has had offers of full scholarships to a number of universities and has considered a career in law, though he is not sure yet what he wants to do in the long run. He has a B average and respectable but not outstanding College Board scores. Meanwhile, the New Jersey Nets have scouted him and have offered a three-year contract as a second-string forward at $150,000 a year right out of high school. What should Oscar do?

Case 2:

Sam and Barbara have two children, ages ten and twelve. Barbara's mother, who is 74, is having occasional health problems that make it unwise for her to continue living alone, although she is still active and alert most of the time. The cost of renting a larger apartment and having her move in with them would be about equal to that of placing her in a nursing home. Barbara's mother has not expressed an objection to either arrangement. What should Sam and Barbara do?

Definition Paragraphs*

Writing a paragraph defining a term means more than giving a dictionary definition. Instead, the writer really discusses the word—what it means and what it does not. More than that, the writer discusses the experience, relationship, object, or idea that the word refers to. Defining *love*, for instance, is a way of discussing how people relate to each other; defining *success* is a way of discussing what people try to achieve in our society. In a good definition the writer includes examples, humor, or analysis to show the reader what the human meaning of the word really is. Erich Fromm wrote a whole book defining love, for example. In *The Art of Loving*, he spent many pages examining the meaning of love, giving examples, explaining types of love, identifying the true characteristics of love, and telling the difference between real love and other feelings. That is an unusually long definition. In fact, whole essays that do nothing but define a term are rare. However, it is important for any writer to be able to define terms, and writing paragraphs defining terms for practice is an important exercise for anyone who wants to have college-level writing skills.

When you define a term, be careful not to make a circular statement. What is wrong with this definition?

Love is the feeling you have when you are very fond of someone.

This is a true statement, but it does not amount to much. This is almost like saying, "Love is the feeling of loving someone," or "Love is love." Think about the *real* meaning of the term, what it is and what it isn't, how you see it applied to real people and situations. Here is how Erich Fromm defined love. He identified four of love's necessary elements:

**See subject-verb agreement in Unit 5.

Beyond the element of giving, the active character of love becomes evident in the fact that it always implies certain basic elements, common to all forms of love. These are care, responsibility, respect, and knowledge.*

A definition usually places the term to be defined in a general category and then makes specific statements about its qualities or the things that it is made of.

Term	Category	Description or Parts
Love	Art	Care, responsibility respect, knowledge

Here we can see how Dr. Fromm defined love: he said it is an *art* to be learned, like music, painting, or writing; then he identified its four main characteristics. Someone else might have called it a *feeling* or a *relationship* instead and described its parts differently. Here are two other definitions of love:

1. Love is a feeling that makes a person want to be with someone else in order to share that person's feelings and experiences.
2. Love is a relationship between two people in which both of them want to help each other grow and enjoy life.

Are these definitions different from Dr. Fromm's or do they agree with his? Write a sentence of your own defining love. Here are some one-sentence definitions of other words. Underline the word or phrase that tells what category the term belongs in.

Example: A *shortstop* is a baseball player who stands between second and third base and catches ground balls and short fly balls.

1. A *soft sell* is a sales technique in which the salesperson uses tricky psychological methods to persuade the customer.
2. A *bomber* is a divorce lawyer who overpowers the exspouse's attorney and wins a lot of money for his client.
3. A *deadbeat* is a borrower who never pays back the money he or she owes to another person or company.
4. A *con artist* is a street person who tricks people into giving money by making up a story or investment scheme.

Definition paragraphs begin with one-sentence definitions and really discuss the characteristics or parts of the thing being defined. You can see how the definitions just given could easily become topic sentences for whole paragraphs. Each calls for examples or explanations to help the reader understand the term better. If we begin by defining *soft sell* as a sales technique in which the salesperson uses tricky psychological methods to persuade the customer, we would continue the paragraph by giving descriptions of some of these methods. We would tell how some salespeople flatter customers, pretend to

*Erich Fromm, *The Art of Loving*. New York: Harper & Row, 1956, p. 22.

agree with anything they say, or make them think their purchase will give them prestige.

Here is a paragraph written by the famous author of a book on baby and child care, Dr. Benjamin Spock. Read the paragraph carefully and underline the term that he is defining.

> Much more dangerous than the open antagonism of one individual toward another . . . is the readiness of a majority of human beings to mistrust or hate whole groups of people with whom we have little or no acquaintance. Psychiatrists call this displaced hostility. It is derived from the antagonism that was first built up in all of us in early childhood toward family members. As we grew a bit older we sensed that since we were utterly dependent on them we must stay on the right side of them. And increasingly our parents and other teachers made us feel deeply guilty about hating them. So we learned to displace. In early childhood we are apt, in our society, to fear and hate witches, ogres, kidnappers, and other fiends that we hear about and that appear in our bad dreams. By the time we are six or eight we are ready to pick up and carry into adulthood the prejudices of the family and neighborhood against groups of real people. The less we know them in actuality the more easily we can imagine them as evil and fear and despise them.*

Dr. Spock's paragraph defines the term *displaced hostility* by explaining the feeling many people have toward groups, races, or nations they consider their enemies. He tells how this feeling comes about as a result of our hostility toward family members in childhood and our redirecting this hostility toward people we don't even know.

EXERCISE: DEFINITIONS

Write one-line definitions for three of these terms:

punk	jock	robot
preppie	break dancing	elective course
superstar	neurotic	gridlock

WRITING ASSIGNMENT: DEFINITION PARAGRAPHS

Use your imagination to write a good definition of one of the following terms. Write a paragraph in which you discuss the meaning of the term by analyzing, giving examples, expressing feelings, using personal experience, or identifying the sources or parts of the idea. Remember, this is not a one-line dictionary definition, but a *discussion* of the term.

---

*From Benjamin Spock, *Decent and Indecent*. New York: Dutton Co., Saturday Review Press, 1969, p. 95.

art	heroism	love
beauty	intelligence	prejudice
courage	insanity	sophistication
friendship	liberated woman	success
happiness	marriage	wealth

Classification Paragraphs

A paragraph can break down a large subject into categories. Writing paragraphs in which you classify subjects is good practice in clear thinking as well as organized writing. Your categories should not overlap but should fit in the same group. Try the following exercises to sharpen your powers of classifying.

EXERCISE I: CLASSIFICATION PARAGRAPHS

Identify three main groups in which all the animals in the following list can be placed. List all of them under the appropriate headings.

bass	woodpecker	monkey
wolf	bear	wren
raccoon	horse	cow
mockingbird	canary	sparrow
trout	wildcat	ox
deer	goldfish	bison
parakeet	salmon	cod
carp	cardinal	catfish
fox	oriole	nightingale
pigeon	bluegill	antelope

EXERCISE II: CLASSIFICATION PARAGRAPHS

Under the main heading of *groceries*, choose headings for four categories of groceries as they are found in the supermarket; then list ten examples for each.

EXERCISE III: CLASSIFICATION PARAGRAPHS

Divide each of the following subjects into three categories—that is, identify three types of colleges, cars, and so on. Do not let the categories overlap.
    Example:
Colleges: 1. private four-year colleges   2. state universities   3. community colleges

Movies	Professors
Cars	Stores
College students	Television programs
Friends	Politicians
Investments	Vacations

WRITING ASSIGNMENT I: CLASSIFICATION PARAGRAPHS

Write a paragraph explaining the three main categories of one subject in the preceding list. Read the following sample paragraph first, noticing the use of transitional words and the clear separation of categories.

Sample paragraph:

There are three main kinds of addiction: dependency on chemical substances, on patterns of activity or behavior, and on people. Addiction of the first type is familiar to everyone in the form of drug addiction and alcoholism. However, it also includes dependency on such substances as tobacco, coffee, and sedatives. Addiction to patterns of behavior includes excessive television watching, playing video games, gambling, eating, exercising, and sleeping. The third form of dependency is the immature reliance on and need for another person or persons, as opposed to a productive relationship in which both partners gain and contribute out of free choice. What characterizes all forms of addiction is an inability to function well without the habit, along with a destructive effect on the person's life and social relationships.

This paragraph explains that there are three kinds of addiction, but that they have certain things in common. The purpose of dividing a subject into categories is to understand it better. In this case, we understand what makes addiction undesirable, even when the addiction is to a good thing, like a relationship or exercise. Sometimes we can only see something clearly when we identify its different types. In biology, we divide animals and plants into many categories by a system called **taxonomy**. Biologists can name what species, genus, family, and so on a particular animal or plant belongs to. Only by such a system is it really possible to understand living things, including human beings.

WRITING ASSIGNMENT II: CLASSIFICATION PARAGRAPHS

For fun, write a paragraph on one of the following topics, dividing people into three or four groups. Be a close observer, like a scientist studying a specimen.

Types of students   Types of automobile drivers
Types of mothers   Types of shoppers
Types of teachers   Types of boxers
Types of television watchers   Types of dentists
Types of friends   Types of dressers

Cause and Effect Paragraphs*

Often in college writing you will have to analyze the causes of something. You will have to explore how some situation in society or world affairs got to be the way it is. In social science courses especially you will study the origins of criminal behavior, inflation, wars, drug addiction, urban decay, problems in the schools, marriage customs, attitudes toward morality, and so on. To do such analyses well, you will have to study the subjects. However, you can practice paragraphs in which you explore the cause of such things by using information from newspaper reports, personal experiences, and what you have learned from parents and teachers. You can explore most issues intelligently without being an expert in sociology, history, criminology, or psychology. Good analysis, however, requires you to do more than simply express your opinion. You must support your opinion with clear reasoning, facts, experience, and examples.

In cause/effect analysis, good writing cannot be separated from clear thinking. Use your common sense and keep an open mind. Remember a few guidelines:

- Don't jump to conclusions. Do focused writing on your topic; brainstorm. Instead of settling for the first explanation that pops into your mind (usually the one that everyone automatically comes up with), test it. Could it be wrong? Could it be only one explanation among others?
- Don't oversimplify. Most important social problems and historical events have many origins. Consider indirect causes as well as direct causes. Remember that something that occurs after something else is not necessarily caused by it. Distinguish between a well-established fact and a controversial opinion.
- Avoid making scapegoats. When discussing the causes of a problem, try not to blame everything on the same old convenient villains. Television, for instance, is blamed for everything from poor school performance to violence in the streets and sex crimes. How do we know that it really is the cause? Could it be one of many causes? Is it the most important one?
- Do your homework. If you write an analytical paper for a specialized course such as sociology or history, back up your statements with facts from the assigned readings or research. The instructor is interested less in your personal *opinion* than in your *conclusions* based on an analysis of what you have read.

*See subordinate conjunctions and fragments in Unit 5.

The following paragraph has a topic sentence and stays on the topic by discussing one cause of crime. In what way, however, does it fail to make a reasonable analysis of the problem?

> Poverty is the cause of crime. Poor people steal because they can't get money any other way. How can the government expect to get rid of crime when there are so many people without jobs or a decent income to live on? The cost of living keeps going up for poor people, and they have to go out and commit crimes to pay the rent and put food on the table. All the government has to do to eliminate the crime problem is provide jobs and housing for the poor. It's the government's fault that the crime rate keeps rising. People who have decent housing, food, and clothing do not commit crimes.

After getting feedback from readers, this writer discovered that he needed to make revisions, since many readers disagreed with some of his points. He realized that he had oversimplified the problem and made a scapegoat of the government. Not that he was completely wrong; he simply had to focus his argument better and support it with better reasoning. Here is his revised paragraph:

> Poverty is often said to be the chief cause of crime. But the real cause cannot be poverty alone, since some very poor communities have little crime and since most poor people are not criminals. The greater problem is poverty in the midst of a rich society, a society in which crime has become a means of making quick money. Some people who become accustomed to a life of drug peddling, car stripping, or working for organized crime syndicates believe that they can rise out of poverty faster and farther through crime than by doing legitimate work. They look around and see many prosperous and some extremely rich people who did not necessarily work hard for their money, and they want to grab the easiest money they can get. Crime has become a major "career," with a nationwide annual income of more than $100 billion. As long as this situation continues, and as long as people born into poverty believe that crime offers a promising an "occupation" as anything else, the United States will continue to have an enormous amount of crime.

WRITING ASSIGNMENT: CAUSE AND EFFECT PARAGRAPHS

Do a page of focused writing on one of the topics from the list on pp. 79–80. Use this exercise simply to explore the range of your ideas on the subject—don't censor yourself. Look over your page and try to identify the precise cause or effect involved. Create a cluster in which you place the main cause (or effect, depending on the topic) in the middle and some secondary causes (effects) in the balloons around the middle. Then identify specific details associated with the secondary causes and write them in smaller balloons.

For example:

Once you have explored the topic in this way, write an exploratory draft of a paragraph beginning with a precise topic sentence. Develop the paragraph in climactic sequence, using reasonable arguments and whatever facts you have. Reread the paragraph and, if you can, get feedback from others by reading it aloud. Revise and correct; write a final draft.

Suggested topics:

1. Why did a particular performer, performing group, or athletic team succeed?
2. Why did a particular product or program catch on with the public?

3. Why is the divorce rate higher now than it was thirty years ago?
4. Why do a large percentage of students drop out of high school (or college)?
5. Why do many people continue to smoke even though they know it will harm their health?
6. Why do people use slang?
7. Why are there so many abortions even though birth control methods are widely available?
8. Why do many people feel unhappy during holidays?
9. What is the effect of television violence on children?
10. How has the women's movement changed young people's attitudes toward marriage?
11. How does being rich affect people's behavior?
12. How does a college education improve the quality of a person's life?
13. How does immigrating to the United States affect a person's attitudes?
14. How does American society benefit from having immigrants from many countries?
15. What effect does being unable to read have on a person's life?

3

WRITING SHORT ESSAYS

Now that you have developed the ability both to write continuously for a page or two and to

develop a specific point in paragraph form, you are ready to compose whole essays.

RECOGNIZING THE ESSAY

The **essay** is several pages of organized writing about one topic and on one main point about the topic. It can be very long, but the essays you will practice will be about five to eight paragraphs, or about five-hundred to twelve-hundred words. Every college student must be able to plan, compose, revise, and proofread such essays.

BUILDING ESSAYS OUT OF PARAGRAPHS

Paragraphs are the building blocks of essays. A successful essay contains the same elements as a good paragraph: *An essay should have a clear, limited main point; a logical arrangement; smooth, varied sentences; and correct spelling and grammar.* Like a paragraph, it should contain transitional words to signal relationships. It should have a recognizable beginning, middle, and end. However, it is not just a series of paragraphs strung together. The first paragraph makes a short introduction, the body paragraphs (there may be three, four, or five) discuss and illustrate separate supporting points, and the last paragraph briefly sums up and reaffirms the main point.

Here is a diagram of a two-page essay containing five paragraphs. This is a model you can use for many of your short essays. Notice its three main parts: the **introduction**, **body**, and **conclusion**.

ESSAY DIAGRAM

Title

First paragraph arouses interest and states main purpose of essay. (3–4 sentences)

Body paragraph #1 discusses first subtopic. (5–12 sentences)

Body paragraph #2 discusses second subtopic. (5–12 sentences)

1

Body paragraph #3 discusses third subtopic. (5–12 sentences)

Short concluding paragraph sums up main purpose. (3–4 sentences)

2

Study the following sample essay. It follows the five-paragraph diagram you just looked at, with an introduction, thesis statement, body, and conclusion. Answer the questions after the essay.

Sample Essay

Trivia Aren't So Trivial

Introduction

Thesis Statement

Many people think of fads as silly ways to waste time and money. This is true of some food and clothing crazes, but the explosion of interest in so-called trivia has some real benefits. *People who spend their time and money on trivia games and books learn a lot about science, history, and the media.*

Three Subtopics Named

Subtopic 1

You may not be able to earn a Ph.D. in nuclear physics by playing trivia games, but *you can pick up some interesting scientific knowledge.* Perhaps not everyone is fascinated to know that a caterpillar has six fully developed legs or that an expert on spiders is called an arachnologist. Maybe some people are not urgently waiting to learn that *robot* comes from a Czechoslovakian word for "work." Still, there are many interesting and useful facts to discover about nature. Did you know, for instance, that the eye is the fastest healing organ in your body? Or that yogurt may help some groups of people live longer? How many people are aware that kangaroos never drink water? Only trivia experts possess such treasures of scientific fact.

Examples of Subtopic 1

Subtopic 2

In the history department, knowledge of trivia makes you more aware of world events. Without the benefit of trivia, most people would have only vague ideas of famous people and events. Most people think that hundreds of women were burned in Salem, Massachusetts, as witches; the truth is that nineteen people were hanged and one pressed to death with stones, but none was burned. Some modern Catholics are not aware that at one time there were two popes, one in Rome and one in Avignon, France. And most Americans are surprised to learn that there were not one but three great civilizations in ancient Mexico—the Olmec, the Zapotec, and the Mayan. Another surprising fact is that at the time of the American Revolution, over eighty-five percent of the people who had come to the New World were Africans. Such bits of information make people

Examples of Subtopic 2

conscious that the real past was quite different from their picture of it.

Subtopic 3

> *Although many people think they know a lot about the media, trivia games can sharpen and broaden their knowledge in that area too.* Most trivia questions in

*Discussion of
Subtopic 3*

the categories of movies and television are much harder to answer than experienced viewers might expect, even though they are related to famous films, television stars, or series. While being an expert on such names and titles might appear to be useless, "useless" knowledge can keep people in touch with common feelings and experiences millions of Americans have enjoyed for half a century. Knowing the name of Ben Casey's hospital or Mr. Kotter's school won't be worth any money, but people who are curious about media facts usually make entertaining company and probably understand our society a little better than others.

*Summary of
Main Thesis*

> *In conclusion, it is obvious that people who dedicate their time to the study of trivia get a lot of enjoyment and educational value out of what they are doing.* Like most fads, books and games about trivia are sometimes silly, but they are not a waste of time.

*Concluding
Thought*

Even if trivial facts are not the same as a serious education they remind us how much we don't know and how different reality is from the way we imagine it. Trivia aren't so trivial!

1. In your own words, what is the main purpose of this essay? _____

   _____

2. What similarities are there between the introductory paragraph and the con-

   cluding paragraph? _____

   _____

3. What differences are there? _____

   _____

4. What method do paragraphs 2 and 3 use to develop their subtopics? _____

   _____

5. What method does paragraph 4 use to develop its subtopic? _____

   _____

6. List five transitional words or phrases that are used to signal connections

   between statements or paragraphs. _____

   _____

PRACTICING THESIS STATEMENTS*

The **thesis statement** is the sentence that explains the main purpose of the essay. Although it can be the first sentence in the essay, it usually follows a few lead-in sentences that arouse interest in the subject. *It often comes at the end of the first paragraph*. It may be just a short, simple statement of opinion, or it may divide the opinion into two, three, or four parts.

Simple thesis statement:
People who spend their time and money on trivia games and books learn a lot.

Developed thesis statement:
People who spend their time and money on trivia games and books learn a lot *about science, history, and the media*.

Although a simple thesis statement is often satisfactory, a developed thesis statement provides a map for the rest of the essay and thus guides the reader more. Science, history, and the media are the subtopics for the body paragraphs in the sample essay. The simple thesis statement in this case would not guide the reader as clearly; the reader would not recognize each subtopic until he or she got to it in the paragraph that discusses it.

Thesis Statements Must Be Broad

Thesis statements must be broad enough to state the whole purpose of the essay. Why would the following sentence not make a good thesis statement for the sample essay?

Trivia games are available in more than ten areas of knowledge.

This is a specific factual statement. It does not provide a main idea or purpose for the total essay.

---

*Since thesis statements often contain two or three items in a series, this is a good time to review parallelism, colons, and the use of commas in a series in Unit 5.

EXERCISE I: THESIS STATEMENTS

Identify which sentence in each pair might make a thesis statement for an essay:

1. A. Los Angeles had a severe water shortage in 1977.
   B. In the long run, California will have to find artificial sources of water to meet the needs of its expanding population.
2. A. The Tigers won the game 3 to 1.
   B. The game between the Tigers and the White Sox was full of suspense and unexpected reversals.
3. A. The current prison system lacks adequate means for rehabilitation and psychiatric counseling.
   B. The state prison at Capital City contains 1400 inmates.
4. A. Levels of alcohol in the blood can be tested by instruments.
   B. Drunken driving can be controlled better by strict enforcement than by new laws.
5. A. My vacation in Venezuela was wonderful, because I met some remarkable people and enjoyed delicious food.
   B. I visited Venezuela for two weeks in March 1989.

Thesis Statements Must Be Precise

Although thesis statements must be broad enough to state the essay's main purpose, they should never be fuzzy or confusing. Remember that catchall words like *bad, good, nice, great, interesting,* and *thing* are not precise. What is good to one person is bad to another; what one person finds interesting another finds tedious. Try to find more precise key words for your thesis statements. Compare these two thesis statements:

   A. *Return of the Goat People* is a bad film.
   B. *Return of the Goat People* is a noisy, violent film with stiff acting and overused camera techniques.

Sentence A does not guide the reader much. It says only that the writer is going to make negative remarks about the film. Sentence B states what kind of objections the writer is going to make to the film.

EXERCISE II: THESIS STATEMENTS

Rewrite these sentences to make them more precise thesis statements:
1. Harry had a good job this summer.

_____

2. The college I attend is a nice place.

_____

3. Working while going to college is a good idea.

_____

4. Vacation Inn is a bad motel.

_____

5. The neighborhood near the college campus is interesting.

_____

6. There are several things I don't like about marriage.

_____

EXERCISE III: THESIS STATEMENTS

Write precise, developed thesis statements for imaginary essays on these topics:

1. Teenagers and their parents
   Thesis statement: _____

   _____

2. Television watching
   Thesis statement: _____

   _____

3. College courses
   Thesis statement: _____

   _____

4. Choosing careers
   Thesis statement: _____

   _____

5. Children and divorce
   Thesis statement: _____

   _____

INTRODUCTORY PARAGRAPHS

The first paragraph in an essay serves several purposes. Its main purpose is to let the reader know what the essay is about, usually in the thesis statement. Most writers, however, find starting with the thesis statement too abrupt. Instead, they lead up to the thesis statement in various ways. The three-step design of lead-in, tie-in, and thesis statement is a useful device for beginning writers.

Starting with the Three-Step Design

Begin your paragraph with an effective **lead-in**. This attention-getter can be one of several types:

- A quotation or question
- A catchy remark
- A general, thought-provoking statement
- A surprising fact or statistic
- A problem or riddle

Be creative when you compose introductory paragraphs. Begin with a lively lead-in, to capture the reader's interest, then find a way to focus that interest on the subject. The two or three sentences in which you do this are your **tie-in**. Finally, move smoothly from your tie-in to your thesis statement. The three-step design—*lead-in, tie-in, thesis statement*—will help you begin your essays successfully. As you become more experienced, you will find other effective ways to arrange your introductions.

The paragraph that follows serves as an introduction to an essay on the subject of computer technology in the office. Notice how it follows the three-step design for introductory paragraphs.

Model introductory paragraph:

> "Future shock," a term from the title of a book by Alvin Toffler, means confusion caused by technological change. Nowhere is future shock more evident than in offices that have not kept up with recent advances in word and information processing. For the first time since the invention of the typewriter and the telephone, drastic changes in office procedures are occurring. Managers who hope to compete in today's business world must stay abreast of word processing software, electronic filing, and new methods of communication.

Organized paragraphs like this do not result from your first efforts to write on a subject. First you must do plenty of prewriting to identify your main purpose and supporting details. Then you will need to write a rough draft of your introductory paragraph, perhaps even two or three, before you compose your final version.

How NOT to Begin

If you try to compose an essay without any prewriting warm-ups, your introductory paragraph may have severe problems. For instance:

1. You may begin by apologizing for not knowing what to write:

In this essay I am supposed to write about the effect of computers. I don't own a computer and I'm not very good at word processing because I don't type very well. All I can say is that computers are very important and are here to stay. Every time I go into a magazine store, I see whole racks of magazines about computers. I wish I could understand everything they write about in those articles.

Compare this paragraph with the previous one about computers in the office. This one reads like a piece of focused writing; you can see the writer searching for something to say about the topic. The paragraph has no organization, no lead-in, and no thesis statement. Don't tell the reader what you don't know; explore what you *do* know through prewriting techniques until you find a good way to begin.

2. You may bore your reader by writing *too* much about what you are going to do in the essay:

I am going to discuss computers in this essay. First, I plan to talk about how important computers are in today's world. My next paragraph will be about how computers are used in the home. Then I will discuss how computers are used in different kinds of businesses. Finally, I will stress how important computers will be in the future.

This writer has a clear plan but calls too much attention to it. No customer in a restaurant wants the chef to bring out all the recipes, pots, pans, and soup spoons used in preparing the food. Your reader also does not want to know the planning details. Leave the homework at home.

3. You may begin with grand, overblown statements that fail to lead into your thesis or contain any specific meaning*:

Since the beginning of time mankind has invented new technological advances that have helped and hindered the progress of society toward perfection. In modern times of today, nothing has had a bigger impact on the way people live than one single invention: a machine called the computer. This machine will be remembered for all time.

EXERCISE: INTRODUCTORY PARAGRAPHS

Read the three sample paragraphs that follow. Identify the one that is carefully organized; find the *lead-in*, *tie-in*, and *thesis statement*. Explain why the other two would fail as introductory paragraphs.

Paragraph A:

Animals are one of the most important things on this earth. Animals have been around since human beings were created, and they come in millions of shapes and sizes. Most people could not live without animals, and many keep

---

*If you find yourself having difficulty with this problem, study the section on wordiness in Unit 4.

them for pets. If human beings ever get rid of the animals, it will be the worst crime in history. We should all be grateful for animals and learn all about them.

Paragraph B:

Do animals have rights? In the past, we have heard about human rights, civil rights, and women's rights, but now for the first time we have groups demonstrating to protect the rights of animals. Such groups may strike some people as eccentric or silly, since we kill millions of animals for food and we must sometimes perform experiments on animals to save human lives. But we should take seriously what the animal rights supporters are telling us: that other species have a right to exist and that we should stop unnecessary killing of animals and cruelty to them.

Paragraph C:

In this essay I am going to talk about the topic of animals. I once had a dog named Florence. It was sort of a poodle but it had big floppy ears. Otherwise, I haven't had much experience with pets, so I talked to my uncle about animals because he used to have a farm where he raised sheep and cows. He told me some funny stories about his animals that made me laugh out loud. Animals can be a lot more interesting than I realized, but I still don't know much about them.

WRITING ASSIGNMENT: INTRODUCTORY PARAGRAPHS

Practice writing an introductory paragraph. First choose an essay topic from the list below. Then create a thesis statement for the whole essay. Remember: an introductory paragraph usually does not begin with a topic sentence the way body paragraphs do. Instead it will contain the thesis statement for the whole essay at or near the end of the paragraph. Once you have written the thesis statement, think of a lead-in that will arouse interest—remember to keep that first sentence short and lively. Now write the whole paragraph, perhaps four to six sentences—shorter than most body paragraphs. Look over the first draft of your paragraph and check for words or phrases that need improvement and for errors. Write a final draft. Identify your lead-in, tie-in, and thesis statement in the paragraph.

1. Extracurricular activities in college: A benefit or waste of time?
2. College curriculum: Should students be allowed to choose any courses they want?
3. Cheating on term papers and exams: Do many students do it, and why?
4. Safe sex: How can young adults protect themselves against sexually transmitted diseases?
5. Single parents: Can one parent raise children just as effectively as two?
6. Today's military: Why do young people join?
7. The etiquette of dating: Should women ask men for dates? Who should pay?

CONCLUDING PARAGRAPHS

Concluding paragraphs, like introductory paragraphs, are usually short. Although you can just stop when you run out of things to say in an essay, good writers usually make some concluding statements that leave the reader with a sense of completeness and a desire to think more about the subject. Like the opening, the ending of your essay should be dramatic, witty, imaginative, amusing, or thought provoking. It might be a question, a prediction, or a paradox. It should remind the reader of something you said at the beginning, but it should not merely repeat the information in the first paragraph. Think of the concluding paragraph as an upside-down version of the introductory paragraph. It may begin by reemphasizing the main idea (but not by restating the thesis sentence word for word) and then broaden out to leave the reader with ideas for further thought on the subject.

How NOT to Conclude

If you have not gone through the writing process sufficiently and really explored what you want to say on your subject, you may find yourself writing a concluding paragraph that is not a conclusion at all. Often you will need to write several pages in your exploratory draft before you discover your really original ideas. If you try to complete your essay in one hasty draft, your "concluding" paragraph may be the one in which these important new ideas finally come out. If this happens, either rethink the whole essay, using material from this "concluding" section as the main point of your essay, or rethink the concluding paragraph to make it fit the essay you have. Do *not* use the concluding paragraph to introduce main ideas that are not supported in the essay.

Consider this attempt at a conclusion to our imaginary essay on computers in the office:

> So we can see that computers have many benefits to offer businesses. This is why colleges should encourage students to take courses in computer programming and make sure all students have computer literacy. In fact, high schools ought to consider computer literacy as a basic skill as important as reading, writing, and mathematics.

This paragraph jumps off the track. The essay is about computers in the office, but at the end the writer suddenly becomes interested in the implications of computers in education. The concluding paragraph is a bad place to broaden your topic, just when you should be stressing the points already made.

Another kind of conclusion that does not succeed in a short essay is the mechanical summary. Sometimes a very long piece of writing such as a book or dissertation, especially if it is complicated, needs a summary to help the reader digest and remember the points made in it. In a short college essay, however, such a summary is an excellent way to bore the reader. Consider this paragraph as an ending to our essay on computers in the office:

> In summary, I have discussed in this essay some of the ways that computers make offices more efficient. The first way I discussed was electronic filing techniques. In the next paragraph I talked about word processing. Then I explained the advantages of high-technology editing. When you have read what I explained about these advantages, you will understand why it is important to know about computers if you work in an office.

This paragraph emphasizes the writer's plan when the focus should be on the topic itself. Give the reader a sense of order, and make some indirect reference to your opening, but don't overdo the repetition.

Model Concluding Paragraph

Here is a more successful concluding paragraph to our essay:

Reemphasis on Thesis

Broadening to Suggest Further Thought

Echo of Opening

> Knowing the equipment, filing techniques, and methods of writing and editing can be a great asset in today's office. Most offices across the country are rapidly replacing their outmoded procedures with computerized methods. Smaller companies may find the initial adjustment expensive, and some managers may feel anxious about giving up comfortable, old procedures. Nevertheless, the change pays off in the long run, and the pangs of change are easier to bear than the misery of suffering future shock while competitors hurry on ahead.

Note the use of the phrase *future shock* here. This phrase brings the essay full circle back to the beginning line of the essay (see page 88).

WRITING ASSIGNMENT: CONCLUDING PARAGRAPHS

Look over the introductory paragraph you composed in the previous exercise. Without actually writing a whole essay at this time, imagine that you have completed the body paragraphs on the topic. Now write an effective concluding paragraph that reaffirms your main thesis and broadens out to suggest directions for further thought on the subject. End with a lively, thought-provoking finale. Consider your first attempt at writing this paragraph to be an exploratory draft. Check it for errors and ineffective words or phrases; revise, then write a final draft.

MODES OF DEVELOPING SHORT ESSAYS

In Unit 2 you practiced writing paragraphs of various types—narrative, descriptive, explanatory, and so on. We will now turn to the development of short essays, using these same modes of writing.

The Narrative Mode: Telling About an Event

As you know from practice with narrative paragraphs, narration means telling a story. Like narrative paragraphs, narrative essays are arranged in time sequence, each paragraph marking one stage of the action. If you are telling about a trip you have taken, for instance, one paragraph might tell about planning for the trip, the next about getting to your destination, the next about what you did there, and another about your return. Although personal experiences happen in a steady flow of time, your paragraphs mark off the important phases of the experience, giving shape to the whole story. In your prewriting and exploratory draft, you may not pay close attention to each paragraph as a separate unit because you are engrossed in telling the story, but in the final draft be sure to divide your paragraphs wherever the story enters a different phase.

First-Person Narration.   You may choose to write in the first person in your narrative essay (I, me, my), telling about your personal experience. When you plan the essay, brainstorm to collect interesting details about each phase of the experience. Narratives generally follow a before/during/after sequence; ask yourself questions about each stage to be sure you have included all the important facts. Here is an example of brainstorming done by a student as her first step in creating an essay about her family's trip to New York City. She arranged her material into questions and answers about each stage of the trip.
    Before:

Question	*Answer*
Why did we go?	We have relatives—my father's cousin and his family—on Long Island. We wanted to visit them and see tourist attractions in Manhattan. I also wanted to check out some of the colleges in New York.
What was it like planning the trip?	Hysterical. My dad's cousin invited us to come in late June when school was out. That was June 15. We had to plan the trip, get clothes ready, and agree on what to do in about a week.

How did we get there?

We drove all the way from Detroit. My brother Steve had just gotten his license, so he wanted to split the driving with Mom and Dad. We stayed overnight in Pennsylvania.

During:

What was it like staying with our relatives?

Terrible at first. All they wanted to do was go bowling and rent home videos, and all we wanted to do was rush into Manhattan. After two days we went into Manhattan by ourselves.

What did we do in Manhattan?

Saw some of the tourist sights—Fifth Avenue, Wall Street, Rockefeller Center, the Statue of Liberty. Went shopping at Saks, saw the Trump Tower, tried to see a musical comedy (sold out). Then we split up. Dad took me to look at N.Y.U., Columbia, Hunter College, and Pace U. Mom and Steve saw a live television show. Went with relatives to a Mets game.

What did I like and dislike?

The people were fantastically varied; some were helpful and friendly but a lot of homeless people. The buildings and shopping were exciting, but too much noise and rushing.

After:

What was the return trip like?

Not as much fun as going there. We argued a lot because each of us wanted to do something we didn't get to do and blamed the others. We also disagreed about what we liked and what we should do the next time. We drove all the way back without stopping overnight.

What did I get out of the trip?

I learned how different each one of us in the family is from the others. I got over my fear of New York and sometimes wish I had gone to college there. I also learned to discuss whatever you plan to do with other people you're going to do it with before you do it.

Like most brainstorming, this exercise produced more ideas and facts than could be used in one unified essay. The next step was to write an exploratory draft that would use some of this material, leave out some of it, and add details where needed.

Exploratory draft:

Three years ago my family took a trip to New York. It was the longest trip we ever took together as a family, although I have been on longer trips by myself, to such places as Los Angeles and Florida. But this trip was especially important because it taught me a lot about myself and my family. The trip was sort of a surprise because we weren't really expecting to go to New York that summer, but my dad's cousin called from Long Island and insisted that we come visit his family at the end of June. That was only one week later. I'll say this about my family—they don't mind doing things at the drop of a hat!

We decided to drive because it would be too expensive to fly, and we would need the car in New York City. Our relatives couldn't be expected to squeeze us all into their car with them, after all. My brother Steve had just gotten his driver's license, and he was dying to prove he could drive better than Mom and Dad, so he got to take turns with them at the wheel. We took it easy driving and stayed overnight in a small town in Pennsylvania. When we finally got to New York, we had to drive through all that traffic to get to the Long Island Expressway and find our way to our relatives' house in Suffolk County, Long Island. We were really tired but eager to see the city. Were we in for a surprise when we found out that nobody in their family ever went into the city themselves! They expected us to stay at their house and go bowling or watch home videos.

This wasn't exactly what we came to New York for, so after two days we politely convinced them that we wanted to drive into Manhattan. That made the whole vacation better, but I wished we had discussed all this before we left. The same problem came up when we started going into Manhattan every day. We realized that each one of us had a different idea of what we wanted to do, and we all just assumed that everybody would agree.

We agreed on some things. We all wanted to see some of the tourist attractions, so we walked up and down Fifth Avenue, saw the Empire State Building, Saks Fifth Avenue, St. Patrick's Cathedral, Trump Tower, and Rockefeller Center. We also took the subway down to Wall Street and the World Trade Center and rode the Staten Island Ferry and saw the Statue of Liberty. Then we had to negotiate what to do next. Dad's idea was for me to visit some of the colleges in New York, so I agreed to go along to look at New York University, Columbia, Pace University, and Hunter College. I didn't really expect to go to college in the East, but I thought it might be interesting. Steve wanted to see a live television show, and Mom wanted to shop, so the two of them managed to see the Giraldo show live and spend an afternoon back on Fifth Avenue. We all wanted to see a musical comedy on Broadway. *Phantom of the Opera* was showing then, but it was impossible to get tickets (more great planning ahead!), so we settled for *Chorus Line*, which was still running after many years.

I liked the excitement of Manhattan, and the people were mostly a lot friendlier than I expected. They would always give directions if you asked them— although not always the right ones. I didn't like the noise of the traffic and the subways, and there were homeless people asking for money everywhere we went.

But I think it would be interesting to live in New York, and sometimes I wish I had gone to college there the way my dad hoped I would. No other place has so many varied types of people.

Before we went back we did have one interesting outing with our relatives. We went to a Mets game at Shea Stadium, which they considered going into the city. Otherwise, not much happened before we headed back. I didn't enjoy the trip back as much as the trip to New York. For some reason, we seemed to argue about everything. Each one of us felt there was something we missed doing in New York, and each of us had a different attitude about the whole trip. I slept most of the way because we decided not to stay overnight anywhere on the way back.

I could say I learned two things from the trip. One is not to take other people's attitudes and wishes for granted, not even your own family's. The other is the importance of communication and planning. If you want to go on a trip or do some other important project with other people, be sure to plan ahead and discuss the plan with everybody else involved. You'll be glad you did.

On rereading this essay in rough draft, the writer decided that she wanted to keep many of the interesting details but needed to organize the story better. Although the rough draft had a loose before/during/after sequence, some paragraphs had too many topics and the main idea did not become clear until the end. She wanted to add more vivid details from her prewriting activities and make the main point clear from beginning to end. She decided to include in her revised essay a title, a thesis, and a clear paragraph arrangement.

An Unplanned Vacation

Lead-in

My family likes to do things at the drop of a hat. Therefore, when my father's cousin on Long Island called to invite us for a visit, it seemed perfectly natural to Dad that we would take off for New York on a week's notice. None of us had been to New York before, and we all wanted to go. The

Tie-in

difficulty was that we made no real plans. We didn't discuss with Dad's relatives what we would do during the week and a half we would stay with them, and worst of all, we didn't discuss with one

Thesis Statement

another what we wanted to see and do in Manhattan. The trip taught us the value of communication and planning.

Paragraph 2: Getting There

Our trip to New York wasn't exactly a disaster, but we learned as soon as we left Detroit what price you pay for not thinking ahead. The car was due for a tune-up, a brake job, and re-alignment. Of course there wasn't time to have any of that done, and of course we had to drive because there wasn't time to reserve a flight. The drive was going smoothly at first; my brother Steve had just gotten his license and was taking turns with Mom and Dad. With three drivers, we didn't plan on stopping over anywhere, but somewhere in a small town in Pennsylvania we had a flat tire. We got to a service station and found out that not only did the tire have to be replaced, but new brake shoes had to be installed and the front end had to be aligned or else we would ruin another set of tires. All that meant an overnight stay in a town that didn't even have a movie theater, far less any night life or tourist attractions.

Paragraph 3: Arrival

Once we were on our way again, the trip was easy except for driving all the way through metropolitan New York to get to Long Island. When we reached our relatives' house in Suffolk County, we were tired but eager to launch out on an exploration of the Big Apple the next day. Were we in for a surprise when we found out that they expected us to stay at their house the whole visit and spend the time going bowling or watching movies on their VCR! Once again, we realized the problems we had created for ourselves by not thinking ahead. We could have discussed our plans with them before we left, but now we had a problem—how to let them know that we were going to spend most of our time in Manhattan without hurting their feelings. Fortunately Mom is a gifted negotiator and managed to convince them politely that it would be better for everybody if we went into the city during the day several times. That made the whole vacation better, but I wished we had made the arrangement ahead of time.

Paragraph 4: What We Did There

Once we started our jaunts into Manhattan, the same problem of inadequate planning came up. We soon realized that each of us had a different idea of how to spend our short time in the city. Since we hadn't talked it over before, we had to begin each day with a round-table discussion. Amazingly, we did agree well enough to see most of the big tourist sights, including the Empire State Building, St. Patrick's Cathedral, Rockefeller Center, and Trump Tower. We also took the subway down to Wall Street and the World Trade Center and rode the Staten Island Ferry so we could see the Statue of Liberty. The rest we had to negotiate. Dad's idea was that I should see some of the colleges in New York, so I agreed to go along with him to look at New York University, Columbia University, Hunter College, and Pace University. Although I didn't really expect to attend college in the East, I thought it would preserve family harmony if I cooperated. Steve wanted most of all to see a live television show, and Mom wanted to shop for gifts for friends and relatives, so the two of them managed to collaborate by spending an afternoon on Fifth Avenue and getting free tickets for the Giraldo show at Times Square in the evening. Our last unpleasant reminder of our lack of foresight came when we tried to get tickets for a musical comedy—something we all agreed on. Our first choice, *Phantom of the Opera*, was sold out for months; the only tickets we could get to a really good Broadway show were for *Chorus Line*, which had been around for more than ten years. And our seats were in the back row.

Conclusion   From beginning to end, this trip taught us the value of communication and planning. Although we enjoyed many experiences on the trip and liked our relatives very much, we decided that from then on, we would discuss any major plans with each other and not take each other so much for granted. The trip back involved a lot of arguing; we didn't agree on much of anything about the trip, but the whole experience forced us to understand one another better. Maybe our unplanned vacation benefited us all.

An unplanned essay is like an unplanned vacation: you can learn a lot from it, but it's not as good as a planned one. You may have noticed that in the final draft the writer added some interesting details that support the main idea, and she took out irrelevant details.* She also divided her paragraphs differently to give a clearer sense of the phases of the trip.

WRITING ASSIGNMENT: NARRATION

Think of a trip you have taken, either alone or with others. Follow the stages of the writing process to create an essay about the trip. First, brainstorm or do focused writing to explore the facts and impressions you remember; group

---

*We have been emphasizing organization and main thesis here, but remember that revision also includes choice of details and improvement of language. At this point, you may want to look ahead to Unit 4, "First and Second Drafts."

the material into stages—before, during, and after. Then look over your prewriting activities. What did the trip teach you? Write an exploratory draft in which you mainly try to tell the important facts and experiences. Put this rough draft away and look at it again a day or two later. Read it aloud to someone else; you and your listener together may be able to recognize your main idea and your attitude toward the experience. (The writer of "An Unplanned Vacation" was obviously somewhat annoyed over what happened, but she ended on a positive note.) Once you have a clear idea of your main point and your paragraph groupings, write the final draft.

Third-Person Narration.   Another kind of narration is third-person narration. This means telling about an event or series of events that happened to someone else. Short stories and novels are (usually) third-person narratives based on fictitious events. News reports are third-person narratives of real events. The paragraphs again serve as steps in the sequence of events. There should be an interesting lead-in and conclusion, and the sentences should follow smoothly one after the other with occasional transitional expressions to guide the reader.

Here is a sample essay in third-person narrative form based on actual events.

Sample Essay: Third-Person Narration

Tragedy in the Potomac

Introduction: Arouses Interest and Sets Scene

For those who are superstitious about numbers, January 13, 1982, proved true to form as an unlucky day in Washington, D.C. After a daylong snowstorm had already punished the city by closing airports and snarling traffic, bad luck turned to total tragedy with a double accident during rush hour. The crash of a jetliner into the Potomac ended the nation's record string of twenty-six months without a fatal air crash. Half an hour later a subway derailment became the first fatal accident in the six-year history of the Washington Metro system. The thirteenth of January, 1982, was indeed a tragic date for the nation's capital.

Body Paragraph 1: The Air Crash

To make the tragedy even worse, the air crash occurred at the worst possible time of day. At the peak of the rush hour, minutes after the runway at National Airport had been reopened for takeoffs, a Boeing 737 bound for Tampa on Air Florida Flight 90 lifted off and headed over the Potomac. Failing to gain enough altitude, it dropped suddenly through the blowing snow over the 14th Street bridge crowded with commuter vehicles. With an overpowering roar it slammed into the bridge, shearing off the tops of four cars and a truck, then plunged toward the river, where it skidded silently across the ice and sank into the water. A topless truck was left teetering on the edge of the bridge, and cars were scattered in all directions.

Body Paragraph 2: Rescue Efforts

Rescue efforts began immediately for the passengers floundering in the icy water and crying for help, as well as for people trapped in their smashed cars. While police and firefighters cut open the cars with acetylene torches, rescue workers threw lines to those in the water and sent out rubber life rafts. A helicopter dropped a rope attached to the life preserver and pulled survivors one by one to the shore. One heroic man caught the preserver five times, always passing it on to someone else; the helicopter pilot, returning finally to pick up the man himself, wept to find that he had disappeared. Two firemen dived into the river and saved a woman who had let go of the wreckage; a young government employee named Lenny Skutnik, seeing a flight attendant lose her grip on the helicopter rope and start to pass out, threw off his coat and swam out to rescue her. When eighteen of the seventy ticketed passengers on the flight had been brought to shore, they were taken to hospitals by ambulances that had to maneuver through the traffic jam.

Body Paragraph 3: The Subway Derailment

Complicating the traffic problem and adding to the confusion was the subway derailment half an hour after the crash. Only half a mile away, near the Smithsonian Institution, a subway train derailed at a switch, killing three people, injuring eighteen and forcing the evacuation of twelve-hundred passengers. Emergency vehicles trying to get through to the subway emergency exits were hindered by the closing of the 14th Street bridge and the resulting traffic jam. Rescue workers at both scenes had to do their job in the midst of swirling snow and approaching darkness.

Conclusion: Looking Back on the Event

It would be many days before the final list of casualties could be compiled and the causes of both accidents found. Firsthand accounts of terror, suffering, and heroism were to be heard from survivors in hospital beds and bystanders interviewed by the media. For everyone involved it was a date not soon to be forgotten for its double tragedy but also for the courage shown by ordinary people in the face of extreme emergency.*

WRITING ASSIGNMENT: THIRD-PERSON NARRATION†

Interview an older relative, preferably a grandparent, or a friend who can tell about life in an earlier generation. Ask this person to tell you about some interesting event that happened in your or the friend's family a long time ago, such as the family immigrating to America; the grandparents meeting and getting married; a family business being set up; the family's experience in war time; the family's survival in hard times; or some other amusing, frightening, or moving experience.

Take plenty of detailed notes. Even better, use a tape recorder. Remember that you always need more material than you will actually use. Once you have all the material, list the facts in a chronological order, such as before, during, and after. Write an exploratory draft of the experience, concentrating on telling the story effectively and using vivid details. Put the draft aside. Read it a day or two later; read it aloud to someone else if possible. Think about the meaning of the experience and compose a thesis statement expressing the meaning. Look over your paragraph divisions and revise them if necessary. Write a final draft.

ALTERNATIVE WRITING ASSIGNMENT: THIRD-PERSON NARRATION

If you do not have convenient access to an older relative or friend, do the following instead. Think of someone you knew when you were younger who did something that caused you to have strong feelings about that person, such as admiration, sympathy, envy, dislike, or love. Perhaps you knew someone who overcame a handicap, won an athletic or artistic competition, assumed a difficult responsibility, or got into trouble.

Since you are working from memory in this assignment, you will need plenty of prewriting to call up everything you know and feel about this person's experience. Keep in mind the fact that your memory contains much more than you can recall at a moment's notice. It may take several sessions of focused writing or brainstorming to explore what you really know and feel. It will help to tell someone else about the experience and have him or her ask you questions about it so as not to omit anything important. Then write an

---

*Adaptations of "A Deafening Roar and Then Icy Silence" by David Shribman, "Plane Hits Bridge over the Potomac: 12 Dead, 50 Missing" by Francis X. Clines, "The Real Hero of This" by Phil Gailey, and "Derailment in Subway in Washington Kills 3" from *The New York Times*, January 14, 1982. Copyright 1982 by The New York Times Company. Reprinted by permission.
†Review the past tense and the *ed* ending in Unit 5 before doing this assignment.

exploratory draft in which you try to tell the whole story of the experience and how it affected your attitude toward the person. Put the draft aside, and then read it aloud to someone a day or two later. Think about the meaning of the experience and discuss it with your listener. Compose a thesis statement on the meaning of the story, and reorganize your paragraphs if necessary. Write a final draft.

The Descriptive Mode

Descriptive essays, although they may contain elements of other kinds of writing, are intended chiefly to give a mental picture of a place, person, or object. As in descriptive paragraphs, be sure to use vivid, specific details and arrange your material in spatial sequence. This means that each paragraph, except the introduction and conclusion, will concentrate on one part or feature of the subject you are discussing. As in all essays, your thesis statement, preferably located near the end of the introductory paragraph, should state an idea that holds the whole description together. It will indicate what parts or features of the subject (the place, person, or object) the essay will discuss, and some point it makes.

Telling About a Place.   Describing a place, whether it is a small area such as your room or a huge land mass such as the continent of Africa (as in the sample essay that follows), requires thought, organization, and supporting details. Therefore you should expect to go through the stages of the writing process. The details will not arrange themselves; you have to group them into spatial categories by either outlining, making lists, or clustering. You should expect to do one or two rough drafts before you get the arrangement and the details right. If you do not have an interesting main idea about the place you are discussing, try focused writing to explore your thoughts and impressions before you try to compose an organized essay. In the sample essay describing Africa, the writer first tried creating a cluster that helped him clarify his mental picture of the subject. In doing this, he also discovered his main thesis: that Africa is not really just one land mass, but is three masses, each with a different ecology and climate.

Sample Essay

The Three Africas

When many people hear the word *Africa*, they picture steaming jungles and gorillas. Hollywood films have shrunk the public image of this immense varied continent into a small segment of its actual diversity. To have a more accurate picture of the whole continent, one should remember that there are, roughly, three Africas, each with its distinct climate and terrain, and with a style of life suited to the environment. The continent can be divided into the northern desert areas, the southeastern grasslands, and the tropical jungles to the southwest.

The northern regions have the environment and living patterns of the desert. Egypt, Libya,

Introduction: Creates Interest and Identifies Three Areas to Be Described

© 1990, 1986 Scott, Foresman and Company.

Body Paragraph 1: Northern Regions

Algeria, and Morocco have hot, dry climates with very little land suited to farming. Therefore, the population tends to be clustered into cities along rivers or the seacoast or into smaller settlements near oases. For thousands of years, people have lived in this vast region, subsisting partly on what crops and animals they could raise and partly on trade with Europe.

Body Paragraph 2: Southeastern Regions

The southeastern grasslands provide a better environment for animal life and for some kinds of crops. Many wild animals inhabit the plains in this region—elephants, giraffes, rhinoceros, antelopes, zebras, and lions. The people in this area have long been expert cattle raisers and hunters. Tea, coffee, cotton, cashew nuts, and tobacco are some of the main products grown in this region. Fishing also provides some food and income for people along the coast. The population here is less concentrated in cities and towns than in the north, but tends to be denser in areas where adequate rainfall and fertile soil make farming possible.

Body Paragraph 3: West Africa

West Africa is the region closest to the Hollywood image of mysterious jungles. As in the other two regions, the way people subsist depends upon their environment. This does not mean that most of the people live in grass huts in the jungle. Such nations as Nigeria have become highly modernized by income from oil, timber, and minerals. Most of the western countries have some farming that provides food and income; sugar cane, coffee, and tobacco are the important cash crops, while bananas, rice, and corn are raised for food. Fishing in the rivers and along the coast also accounts for food and income, and precious stones, especially diamonds, enhance the economy of Angola and the Ivory Coast.

Conclusion: Restates Main Idea

Even a superficial look at the major regions of Africa shows that it is a varied continent with several environments. Although most of the continent is tropical in its range of temperature, the climate ranges from deserts to rain forests. Similarly, human life-styles vary from the simplest rural villages to industrial cities, both new and ancient. Contrary to the myth, however, jungle life makes up only a very small portion of the whole of Africa.

WRITING ASSIGNMENT I : DESCRIPTION*

Write a short essay describing one of the pictures below and on the following page. Divide your description into three parts: foreground, middle ground, and background; or left, middle, and right. Remember to brainstorm, noting as many details as you can before you actually write the essay. Try to use precise, vivid adjectives to describe what you see.

WRITING ASSIGNMENT II : DESCRIPTION

Write a short essay of about five paragraphs describing the town where you live or the college campus where you study. Remember that you must limit such a broad topic by focusing on one controlling idea about the place. (Notice how the essay on Africa concentrates on disproving the myth that Africa is merely a jungle.) Divide your description into two, three, or four body paragraphs, each one describing one section of the place you are writing

---

*This is a good point at which to study the use of descriptive words such as adjectives and adverbs in Unit 5.

about. Remember to practice what you have learned about introductory and concluding paragraphs.

Portraying a Person.   Another important kind of descriptive essay is the portrait of a person. While resembling the one-paragraph description of a person that you have practiced, the essay portrait is longer and fuller. It will succeed best if you discuss several characteristics of the person, one in each body paragraph. The thesis statement should introduce these characteristics. A descriptive thesis statement might read, "Mary is one of the most sensible, ambitious, and resourceful members of the freshman class." One body paragraph would discuss how sensible she is, one would discuss how ambitious she is, and the final one would discuss how resourceful she is. Although the reader can follow your plan more easily if you name the subtopics in your thesis statement, it is not necessary to do so. You may sometimes prefer a simpler thesis statement such as "I admire Mary for three outstanding traits." Either way, be sure to have the two, three, or four subtopics in mind before you begin the body paragraphs. Also, remember to have a controlling central idea that all the subtopics will support, such as your admiration for the person in his or her successful pursuit of a career, or some such general concept. Notice how in the following sample essay the main idea, that Sam is a survivor, is supported by three subtopics—that he reacts quickly, that he is persistent, and that he has a sense of humor. To discover this arrangement of subtopics and to find supporting details for each one, the author developed the following cluster:

Sample Essay: Describing a Person

Sam the Survivor

Introduction: States Main Idea and Three Supporting Points

Although many people admire personality, looks, or intelligence more, I think that the instinct for survival is one of the most valuable human traits. Having witnessed my cousin Sam pull through dangers, difficulties, and stresses, I have come to put a high value on the qualities that help people survive. I admire Sam particularly for his quick reflexes, his dogged persistence, and his sense of humor.

Sam takes pride in being able to respond quickly in any crisis. Once as a teenager he escaped

*Body
Paragraph 1:
Discusses Sam's
Quick Reflexes*

from two muggers by his quick thinking. When cornered on a dark side street by two young toughs with knives, he caught them off guard by leaping in the air, aiming a karate kick at them, and shouting as loudly as he could. This sudden action frightened them just long enough for him to make a getaway by dodging between parked cars. The same kind of quick thinking carried him through many situations later, such as talking his way out of a gang that was trying to force him to join them and sell drugs. Once he even saved a friend from choking to death in a restaurant by using the Heimlich maneuver.

*Body
Paragraph 2:
Discusses Sam's
Persistence*

These exciting incidents are less important in the long run than his ability to keep going when others give up. Even though he is lazy about many ordinary tasks, when a goal matters to him he keeps working toward it with the endurance of a marathon runner. He trained himself in this ability years ago by constructing model airplanes and ships so intricate they would have driven most people to a nervous breakdown. From there he went on to absorb everything there was to know about electronics and computers. His professors in college were astonished at how thoroughly he mastered these subjects, while he was barely passing courses that did not interest him. He was never an outstanding student overall, but because of his determination to excel in electronics, he not only graduated but landed an excellent job.

*Body
Paragraph 3:
Discusses Sam's
Sense of Humor*

In my opinion, Sam's most important strength as a survivor is his sense of humor, especially about himself. Whereas others tell jokes and laugh when they are relaxed, Sam's humor shines most brilliantly when he is under stress. Twice he has been close to death, and both times his humor kept him going. The first was an accident in which he was severely burned and had to spend two months in the hospital, where he entertained the other patients and even the staff with endless jokes and stories despite the pain he suffered. The other incident occurred aboard a fishing boat in the Gulf of Mexico. A tropical storm had driven the boat farther out from shore than it should have been, and the waves threatened to overturn it. Sam buoyed up the spirits of the other passengers, some of whom could not even swim, until a large steamer was able to reach them. Sam's friends could name dozens of smaller incidents where his humor, which hardly ever shows itself at parties or other social occasions, eased a stressful situation. Those who know him best insist that this trait comes from his growing up in a poor family with an alcoholic father and learning to overcome troubles by means of humor.

Conclusion: Discusses Main Idea in New Words

Sam's three outstanding traits would not be evident to someone meeting him for the first time. He often strikes strangers as dull and ordinary, since he gives no impression of being particularly smart or entertaining. He is one of those precious individualists whom we eventually learn to value more than others born with more noticeable talents or good looks.

WRITING ASSIGNMENT: DESCRIBING A PERSON

Choose a person you have strong feelings about—someone you admire very much or someone you dislike strongly. This person may be someone close to you, such as a family member or friend you have known for a long time, or it may be a famous person. If you choose a celebrity, however, be sure you know a lot about the person, since you will have to back up whatever you say about him or her.

First do some focused writing beginning with the phrase "I admire (or do not admire) _____ because...." Continue writing nonstop about this person, trying to express all your feelings about him or her and your reasons for feeling that way. Next, make a list of ten qualities this person possesses. You will not discuss that many traits, but you should explore as many possibilities as you can. If you can't think of more than one or two traits you probably do not know this person well enough to write a good description. Start over with someone else.

Once you have a pretty good idea of your attitudes about the person and have a list of traits, do a cluster similar to the preceding one on Sam the Survivor. Then write an exploratory draft. Read it aloud to someone for feedback. Be sure you have a clear thesis: What is the overall point you wish to make about this person? Reorganize your draft if necessary for clear paragraph divisions. Write a final draft.

The Explanatory Mode: Discussing an Issue

In English composition courses and in other college courses as well, you will have to write essays about social issues. These will allow you to make use of what you know about writing "how" and "why" paragraphs. Such essays usually include several modes that you have practiced in your paragraph writing. Although chiefly explanatory (or expository, another term used for the same category), such essays may also contain narration, description, definition, comparison, and persuasion. You have been practicing these modes separately, but it is well to remember that in explanatory writing you will often combine several of them to support your points.

Explanatory essays on social issues may cover any number of topics, but they tend to fall into several broad categories:

- Schools and education
- Crime and the justice system
- Children and child rearing
- Marriage, divorce, and living together without marriage
- The media and their effect on our lives
- Moral questions, for example, abortion, mercy killing, sexuality
- Medical problems such as AIDS
- Alcoholism and drug abuse
- The economy
- Environmental issues (chemical and nuclear waste, air and water pollution)
- Conflicts between the older and younger generations
- College and professional sports
- Civil rights
- The women's movement
- Foreign policy
- Technological change and its effects

These are, of course, broad categories, not topics for essays. The topics you write about, whether you choose them or they are assigned to you, will be much more specific. You have been exposed to all of these general concerns through news broadcasts, editorials, television documentaries, magazine articles, books, and general conversation. In some advanced courses you will study such issues systematically and have to write about them using source material. For now, however, we are concerned with your ability to write intelligently about social issues using your knowledge from your own experience and your general knowledge as a concerned citizen.

A reasonably well-informed citizen should be able to write an effective essay on any one of the foregoing subjects without any specialized research. We are speaking here of the kind of article or letter to the editor that appears frequently in newspapers and magazines, not the heavily documented research paper that might appear in a scholarly magazine or be assigned in an advanced seminar. You do not need to be an expert to express an opinion and back it up with evidence. What you *do* need is a clear main point and the ability to organize your ideas effectively. How you organize depends on the kind of essay you are writing. There are several common patterns for explanatory essays; we will look at a few.

Essays Based on Examples.   One of the simplest methods of developing and organizing explanatory essays is **multiple illustration**, or **enumeration**. This means supporting the main point in a series of examples that illustrate it. This method allows you to draw on your own experience or on the experience of people you know, or to furnish examples from your reading. Each example may be a small story or description of a situation that proves your main point. College examination questions often call on students to provide examples from their reading in the course to illustrate some thesis. In composition courses as well as popular magazines, lively personal essays may use multiple examples to discuss a social issue like single parenthood, computerized dating, forced retirement, or teenage runaways in an amusing or emotionally moving way.

Remember a few pointers when writing essays of this kind:

- Be sure that your examples all support the point—it is easy to get into an interesting story and lose the point you are making, ending up with a long piece of gossip.
- Think about the order of your examples, putting the most important, dramatic one last.
- Vary your examples—although they all support one *main* idea, the way they do it should differ in order to hold the reader's interest.
- Make connections between the examples by using transitional phrases like "another example," "a still more exciting case," "a third incident that illustrates the point," and so on.

Here is a short plan for an essay using multiple examples:

Main point: People sometimes achieve greatness by overcoming physical illnesses or handicaps.

Examples:

1. Demosthenes, the ancient Greek leader, became a great speaker by overcoming his speech handicap.
2. Theodore Roosevelt became a great military and political leader by overcoming his childhood asthma.
3. Helen Keller, though born deaf, mute, and blind, overcame these handicaps to become a great public figure.
4. Jim Abbott, although born with only one hand, became a pitcher for the California Angels.

EXERCISE I: MULTIPLE EXAMPLES

Write sentences about famous people whose lives make good examples of the main point.

Main point: Young celebrities such as rock stars, television actors, and athletes sometimes cannot handle sudden fame and destroy their careers through drug abuse, alcohol, or self-destructive behavior.

Examples:

1. _____

2. _____

3. _____

4. _____

EXERCISE II: MULTIPLE EXAMPLES

Read the following essay and answer the questions.

Computer Addicts

There is a strong camaraderie and sense of belonging among hackers. They have their own subculture, with the usual *in* jokes and even a whole vocabulary based on computer terminology (there is even a hacker's dictionary). But to outsiders, they are a strange breed. In high schools, the hackers are called nerds or the brain trust. They spend most of their free time in the computer room and don't socialize much. And many have trouble with interpersonal relationships.

Bob Shaw, a 15-year-old high-school student, is a case in point. Bob was temporarily pulled off the computers at school when he began failing his other courses. But instead of hitting the books, he continues to sulk outside the computer center, peering longingly through the glass door at the consoles within.

Pale and drawn, his brown hair unkempt, Bob speaks only in monosyllables, avoiding eye contact. In answer to questions about friends, hobbies, and school, he merely shrugs or mumbles a few words aimed at his sneakered feet. But when the conversation turns to the subject of computers, he brightens—and blurts out a few full sentences about the computer he's building and the projects he plans. . . .

Are the hackers just a group of social outcasts who hook up with machines because they can't make it with people? That would probably be a gross exaggeration—and yet, "Most hackers do have problems adjusting socially," admits J. Q. Johnson, a graduate student at Stanford. "Perhaps because they don't have much social life, they spend more time at the computer center."

Joel Bion, a sophomore at Stanford, explains how he got hooked: "I've been working with computers since I was eight. I grew up in Minnesota and I didn't have many friends. I wasn't into sports and couldn't participate in gym class because I had asthma. Then I found a computer terminal at school. I bought some books and taught myself. Pretty soon I was spending a few hours on it every day. Then I was there during vacations. Sure, I lost some friends, but when I first started I was so fascinated. Here was a field I could really feel superior in. I had a giant program, and I kept adding and adding to it. And I could use the computer to talk to people all over the state. I thought that was great social interaction. But, of course, it wasn't because I never came into face-to-face contact."

Joel managed to break his addiction after a few years and is now a peer counselor at Stanford. But his lack of interpersonal relationships during the hacker period is common, and this problem has led Stanford psychologist Dr. Philip Zimbardo to take a closer look at the hacker phenomenon.

Zimbardo describes the case of a computer student who was working with him on a special assignment. The student interacted with excessive formality. He couldn't deal with small talk, and all his conversations were task-oriented: "You will do this. This must be done." He gave commands rather than making requests or suggestions. And he couldn't deal with the "fickleness" of human nature. All this, according to Zimbardo, was a reflection of the way the student interacted with the computer. Ultimately the student was dismissed because of his inability to get along with others.

"In some extreme cases, hackers exhibit elements of paranoia, because people can't be trusted the way computers can," says Zimbardo. "When people don't do just what he orders them to do, the hacker begins to perceive hostile motives and personal antagonism."

It would be absurd to label all hackers paranoid or even deviant. But it would also be naive to shrug off the hacker phenomenon as meaningless."*

1. In your own words, what is the main point the author is making

   about hackers? _____

   _____

2. How many students does she name or describe in detail who suffer

   from this problem? _____

   Name or describe them: _____

   _____

3. Where does the author get her examples? _____

---

*From "Computer Addicts" by Dina Ingber, *Science Digest*, July 1981. Copyright © 1981 by The Hearst Corporation. Reprinted by permission of the author, Dina Ingber Stein.

4. What do the students used as examples all have in common? _____

_____

5. What differences are there between the ways the author presents

the examples? _____

_____

_____

WRITING ASSIGNMENT: MULTIPLE EXAMPLES

Look over the following list of topics and choose one for a five-paragraph essay:

1. Discuss the qualities of an effective leader by describing three people who, in your opinion, were effective leaders.
2. Discuss the qualities of a great film by analyzing three examples.
3. Discuss effective parents by giving three examples among people you know.
4. Discuss success by means of three examples of people you consider to be successful.
5. Discuss happy marriages by describing three examples from among your friends, relatives, and acquaintances and from television programs and movies.

Once you have chosen a topic, do three focused writing exercises, one on each of the examples mentioned. Don't try to fit them together; just write as much as you can about each one. Once you have explored your impressions of all three, write a list of all the qualities the three have in common. Look over your list and create a thesis statement such as "Judging from three examples I know, a happy marriage depends on a sense of humor and an ability to empathize with the other person's feelings." Write a rough draft using your thesis statement to hold your examples together. Remember to describe each example in a different paragraph. Put your first draft aside for a while, then look it over to see if it is organized effectively and stays on the topic. Arrange your examples in climactic sequence, putting the best one last. Revise as needed; write a final draft.

*Problem/Solution Essays.** Our society has many problems—large and small, serious and not so serious. As a student you will certainly be asked at some

---

*Review subject/verb agreement and the *s* ending in Unit 5.

time to write an essay proposing a solution to one of these problems. The purpose of such an assignment, of course, is not to have you solve the problem but to encourage you to think creatively and realistically about the problem and its solution. You are to determine what you think is the best solution and then effectively support your proposal.

Problem/solution essays generally can be organized into three parts:

1. Establishing the need
2. Considering various proposals
3. Stating and defending one proposal.

Leaving out any of these parts will inevitably weaken your essay.

An outline for a problem/solution essay might look like this:

I. Introductory paragraph stressing the urgency of the problem and indicating the kind of solution you will propose
II. Body paragraphs
    A. Paragraph explaining the need at length and possibly analyzing how the problem arose
    B. Paragraph discussing other proposed solutions and showing why they will not work
    C. Paragraph (or two) explaining your solution in detail and showing why it will work
III. Concluding paragraph reemphasizing the need for change and stressing the effectiveness of your solution, possibly warning what will happen if your proposal is not implemented

This, of course, is just one possible way to organize such an essay. Any outline should be the result of plenty of brainstorming about the subject. Do not try to set up an outline for your essay without first exploring the range of your knowledge and opinions on the problem you will discuss.

Read the following sample essay, noticing how the writer follows the above outline:

Hope for the Homeless

Introduction: Dramatizes Problem

Homeless people differ in many ways. Some are drug addicts or alcoholics; some are victims of personal catastrophes. Many are mentally ill. Nearly all are unemployed and some seem unemployable. Some are handicapped. A large number are literally homeless in that they have been evicted from their previous home and cannot find affordable shelter. For such a diverse group of people with such severe and differing problems, no one source of aid would seem to be enough. One attribute the group shares however, is lack of hope. The only solution that will make a permanent difference is one that gives homeless people the hope that they can find a better life than the life of sleeping in subway stations and panhandling on the streets.

In most cities, efforts to aid the homeless have not reduced the numbers significantly. Shelters have been established in most large cities and many smaller communities, but people living in them remain as homeless as ever. Many of the shelters even add to the problem, by becoming centers for drug trafficking; homeless people may fear the crime and violence in the shelters. Attempts to round up, house, and care for homeless people who appear to be mentally ill have sometimes been foiled by civil libertarians who support the "rights" of the homeless to live in the streets and behave as they choose. Putting people in welfare hotels has proved an expensive disaster — local governments end up paying exorbitant rents to house families in dangerous and barely livable conditions. As a result of current policies, the homeless population seems to keep expanding, and their living conditions keep getting worse.

Paragraph 2: Explains Need For New Approach

Other solutions have been proposed. People often point to abandoned buildings in the inner cities and say they should be renovated to provide housing for the homeless. Certainly shelter *is* part of the problem, and any cities that can afford to renovate abandoned buildings that they own should do so. But many homeless people are also without hope. If they are just assigned apartments, their personal problems of joblessness, alcoholism, drug addiction, or mental illness remain. Some may go back to living in the streets, even when given a place to live. People need identities and self-confidence, not just four walls around them. Job-training programs also sound good, and should be available. But many of the homeless need much more than job training. In fact, some once had good jobs, and a few were even highly trained professionals. Any effective improvement in their lives can come only if they acquire real hope — not fanciful promises, but the realistic inner confidence that their lives are going somewhere.

Paragraph 3: Dicusses Other Proposals

If we put ourselves in the position of the homeless, we can better understand what it will take to solve their myriad problems. To regain confidence about your life when you have reached the

Paragraph 4: Discusses Writer's Proposal

bottom, you need plenty of human contact. You need to know that somebody cares and is going to keep on caring. You also need to know that the fight for a better life is worth the effort—that there is a real possibility of a well-paid job, a decent home, and a safe social environment. To provide people with hope means to provide all of this— and no program for helping the homeless has yet gone this far. There must be much more help by social workers and psychologists, and treatment centers for alcohol abuse and drug abuse, to begin with. Nothing can be accomplished without this first step. Then there must be decent temporary housing that does not herd people together like animals. Finally, there must be job counseling, training, and placement, along with follow-up services so that those who get back on their feet do not give up at the first sign of difficulty.

Conclusion: Reemphasizes Urgency of Problem

Like anything, hope costs money. It is useless to pretend that we can even touch the problem of homelessness without spending more on housing, counseling services, and employment assistance than has been spent so far. Emergencies of this size demand emergency relief. The federal and state governments should treat the problem of homelessness the way they treat emergencies like floods, earthquakes, and droughts, and spend the money where it is needed. The cost will be high, but not as high as the cost of ignoring the problem. When we face hopelessness all around us—huddled in doorways, lying in train stations, reaching out for coins in the streets—we pay a price in the loss of hope for our own lives and our society.

WRITING ASSIGNMENT: PROBLEM/SOLUTION ESSAYS

Identify a problem at your college, such as racism on campus, the rising cost of tuition, fraternity hazing, cheating on exams and term papers, snobbishness between different groups of students, a high dropout rate, problems with registration and financial aid, problems with course selection and curriculum, or problems with extracurricular activities or the athletic program. Discuss this problem with friends to explore the range of opinions about it. Do two pages of focused writing expressing your thoughts about the problem— what is causing it, who is responsible, and what should be done about it.

Once you have explored your thoughts, brainstorm the separate aspects of the problem. First, list everything you can about the problem itself—its causes, why it has to be dealt with, whom it affects, whether it is getting worse, and so on. Then list all the possible solutions, including any suggested by friends. Finally, identify the one solution that seems most likely to work, and write down everything you can about it.

At this point you should have the basis for a working draft of a problem/ solution essay. Make a rough outline of your paragraph plan before you begin. You may not follow this outline exactly, because new ideas may come as you compose (always be open to new ideas even if they force you to reconsider your outline). Write your exploratory draft using the outline as a general guide only. Put the essay aside for a day or two; then look at it again. Read it aloud to friends for their feedback. If they disagree, use their disagreement as an opportunity to dig deeper into the subject, either to strengthen your point with better evidence or to modify your point. Revise your organization if revision is needed. Write a final draft.

*Essays Based on Autobiographical Example.** Another method of developing an explanatory essay is by means of your own experience. An autobiography is a story you write about your own life. Development by autobiographical example means using experiences from your own life to support a point. If you have ever been the victim of discrimination because of race, sex, or religion, you could use the experience to illustrate how prejudice manifests itself in our society. If you have had experience with the courts, you could use it to discuss the legal system. Many topics are suited to this method. Adoption, divorce, immigration, upward mobility, hospital care, problems in the schools, and issues regarding jobs and unemployment can all be discussed effectively by means of autobiographical examples. Of course, you have to have enough experience to discuss the issue effectively. Everyone, for instance, has plenty of experience with the schools, but not everyone can use personal experience to discuss adoption or immigration.

Such essays can be vivid and forceful, sometimes humorous. However, it is easy to get off the track and forget that your main purpose is to discuss only one issue. *Be sure to state your main point early in the essay, and use topic sentences to focus your paragraphs on supporting points.*

Read the following essay, noticing how the writer states a clear main idea and develops it in separate paragraphs that follow the stages of her life.

Sample Essay: Autobiographical Example

Women in Sports

As a little girl, I used to watch the World Series
with my father. Other children would tease me for

———————

*If you have not done so already, review verb tenses in Unit 5.

*Introduction:
Arouses Interest
and Announces
Main Idea*

being fascinated by a "boys' game," and my mother would sometimes get impatient with me for watching television when she thought I should be helping her in the kitchen. Instead of listening to other people's objections, I decided to become a great athlete myself. I thought that when I proved I could do it, they would all be amazed and pleased. I didn't know then that even in our liberated society, I would face discrimination as a female athlete.

*Body
Paragraph 1:
Discusses
Discrimination
in Grade School*

Grade-school sports were fun because no one objected to girls playing rough games like kickball, tag, or softball. It was only when our fourth grade sent a softball team to play against another school that I realized the world was not designed to encourage my athletic ability. Although I was the best second baseman in the class, I was excluded from the team because only boys were allowed to play against other schools. I was enraged; it never occurred to me that such a silly rule would keep me from playing. At the same age, I started to experience some of the discrimination built into the system when boys in my class joined Little League teams in the summer, while I had to confine myself to swimming and roller skating. They could do my sports, but I couldn't do theirs. My family and friends didn't argue with me when I complained; they just wouldn't take me seriously. Little girls could be good at sports, but they weren't supposed to care very much about them.

*Body
Paragraph 2:
Discusses
Discrimination
in Junior High
School*

In junior high school the problem became more serious. I had become a good runner and had begun to excel in tennis. Although I still cherished an ambition to be a baseball star, I had learned to keep that dream to myself. Some of the other girls also did well in tennis, and a few were interested in track and field events, but now the problem was that most of the girls were really more interested in boys and going steady than in anything else, particularly sports. They thought that being athletic would ruin their image in the boys' eyes and keep them from having steady boyfriends. A few of us overcame this prejudice and discovered that tennis was an exception. Being a good tennis player did not hurt our chances with boys, and it was a great way to meet boys. I met my steady boyfriend on a tennis date, and we often played tennis together. This situation, however, raised a new difficulty. I was becoming an outstanding player, which meant that I could usually win in singles against most of the boys. Should I lose on purpose so that I didn't make the boys feel bad or become unpopular? I was too ambitious not to compete seriously, so I won and took my chances. Luckily, my boyfriend was a star football player so he didn't mind losing at tennis once in a while.

Body Paragraph 3: Discusses Discrimination in High School

High school sports were very competitive, even for girls. In a way this seemed to show that there was now less discrimination than at earlier stages. The lacrosse team played against other girls' teams, and our championship tennis team attracted large, enthusiastic crowds. No one even hinted that girls shouldn't take these games seriously. In public I was the center of attention and I enjoyed the competition. I discovered, however, that the girl athletes were not idolized socially the way the boys in football and basketball were. The girl athletes were considered a special group of their own—not looked down on exactly, but always outside the circle of the most popular kids in school. When I talked with counselors about making a career of athletics, once again I faced the total lack of enthusiasm I encountered when I objected to being excluded from Little League.

Conclusion: Discusses Later Results Discrimination

As a result of my experiences, I have decided to continue sports in college only as an extracurricular activity that I enjoy but not as a serious undertaking. I have learned that unless I expect to be a world-famous superstar, I will face too many forms of silent prejudice to be happy trying to make a career out of my athletic ability. Fortunately, I have equally strong ambitions in business administration, but I wonder how many other women in our "liberated" society are persuaded not to take their abilities seriously.

WRITING ASSIGNMENT: AUTOBIOGRAPHICAL EXAMPLE

Basing your choice on your own experience, select one of the following topics for an essay using autobiographical example to support the main idea.

1. Discrimination in our society is still present.
2. Women still have to do most of the work around the house.
3. Military service changes people's lives.
4. The schools are not what they should be.
5. Hospitals are not as safe and efficient as we think.
6. Becoming a father (mother) changes your life.

Since this essay will be chiefly in narrative form, start with a focused writing exercise in which you tell everything that comes to mind about your experiences with this subject (hospitals, schools, parenthood, and so on). Once you have as much material as you can gather, think about what you want to say. What have you learned from your experience? Be as specific as you can. To say that the schools are bad, for instance, is an overgeneralization. In what way are they bad? Is your experience typical?

Once you have a thesis statement, write an exploratory draft. Try to stay on the point throughout the draft, and divide your experience or experiences into clearly identifiable phases or events. Put this draft away for a day or two. Then read it aloud to someone else to see if that person responds with similar experiences from his or her life. If that person disagrees with your point, perhaps you need to sharpen the point or modify it. If you have a strong point, you will probably get an "I know what you mean" response. Using feedback from your listener and your own critical eye, revise your draft as needed to make the main point clear and the paragraphs distinct and unified. Write a final draft.

The Persuasive Mode: Enumerating Reasons*

One reliable pattern of organization for argumentative essays is the series of reasons. You express your main idea in the thesis statement, then give three or four reasons why you hold that opinion. One reason should be discussed in each body paragraph. This method produces an extremely clear arrangement, but it is not necessarily simple. You may want to support each reason in a different way—a small story for one, facts for another, analysis of cause and effect for a third. The overall plan, in other words, is simple, but there is plenty of room for variety in the ways you develop the parts. As a result, you will need to be careful about making smooth transitions between body paragraphs and seeing to it that all three or four reasons really do support your thesis. A final concern is the sequence of reasons: which comes first? second? last? Usually, the most convincing reason should come last, in the most emphatic position.

The following sample essay gives three reasons to back up the opinion expressed in the thesis statement. Can you explain the method used to develop each body paragraph?

---

*You may want to review the discussion of persuasive writing in Unit 2 at this point.

Sample Essay: Enumerating Reasons

Working Mothers

Introduction: Arouses Interest and States Main Thesis

A generation ago, any woman who went out to work and left her children with a babysitter felt guilty unless she had no other source of income. Attitudes have changed: now a large percentage of mothers with small children hold jobs, many of them full-time. Although there are problems involved in being a mother and career woman at the same time, I believe there are three good reasons why mothers who want to go out and work should do it.

Body Paragraph 1: Discusses First Reason by Process Analysis

First, working outside the home is good for the mother herself. Motherhood is an exciting experience, but the endless hours of minding infants and small children can lead to depression. The mother needs another dimension to her life in order not to feel trapped in her home and buried under tons of baby food, diapers, and laundry. Furthermore, if she had begun a career before her children were born, an interruption of several years—which often stretches into many years—will set her progress back at a crucial time. In later years she will feel frustrated and insignificant when she tries unsuccessfully to regain the momentum she had at the beginning of her career. As the frustration builds, she may unconsciously blame her children or her husband for the lack of fulfillment in her life. Had she continued to grow in her career, she would have maintained a more positive attitude toward both herself and her family.

Body Paragraph 2: Discusses Second Reason by Example

Another reason why she should continue working is that it can be good for her children. Of course, she must coordinate her work and her time with the children in the right way. My friend Anne, for example, has shown me how successful a working woman can be as a mother. Anne was a full-time nurse before she had children, and she continued her career after a son and daughter were born, two years apart. Her first step after the birth of the first child was to find a first-rate babysitter to look after the baby during the day. She also worked out a schedule with her husband, who was a security guard during the afternoon and evening, so that he could watch the baby during part of the morning. Then she figured out many ways to keep up a close relationship with her children, calling them from work during the day, and planning evening and weekend activities that made the quality of the time spent with them very high. Her children are now seven and nine years old and appear to be healthy, well adjusted, and well behaved.

Body Paragraph 3: Discusses Third Reason by Use of Definition

Finally, it is good for society if women know that motherhood will not close off their options or force them to accept inferior status. A truly democratic society might be defined as one in which every person is able to achieve as much as his or her talents allow. The women's movement has done much to open doors that once were closed to women, thus creating a more democratic society. Women in a sense won participation in our political democracy when they won the constitutional right to vote in 1920, but social democracy is an ideal that includes more than the right to vote. It encompasses equal opportunities in careers, equal legal rights, and equal moral obligations. Giving women the opportunity to choose motherhood and a career without jeopardizing either is certainly a big step toward full democracy.

Conclusion: Summarizes Main Argument

For the good of the mothers themselves, their children, and society, women with small children should be encouraged to work outside the home. Current trends have been in the direction of more working mothers, and the change is mostly for the better. While we may have to give up some of the simpler, settled family styles of our grandparents' day, we should enjoy the advantages that go along with the change.

WRITING ASSIGNMENT: ENUMERATING REASONS

Choose one of the following statements as a thesis for an essay. (You may take the opposite side if you prefer.)

1. Homeowners should be required to own guns to protect their families and property.
2. Colleges should not have required courses—students know what courses they need and are interested in.

3. Parents should raise boys and girls the same way, giving them the same toys, games, advice, rules, and discipline.
4. Women should wait to get married and have children until they have had time to enjoy life and have established their careers.
5. Men and women should sign prenuptial agreements before they get married.

After you have chosen the topic, list all the reasons you can think of to support your opinion. Try to list five to ten. If you cannot think of more than one or two, try doing focused writing on the subject to loosen up your thinking. You might also try listing reasons why people have the opposite opinion and then list your responses to those reasons.

When you have gathered more than enough reasons, analyze the list. Pick out the three or four that seem to you the most important. List them in climactic sequence, with the most important—the clinching one—last. Write an exploratory draft using this list, with one paragraph for each reason. Explain each reason clearly and use examples to illustrate some of them. Read your rough draft aloud to get feedback on your ideas. If the other person disagrees at any point, see if you need to strengthen your argument with a better explanation or examples. Be sure you have an effective introduction and conclusion. Write a final draft.

The Persuasive Mode: The Dialogue Pattern

Still another effective method of developing an opinion on a social issue is the dialogue pattern. You will often see this method in editorials. The writer will state an opinion held by some person or group that he or she disagrees with; then the writer will use the rest of the editorial to reply to that opinion. The result is either a long answer to one opinion or a pro-and-con discussion in which the writer takes up several opinions of the opposition and answers them one by one.

This method is especially effective for the most controversial issues, ones that demand open-mindedness and fairness. By taking up the arguments of the other side, the writer demonstrates reasonableness and a grasp of the issue. To write this kind of essay well, you must be able to answer the best objections from the other side. It is tempting to use the "straw man" technique of mentioning only opinions that you can easily knock over, while ignoring really convincing ones.

Organizing an essay of this kind is not difficult if you include three or four opinions held by the other side. Include one in each body paragraph and refute each one effectively. The pattern is much like the series-of-reasons method: arrange the body paragraphs so that the arguments build up from the least to the most important. Each paragraph can be developed in its own way. When you answer one objection from the other side, you may find a personal example to be your best means of support; when you answer the next, you may use logical analysis, and so on.

Read the following sample essay, noticing how the writer replies in different ways to three opinions held by those who disagree with him. Notice also that the introductory paragraph in this kind of essay does more than state the writer's own opinion; it also identifies the person or group on the opposing side.

Sample Essay: The Dialogue Pattern

The Case for College

Introduction: Identifies Opposing View

Is a college degree worth the time, effort, and above all, the expense? As tuition rises to frightening levels, more and more students and parents are asking this question. Some critics have answered it with an emphatic no. In a book called *The Case Against College*, for instance, Caroline Bird argued that many students would be better off not going to college. To appreciate the real value of a college education, we need to consider some of the strong charges made by such critics.

Body Paragraph 1: Answers One Charge Made by Opponents

One accusation is that college students seldom acquire an education that has value in itself. Critics point to fancy courses in science fiction, filmmaking, and water skiing and ask whether college can be taken seriously. Some critics claim that the level of most courses is no higher than a high-school level, and the college degree does not certify real higher education. These charges are serious, and if they are true, something needs to be done about the problem. Keeping students out of college, however, would not solve the problem. The real goal should be to see to it that colleges do provide higher education by improving the curriculum of colleges where it is weak and raising the level of skills high-school seniors bring to college. It may be true that some colleges offer a few courses designed only to attract students without much thought to education. But consider the courses required at most colleges—mathematics, science, history, English, foreign languages. These must still have value.

Body Paragraph 2: Answers Another Claim

Another charge often made against colleges is that most modern students don't really want to be in college, that they attend only because everyone else does. This claim is also hard to prove or disprove. It may be that with a much higher percentage of high-school seniors entering college than was the case thirty years ago, more students are uncertain about their goals than previously. However, deciding on a career and other life goals has always been a part of the college experience. Many famous men and women found their paths in life while attending college; Dr. Martin Luther King, Jr., for example, left a premedical curriculum to join the ministry while he was in college. What some critics call unhappiness at being in college may be a general uncertainty about the future. And what better place to consider one's future than in college, surrounded by teachers, counselors, and other students?

Body Paragraph 3: Answers the Strongest Objection

Finally, the crucial question of course is money. Is college really going to pay back the dollars spent? Critics have tried to prove that a typical college student would be richer in the long run if, instead of going to college, he or she invested the same money in a business or merely went to work and put it in a savings account. A young man might, for instance, invest money in a truck and begin hauling for hire, then eventually buy a larger rig and earn a higher income than he would with a college degree. For some students who wouldn't mind spending their lives driving a truck, these estimates may be true, but how many does this apply to? The trend in the 1980s was for the income gap to widen between those with and without college degrees. Highly trained personnel in areas like computer technology became more in demand, and the number of high-paying unskilled jobs decreased. The gap for women is even wider. In the late 1980s men with college degrees earned over thirty-five percent more than men without college degrees, and women with college degrees earned over forty percent more than women without college degrees.* This trend will probably continue in the 1990s. There have always been a few multimillionaires with little formal education, and there may continue to be. However, for the large majority of college-age men and women, sacrificing a college education to

---

*Facts from "Benefit of B.A. Is Greater Than Ever," *Wall Street Journal*, August 17, 1988, sec. 2, p. 1.

invest in a risky business (where the money could be lost) or to take an unskilled job with little chance of advancement would be a foolish move.

Conclusion: Reaffirms Author's Point

The critics of college have a persuasive case, yet they do not seem to be winning the argument if we judge by the percentages of high-school graduates continuing to enter college. The reason must be that there are benefits to be gained from a college degree and that college education still has some value in itself. Is college worth it? Those who answer no must tell us what else is worth more.

WRITING ASSIGNMENT I: THE DIALOGUE PATTERN

Find a magazine or newspaper article, preferably an editorial, that expresses a strong opinion you disagree with. List the main point of the article and the supporting reasons. Across from these write your own opposing opinions on each point. Add to your list any further points you can think of on *your* side. If you have difficulty thinking of sufficient reasons to support your opinion, try a nonstop writing exercise to explore your thoughts on the subject.

Once you have sufficient ideas, write a first draft of an essay using the dialogue method. Begin with an introduction identifying the writer and article you are opposing, as well as its main point. State your opposing point. Base the body of your essay on a series of rebuttals to the main arguments given in the article. Add any important points on your side not considered in the article, and write an effective conclusion. As always, read your rough draft aloud to someone else, preferably a small group of other students, to get as much feedback as you can. Use the feedback to strengthen arguments that need more support and to better explain arguments that are unclear. Do not be afraid to modify your arguments if they contain errors—the point of dialogue, after all, is to seek the truth. Reread your first draft to be sure you have represented your opponent's opinion correctly and organized your material effectively, saving your strongest argument for the last. Write a final draft.

WRITING ASSIGNMENT II: THE DIALOGUE PATTERN

Each of these exercises contains a main thesis and some supporting points. Across from each point, write in arguments on the opposite side. After completing the exercises, choose *one* of them as the basis for an essay, following the same writing stages as in Writing Assignment I. You may take either side of the question.

1. Thesis Statement: Drugs should be legalized in the United States.

   Opposing Thesis Statement: Legalizing drugs would make the drug problem worse in the United States.

   Supporting Points:

   Opposing Points:

   A. Legalizing drugs would reduce drug-related crimes and violence.

   A. _____

   _____

   _____

   B. We can't stop drug traffic—it is too widespread.

   B. _____

   _____

   C. People have a right to make their own choices, even harmful ones.

   C. _____

   _____

   _____

   D. Legalizing drugs would make drug use less exciting; there would be less addiction.

   D. _____

   _____

   _____

   E. We tried making alcohol illegal in the 1920s; that did not work, and keeping drugs illegal does not work either.

   E. _____

   _____

   _____

   _____

   F. The government would collect taxes on the legal sales of drugs.

   F. _____

   _____

   _____

2. Thesis Statement: Women should not serve in the military.

Opposing Thesis Statement: Women improve the military significantly.

Supporting Points:

Opposing Points:

A. Women are not as strong as men in combat and other military work.

A. _____

_____

_____

B. Women are needed at home during wartime.

B. _____

_____

C. Women would be more emotional in war situations.

C. _____

_____

D. Women might get pregnant and drop out.

D. _____

_____

E. Having women around would distract men from their duties.

E. _____

_____

3. Thesis Statement: Pornographic videos, magazines, and telephone services are harmless forms of entertainment and should be permitted.

Opposing Thesis Statement: Pornography promotes violence and harms society by degrading both sex and women.

Supporting Points:

Opposing Points:

A. People have a right to whatever forms of entertainment they choose.

A. _____

_____

_____

B. Pornography has not been proven to be harmful.

B. _____

_____

C. Many serious films, books,
   and works of art are "pornographic."

C. _____

_____

_____

D. Denial and ignorance of
   sexuality does more harm
   than pornography, which
   helps educate people.

D. _____

_____

_____

4. Thesis Statement: Young
   people should not have sex
   before marriage.

Opposing Thesis Statement: Sexual experience before marriage is
morally and socially acceptable
today.

Supporting Points:

Opposing Points:

A. The only safe sex today is
   celibacy before marriage.

A. _____

_____

B. Sex is right only with the
   person you want to spend
   your life with.

B. _____

_____

_____

C. The purpose of sex is to bear
   children, which should
   happen in marriage.

C. _____

_____

_____

D. Sex before marriage is often
   psychologically harmful,
   especially for young teenagers.

D. _____

_____

_____

E. Premarital sex tends to make
   marriages fail.

E. _____

_____

5. Thesis Statement: College Board (SAT) scores should not be used by admissions offices.

Opposing Thesis Statement: College Board scores serve a useful and fair purpose.

Supporting Points:

Opposing Points:

A. SAT scores put too much pressure on students to excel in exams.

A. _____

_____

_____

B. SAT scores discriminate against some groups of people.

B. _____

_____

_____

C. Students tend to "prep" for College Board exams instead of learning course material.

C. _____

_____

_____

D. SAT scores put too much emphasis on raw ability and downgrade hard work.

D. _____

_____

_____

Twenty Current Topics for Additional Practice in Persuasive Writing

1. Should smoking be banned in all public places?
2. Should surrogate motherhood be allowed by legal contract?
3. Should drug testing be compulsory on all jobs?
4. Should teenage girls be allowed to get contraceptives and abortions without their parents' permission?
5. Should athletes be allowed to compete if they use steroids?
6. Do homeless people have the right to live on the streets?
7. Should a teenager who gets pregnant have an abortion, keep her child, or put it up for adoption?
8. Should college athletes be paid salaries?
9. Should teenagers who murder be tried and sentenced as adults?
10. Should minorities and women be given preferential treatment in hiring?

11. Should mothers stay home with preschool children or go out to work?
12. Would the United States benefit from taking in more immigrants?
13. Should college administrations censor student publications?
14. Should prostitution be legalized?
15. Should telephone and television pornography be outlawed?
16. Should people live together before getting married?
17. Should divorced men get custody of children?
18. Should welfare recipients be required to work?
19. Should parents be forbidden by law to hit or spank their children?
20. Should the United States spend more money on space exploration?

REVISING AND IMPROVING YOUR WRITING

You have now learned and practiced prewriting skills and have practiced writing paragraphs. You have also composed short essays and have done minor revising. So far you have worked on the plan, content, and organization of your work. Now we will turn to techniques for improving the effectiveness of your language, especially your choice of words and your sentence patterns. To write vividly and forcefully you must be able to turn monotonous, flat prose into writing that catches and holds the reader's interest. This means taking what you thought was already a "final draft" and making it still better.

FIRST AND SECOND DRAFTS

In the previous units you have learned to work with a topic through several phases of the writing process. Moving from prewriting to formal composition, you have written paragraphs and essays and have revised many of their features. In this unit you will concentrate on improving completed first drafts, one of the most difficult but crucial stages of the writing process.

Revising means more than making a neater copy in more legible handwriting. Neatness is not the goal; revision should be messy. You may go through several very messy drafts before you arrive at exactly what you want. Real revision means re-vision, or re-seeing—taking another look. Use the feedback from your listeners to guide you, just as you used it in prewriting to explore the topic. Now, however, think about cutting, adding, rephrasing, and polishing.

Write the best first draft that you can. Then assume that it is not good enough and make it better. Effective revision requires cutting for greater force and conciseness as well as adding details to develop your topic. If you want to write 500 words, aim for 700 and cut out the deadwood. Remember that *the difference between mediocre writing and superior writing usually lies in revision*. Treat your first draft as a rough, loose working model of the essay you want, and keep revising to bring it to perfection.

Here is an example of a reasonably good first draft that needs alterations to bring it to life. Where does it leave out facts? Where is it too vague? Where is the language not vivid enough?

First draft:

> Moving out of my parents' house was a big problem. I had to find a place to live, look for a job, and take charge of my daily responsibilities. I never realized until then how much my parents had provided for me. Then I got a car since I couldn't use the family car anymore and I soon discovered how many expenses owning a car involves. Getting myself moved, which meant packing the stuff that I owned, was a huge mess. But once I was settled in my new life-style I was glad I decided to move.

Revised draft:

> Moving out of my parents' house was a big ordeal, but it helped me mature. I took on many new responsibilities. For instance, I found my own apartment in Queens, and I packed my clothes, books, and stereo equipment into a U-Haul van and transported all of it to my new residence. My next step was to apply for a job. I interviewed for a position as a security guard at a department store and began working the night shift. I also learned how to cook hamburgers, spaghetti, and steak for myself, and I took care of my own laundry. Since I could no longer use the family car, I bought a 1980 Plymouth and was suddenly shocked to find how much extra auto expenses are: $400 a year for insurance, $50 a month for parking, and $20 a week for gas. All of these adult responsibilities made me realize how much I had taken my parents for granted and how much they had provided for

me. Once I had made all these adjustments and was settled into my new life-style, I was proud of my adult responsibilities and glad I had made a mature decision. And of course my parents breathed a big sigh of relief!

What are the main differences between the first draft and the revised version? What makes the revision better than the first draft? What makes the revised version longer than the first? What could the writer do to improve the revised version?

Read the following draft. This short essay is on a subject the writer had been reading about and thus knew something about. It is much more developed than the first draft you just read; however, it too can be improved a great deal by revision.

Sample first draft:

Silicon Valley

Silicon Valley is an important place in modern America. Lots of companies have started there. Some of them began very small and became huge in a few years. Most of these companies make computers or things related to computers. Silicon Valley is in California, located between Palo Alto and San Jose. It got its name from the material silicon, which is used in making computer chips.

For the last twenty or thirty years, companies have been started there. Some of them became big and successful, some of them didn't. This makes the place exciting to think about. California has always been the place for people with big dreams and ambitions. Nowadays, Hollywood isn't the place for such people the way it used to be. Now people with big ideas dream about starting a company in Silicon Valley and watching it grow into an enormous corporation.

Computers are important in our lives. This makes Silicon Valley important as a new capital of technology. The Japanese are also making computers. Silicon Valley is the place where the United States competes with the Japanese companies.

Now Silicon Valley is getting very crowded. So many companies have started there that there is not much room for new ones. Other places may begin to have a lot of computer companies being built there. If that happens, Silicon Valley may become just one of many high-technology areas. Or maybe it will be where the headquarters of these companies stay, while a lot of their other business is done somewhere else.

The writer of this essay has done a good job in many ways. She has found out a lot about her subject and has expressed some thought-provoking ideas about it. She has given the reader factual information and stayed on the general topic. Her sentences are clear and easy to read, and her vocabulary is college level, even including such phrases as "high technology."

Why is this not a first-rate finished essay? If this writer asked for readers' feedback on the essay, she would find that quite a few ideas are not developed with specific examples and that her organization is not very clear. Readers might tell her as well that her sentences tend to be rather short and choppy and that she repeats some words (especially Silicon Valley) and phrases too often. To make the essay better, she would have to revise her phrasing and organization, as well as dig up some interesting examples of her important ideas.

Revised version:

Silicon Valley Fever

Between Palo Alto and San Jose, California, lies the high-technology capital of the world. In Silicon Valley, named after the material used in making computer chips, thousands of companies that design and manufacture computers, video games, software, and electronics equipment have sprung up. Giants like Apple Computer, Atari, Hewlett-Packard, and Intel have their main operations there.

From the Gold Rush of 1849 through the golden years of Hollywood, California has always lured dreamers to the West Coast with promises of wealth and success. So it is that in the last thirty years, Silicon Valley has held out the promise of fantastic success to young business people. Some have watched their small companies with a handful of employees mushroom in three or four years into corporations with annual sales above $100 million. Instead of the hundreds of small concerns that struggle every year and fail to compete in a field dominated by IBM, the public notices the big success stories like Apple and Intel. Silicon Valley has captured the imagination of Americans as a symbol of overnight success and as the competition with Japan's outstanding computer and electronics firms.

Now, however, some changes are occurring. So many companies have begun there that almost no building space remains. Other suburban areas may become the sites of high-technology complexes. The Boston area, with MIT and Harvard University nearby, and Austin, with the University of Texas, have already attracted many companies that design computers and related products. Silicon Valley could lose its leadership as the chief center of computer manufacturing. On the other hand, the large companies may decide to do their manufacturing, packaging, and marketing in areas where space is cheaper and more available, while keeping their headquarters in Silicon Valley. The application of computers to education, business, banking, the military, and scientific research has turned the area into the computer center of the world, and that's what it will probably remain.

This version is much better than the first draft in several ways. First, its organization is clearer: it has three paragraphs with clear topics:

Paragraph 1: Introduction telling about the importance of Silicon Valley
Paragraph 2: How Silicon Valley has become the symbol of success
Paragraph 3: What may happen as a result of current changes

The writer has also included specific examples to illustrate important points:

General idea:	Many companies are located there.
Specific examples:	Apple Computer, Atari, Hewlett-Packard, and Intel

General idea:	These companies make things related to computers.
Specific examples:	computers, video games, software, and electronics equipment
General idea:	Some companies were very successful.
Specific examples:	companies with a handful of employees that mushroomed in three or four years into corporations with annual sales of over $100 million (Apple and Intel)
General idea:	Other areas may compete with Silicon Valley.
Specific examples:	Boston, Austin
General idea:	Computers are important in our world.
Specific examples:	the application of computers to education, business, banking, the military, and scientific research

Furthermore, the sentences in this version are more developed and varied than the short, simple sentences in the first draft. Compare these sentences for their length and form:

First Draft: Lots of companies have started there. Some of them began very small and became huge in a few years. Most of these companies make computers or things related to computers.

Revised Version: In Silicon Valley, named after the material used in making computer chips, thousands of companies that design and manufacture computers, video games, software, and electronic equipment have sprung up.

First Draft: California has always been the place for people with big dreams and ambitions.

Revised Version: From the Gold Rush of 1849 through the golden years of Hollywood, California has always lured dreamers to the West Coast with promises of wealth and success.

First Draft: Other places may begin to have a lot of computer companies being built there.

Revised Version: The Boston area, with MIT and Harvard University nearby, and Austin, with the University of Texas, have already attracted many companies that design computers and related products.

Finally, the writer, in revising the first draft, has remembered that good writing depends on vivid, forceful, specific words instead of vague, weak ones. Notice the differences:

First Draft	*Revised Version*
is an important place	lies the high-technology capital
lots of companies	thousands of companies
things related to computers	video games, software, and electronics equipment
have been started	have sprung up
watching it grow	watched their companies . . . mushroom
other places	other suburban areas

EXERCISE: REVISION

The following essay contains some weaknesses in organization, use of examples, sentence patterns, and choice of words. Rewrite the essay, improving it in as many ways as you can.

Job Interviews

Job interviews are very important. Going for a job interview, it is important to know how to behave and how to look. Knowing how to take a good interview is important because you may get a good job.

When you go for an interview, you should look and act right. You shouldn't act too loose, like you just came off the street. You shouldn't dress wrong either. If you dress and act right, you may get the job. If you don't, you won't get the job. Acting right means talking the right way and being polite. Friendly but not pushy. You should also be confident. You should say the right things and can ask good questions. Men should dress well, usually in suits and ties. Women should also dress well, not in jeans. Some people don't make a good impression because they are too shy or uninteresting. Some people don't know how to talk well. Others do all the talking and don't leave anybody else a chance to talk. Most people don't know what to say to an employer, and a lot of people don't know how to dress right. The important thing is to make a good impression that makes the employer feel that you are right for the job and the company.

NOTICING EFFECTIVE SENTENCE PATTERNS

Have you ever read a story, article, or book that had an unusual effect on you—left you touched, delighted, angered, or convinced? What do you think made that writing come alive with feeling and purpose? In part, it was the mysterious element of originality. Each writer's imaginative gift is his or her own, and not everything good about the best writing can be taught in the classroom. However, you can learn some important things about making your style forceful and direct. And you can learn to avoid the common faults that cause many beginning writers' prose to limp weakly along or set the reader snoring after a few sentences.

Good writing depends on sentence variety. Learn to vary both the length and the patterns of your sentences. One pitfall to avoid is "playing it safe"—escaping grammatical errors by writing only in short, simple sentences. Just as bad is the opposite extreme: using long, tangled, shapeless sentences because you didn't plan or revise. When writing about complicated ideas, either plan each sentence before you write it or be prepared to do extensive revising. Be realistic: it takes both experience and revision to shape graceful, emphatic statements. Hiding behind tiny, choppy sentences will prevent you from learning to write well. You need to experiment. Launching out into complicated statements without practice or planning will leave you with ten- or twelve-line sentences that you cannot end and that no one can read.

COMBINING SENTENCES TO IMPROVE YOUR STYLE*

Sentence combining is something all writers do, often unconsciously, to show relationships between ideas and to make their writing more effective. Combining can be simple or complicated. It includes both adding elements to simple statements by using connecting words like *and* and inserting within simpler statements modifying words or phrases (a procedure called **embedding**). Advanced writers learn to pack much material into their clauses and sentences; beginners tend to write in short, simple statements or to string long ones together loosely.

Sentence-combining exercises can start you on the road to acquiring this density and complexity. In simple terms, *sentence combining means taking short kernel (or core) sentences and fitting their essential facts together into more developed statements.*

For example:

Kernel sentences:	The painter did a job.
	The job was careless.
	The job was messy.
	The messiness and carelessness were embarrassing.
Developed sentence:	The painter did an embarrassingly careless and messy job.

We have packed in the facts from the kernel sentences to make one mature statement. We embedded *careless* and *messy* as adjectives before the noun *job* and *embarrassing(ly)* as an adverb describing the adjectives *careless* and *messy*. Being able to do this kind of combining is indispensable to writing varied, mature, and readable English. Studying grammar alone will not give you this

---

*You may want to review fragments; run-together sentences; comma splices; and simple, compound, and complex sentences in Unit 5 to be sure you combine sentences grammatically.

skill. It comes partly from your familiarity with the phrasing and rhythm of English, which you have gained from speaking, reading, and hearing the language. You can improve the skill you already possess by doing sentence-combining exercises that help you recognize the varied possibilities for expressing a thought.

There is never just one way to combine a series of kernel sentences, although in some exercises one way may seem much better than the others and some possibilities may sound awkward. In the previous example, there are other possible combinations. Are these two as good as the first?

1. The painter did a job that was embarrassingly careless and messy.
2. The job done by the painter was careless and messy to the point of being embarrassing.

These took more words to say the same thing as the first sentence. While this does not necessarily mean that the first way was best, we all like economy. The shortest, most compact way is often the best, as long as it is not awkward or unclear.*

EXERCISE I: COMBINING SENTENCES

The following kernel sentences have been combined into pairs of developed sentences. Circle the letter of the sentence you prefer in each case. Explain to a classmate why you prefer it. Is it smoother, more condensed, or freer of grammatical errors than the other one?

1. The dancer gave a performance.
   The performance was graceful.
   The performance was skillful.
   The grace and skill were remarkable.

Developed sentences:

   A. The dancer gave a remarkably graceful and skillful performance.
   B. The performance the dancer gave was graceful and skillful to the point of being remarkable.

2. The student wrote an essay.
   The student was ambitious.
   The essay was long.
   The essay was involved.
   The writing was rapid.

Developed sentences:

   A. The student who was ambitious wrote an essay that was long, involved, and rapidly written.
   B. The ambitious student rapidly wrote a long, involved essay.

*You may want to review adjectives and adverbs in Unit 5 before doing the next exercises.

3. The road changed.
   The road was bumpy.
   The road was made of dirt.
   The change was unexpected.
   The change was into a broad highway.

Developed sentences:

   A. The bumpy dirt road unexpectedly changed into a broad highway.
   B. The dirt road, which was bumpy, changes suddenly into a broad highway.

EXERCISE II: COMBINING SENTENCES

Write your own developed sentences using the kernel sentences given. Write two possible sentences for each group; circle the letter of the one you find reads more smoothly.

1. The teacher gave a test.
   The test was short.
   The test was easy.
   The shortness and easiness were surprising.

Developed sentences:

A. _____

B. _____

2. The campers erected a tent.
   The tent was green.
   The tent was made of canvas.
   The tent was large.
   They erected it carefully.

Developed sentences:

A. _____

B. _____

3. The story came to an end.
   The story was about ghosts.
   The story was thrilling.
   The end was abrupt.
   The end was shocking.

Developed sentences:

A. _____

B. _____

4. Travis learned breakdancing.
   He learned from other teenagers.
   The teenagers performed on the streets.
   They performed in films.
   Travis watched them perform.

Developed sentences:

A. _____

B. _____

5. Jennifer selected an umbrella.
   She selected it carefully.
   The umbrella was beautiful.
   The umbrella was plaid.
   The umbrella looked expensive.

Developed sentences:

A. _____

B. _____

In these exercises you have either *added* parts by joining them with *and* to the main sentences or *embedded* parts by fitting them tightly into the sentences as modifiers. You should also be able to use **free modifiers** sometimes to make your sentences more varied. A free modifier is a descriptive word or phrase that reads as an extra element, interesting and informative but not essential. The same descriptive elements can sometimes be used either way:

Embedded: The dancer gave a *remarkably graceful, skillful* performance.
Free: The dancer's performance, *remarkably graceful and skillful,* received tremendous applause.

The second way sounds more sophisticated, doesn't it? That does not mean that it is better, but by knowing how to use options you can make your style more interesting.

For practice, convert the embedded modifiers to free modifiers in this sentence:

1. The *heavy, lumbering* dump truck rolled gradually to a stop.
2. The dump truck, _____ , rolled gradually to a stop.

Free and Embedded Modifiers

Free modifiers are groups of words—nouns, verbs, or adjectives—that can be placed in different parts of the sentence. They are called free because they are movable; the same cluster may be located before the main statement, in the middle of the main statement, or after the main statement. A free modifier is added to enliven or add color to the main statement.

Suppose we begin with a main statement:

> Michael took extra courses in the summer.

Now we add a free modifier:

> hoping to graduate in three years

This modifier can be placed at the beginning:

> Hoping to graduate in three years, Michael took extra courses in the summer.

Or it can be placed in the middle:

> Michael, hoping to graduate in three years, took extra courses in the summer.

It can also be placed at the end:

> Michael took extra courses in the summer, hoping to graduate in three years.*

EXERCISE I: COMBINING SENTENCES WITH MODIFIERS

Write two developed sentences for each exercise. Use embedded modifiers in one sentence, free modifiers in the other.

Example:

> Ted's girlfriend was waiting.
> She was waiting at the cafe.
> His girlfriend was pretty.
> His girlfriend was charming.
> She waited patiently.

---

*See dangling and misplaced modifiers in Unit 5. Sometimes a free modifier will not fit correctly in one of its possible positions.

Embedded modifiers: Ted's *pretty, charming* girlfriend was waiting patiently at the cafe.

Free modifiers: Ted's girlfriend, *pretty and charming*, was waiting patiently at the cafe.

1. The poodle came running.
   The running was toward his owner.
   The poodle was trimmed.
   The trimming was exquisite.
   The poodle was perfumed.

   Embedded modifiers: _____

   Free modifiers: _____

2. The car was parked.
   The parking was near the school.
   The car had been stolen.
   The car had been stripped.
   The car was new.

   Embedded modifiers: _____

   Free modifiers: _____

3. The wedding took place.
   It was in a ballroom.
   The wedding was large.
   The wedding was planned.
   The planning was careful.

   Embedded modifiers: _____

   Free modifiers: _____

4. The sequoias towered.
   They were in the forest.
   They towered above the other trees.
   They were ancient.
   They were awesome.

   Embedded modifiers: _____

   Free modifiers: _____

EXERCISE II: COMBINING SENTENCES WITH MODIFIERS

On a separate sheet of paper, combine these kernel sentences into developed sentences; write two versions of each set.

1. The parties lasted.
   The lasting was often.
   The lasting was until 3:00 a.m.
   The parties were given.
   The giving was by Scott and Zelda Fitzgerald.
   The parties were wild.
   The parties were unforgettable.

2. The stories appeal.
   The stories are by Edgar Allan Poe.
   The stories are short.
   The stories are bizarre.
   The stories are macabre.
   The appealing is to readers.
   The readers are in the millions.
   The readers are today's.

3. The stories contain crimes.
   The crimes are grotesque.
   The stories contain events.
   The events are supernatural.
   The stories are among thrillers.
   The thrillers are the earliest.
   The thrillers are psychological.
   The thrillers are about detectives.

4. Child abuse is a problem.
   The problem is widespread.
   The problem is in our society.
   The problem requires action.
   The action is from our communities.
   The action is from our legislatures.

EXERCISE III: COMBINING SENTENCES WITH MODIFIERS

Rewrite this paragraph in better style by combining the choppy sentences into more developed ones.

My friend Laverne is an impressive person. She is impressive because of her style. She is impressive because of her activities. She is impressive because of her goals. Her style of dressing is beautiful. It is also up to date. Her clothes always look elegant. They also look expensive. But they really aren't expensive. That is because she knows how to shop. She also has many activities. She knows how to do silkscreens. She also knows how to do landscape photography. She can play golf. She can play racquetball. She can play tennis. She does all of these like an expert. It is not surprising that she has high goals. She wants to graduate from college. She wants to do this with honors. She wants to graduate with a major in biology. She later wants to earn a master's degree. This will also be in biology. Later she wants to become an oceanographer. This job will allow her to travel. It will also keep her interested for many years. It will also give her satisfaction. This is because such work is important. It is important to the future of the environment.

Who, Which, and That Clauses*

Clauses that begin with *who, which,* or *that* are called **relative clauses**, meaning that they *relate to,* or describe, some person or thing just before them in the sentence. Two kernel sentences can sometimes be combined by turning one of them into a relative clause:

Kernel sentences:	Some people drive to work every day.
	These people don't want the price of gasoline to rise.
Developed sentence with relative clause:	People *who drive to work every day* don't want the price of gasoline to rise.

The same thing can be done with things instead of people using *which* or *that* instead of *who*:

Kernel sentences:	Some companies receive government contracts.
	These companies face bureaucratic regulations.
Developed sentence with relative clause:	Companies *that receive government contracts* face bureaucratic regulations.

Some clauses use prepositions like *in, to, for, of,* and *from* before *which* or *whom.* Learn to use these patterns as well:

Kernel sentences:	You spoke to a lady in the elevator.
	That lady is our Saturday afternoon newscaster.
Developed sentence with relative clause:	The lady *to whom you spoke in the elevator* is our Saturday afternoon newscaster.

*You may want to review the use of commas to separate *who* and *which* clauses in Unit 5.

EXERCISE I: COMBINING SENTENCES WITH RELATIVE CLAUSES

Combine these kernel sentences into developed sentences using *who, which,* or *that* clauses:

1. Some students wait until the last minute to study for exams.
   These students rarely earn high grades.

   Developed sentence:

   _____

2. Some colleges have developed work-study programs.
   These colleges have flourished in a tight economy.

   Developed sentence:

   _____

3. Robert Frost is known as a New England poet.
   He was actually born in San Francisco.

   Developed sentence:

   _____

4. Some people appear on television talk shows.
   These people often have a film or book to promote.

   Developed sentence:

   _____

5. For some people correct spelling is easy.
   These people often learned to read early.

   Developed sentence:

   _____

6. From some countries raw materials are exported to the United States.
   These countries suffer economic losses when the dollar increases in value.

   Developed sentence:

   _____

7. Brochures were sent to some customers.
   These customers can receive free six-month subscriptions.

   Developed sentence:

   _____

8. Some mayors have been in office for over ten years.
   These mayors have seen a change in urban policies.

Developed sentence:

_____

9. Some stars suddenly become intensely bright.
   Later they turn into black holes.

Developed sentence:

_____

10. The public places a lot of trust in some political leaders.
    These leaders should set an example of honesty.

Developed sentence:

_____

EXERCISE II: COMBINING SENTENCES WITH RELATIVE CLAUSES

Combine these kernel sentences into developed sentences using *who*, *which*, and *that* clauses. Write each one two ways, underlining the relative clause in each. Example:

Kernel sentences:

Some girls want to study medicine.
These girls take biochemistry in high school.

Developed sentences:

A. Girls who *want to study medicine* usually take biochemistry in high school.
B. Girls *who take biochemistry in high school* often want to study medicine.

1. Some people like to shop at Fashion City.
   These people have good taste in clothes.

Developed sentences:

A. _____

B. _____

2. Some motorists park outside the city.
   These motorists prefer to avoid rush hour traffic.

Developed sentences:

A. _____

B. _____

3. Some regulations did not make sense.
   These regulations have been eliminated.

Developed sentences:

A. _____

B. _____

4. Some stories have violence in them.
   These stories have been analyzed by psychologists.

Developed sentences:

A. _____

B. _____

5. Citizenship was granted to some immigrants.
   These immigrants had lived in the country for five years.

Developed sentences:

A. _____

B. _____

How, When, Where, and Why Combinations

You can often combine kernel sentences by **subordinating**,* which means turning one kernel sentence into a **subordinate clause**. Here is an example:

Kernel sentences: Utility bills are high during the summer.

Air conditioning consumes a large amount of electricity.

---

*Clauses using *who, which,* and *that* also subordinate by using these relative pronouns; they are called **relative clauses**. To check your grammar while using subordinate clauses to combine sentences, you may want to review subordinate conjunctions and fragments in Unit 5.

The first statement is the base sentence; the second explains *why* the first is true. Transform the second into a subordinate clause by using *because*.

Developed sentence: Utility bills are high during the
                                       summer *because* air conditioning
                                       consumes a large amount of
                                       electricity.

In such combinations, the base statement is a **main clause**. It contains a subject and verb (bills *are*) and stands by itself as a complete statement. The other statement becomes a **subordinate clause**. It also has a subject and verb (air conditioning *consumes*) but cannot stand by itself. Rather, it tells how, where, when, or why the main statement is true. Subordinate clauses begin with introductory words called **subordinate conjunctions** like these:

after	if
although	since
as	until
as if	when
because	where
before	while

Notice that more than one subordinate conjunction may be possible in the same combination:

Utility bills are high during the summer, *when* air conditioning consumes a large amount of electricity.

Utility bills are high during the summer, *since* air conditioning consumes a large amount of electricity.

EXERCISE I: COMBINING SENTENCES BY SUBORDINATING

Combine these kernel sentences into developed sentences by subordinating.

Example:

Kernel sentences: The original date of the perfor-
                                       mance was changed.
                                       The original date conflicted with
                                       commencement exercises.

Developed sentence: The original date of the perfor-
                                       mance was changed *because* it
                                       conflicted with commencement
                                       exercises.

1. Politicians lose their credibility with the public.
   Politicians make wild promises.

Developed sentence:

_____

2. Drivers should be especially alert.
   Drivers approach busy intersections.

Developed sentence:

_____

3. Actors in soap operas are sometimes attacked in public.
   The characters they play do ugly or immoral things on the screen.

Developed sentence:

_____

4. The marathon run is named after an ancient Greek city.
   The Athenians defeated the Persians at that place.

Developed sentence:

_____

5. This trampoline is not difficult to assemble.
   You follow the instructions step by step.

Developed sentence:

_____

6. Reading modern poetry is difficult.
   Its meaning is usually hidden.

Developed sentence:

_____

7. You can learn a lot about the process of your writing.
   Other people share their impression of it with you.

Developed sentence:

_____

8. Cordless telephones are very convenient.
   People nearby can sometimes listen in on your conversation.

Developed sentence:

_____

9. Sandra has decided to wait to get married.
   She will be thirty-five years old at that time.

Developed sentence:

_____

10. Most presidents lose popularity in the polls.
    They have been in office a year or two.

Developed sentence:

_____

EXERCISE II: COMBINING SENTENCES BY SUBORDINATING

Combine these kernel sentences by means of subordination. Write each developed sentence two ways, reversing the order of the statements the second time.

Example:

Kernel sentences:

Sally was twenty pounds overweight.
She went on a sugar-free diet.

Developed sentences:

A. Sally was twenty pounds overweight *when* she went on a sugar-free diet.
B. *When* Sally went on a sugar-free diet, she was twenty pounds overweight.

1. Traveling beyond the solar system is unlikely.
   The nearest stars would take lifetimes to reach.

Developed sentences:

A. _____

B. _____

2. Hypnosis can produce startling effects.
   It is practiced by a well-trained professional.

Developed sentences:

A. _____

B. _____

3. Recruits are sometimes nervous and irritable.
   They enter basic training.

Developed sentences:

A. _____

B. _____

4. Most men and women should exercise regularly.
   They reach the age of forty.

Developed sentences:

A. _____

B. _____

5. You should learn to read and write effectively.
   You want to become a lawyer.

Developed sentences:

A. _____

B. _____

EXERCISE III: COMBINING SENTENCES BY SUBORDINATING

These groups are more complicated than the preceding ones. All of them need subordination, but you may want to use other forms of combining as well.

Example:

Kernel sentences:

Some elderly people are at a disadvantage.
They are on fixed incomes.
Inflation keeps reducing their spending power.

Developed sentence:

Elderly people who are on fixed incomes are at a disadvantage because inflation keeps reducing their spending power.

1. Teenage pregnancies can be tragic.
    The mothers have babies to care for.
    They are not much more than babies themselves.

Developed sentence:

_____

2. Alcoholism has been a menace for decades.
    It has increased sharply in recent years.
    It now affects one out of ten American adults.

Developed sentence:

_____

3. Marijuana used to be considered harmless.
    Recent studies have shown its serious long-range effects.
    These include damage to the lungs, heart, and reproductive system.

Developed sentence:

_____

4. Pornography has become offensive in big cities.
    It overwhelms the business districts with signs and pictures.
    These pictures are of explicit sexual acts.
    Sometimes these acts include children.

Developed sentence:

_____

5. Gambling can be a form of light entertainment.
    For some people it is an addiction.
    This addiction destroys their personal lives.
    It reaches a certain point.
    At this point they cannot control it.

Developed sentence:

_____

EXERCISE IV: COMBINING SENTENCES BY SUBORDINATING

These combinations are still more complicated than those in the previous exercise. Again you should use subordination along with other ways of combining kernel sentences.

Example:

Kernel sentences:

A prospective doctor goes to medical school for four years.
Then he or she becomes an intern.
Next he or she serves several years as a resident.
Finally he or she goes into independent practice.

Developed sentence:

After going to medical school for four years, a prospective doctor becomes an intern, then serves several years as a resident, and finally goes into independent practice.

1. Heroin is derived from morphine.
   It is stronger than morphine.
   It is also more addictive.
   It takes effect faster.

   Developed sentence:

   _____

   _____

2. You want to help a choking victim.
   Stand behind the person.
   Place your fist above his or her navel.
   Suddenly press your fist in and up with your hand.

   Developed sentence:

   _____

   _____

3. A. Philip Randolph was a hero.
   He was in the labor movement.
   He challenged authority by his activism.
   His activism was for civil rights.
   He also organized unions and marches.
   The marches were on Washington.

   Developed sentence:

   _____

   _____

4. Most unidentified flying objects can be explained.
   The explaining is scientific.
   Others defy explanation.
   The others are not weather balloons.
   The others are not optical illusions.

Developed sentence:

_____

_____

5. Michael loves to play trivia games.
   He always wins.
   The winning is against his friends.
   The winning is against his classmates.
   He knows more facts than anyone else.
   The facts are about geography.
   The facts are about history.
   The facts are about sports.

Developed sentence:

_____

_____

EXERCISE V: COMBINING SENTENCES BY SUBORDINATING

Combine these sentences so that you make one developed sentence out of each group of kernel sentences. Then rewrite your developed sentences in order as a paragraph.

1. There are differences between boys and girls.
   These differences are many.
   These differences are apparent.
   These differences are based on stereotypes.
   The stereotypes are created by society.

Developed sentence:

_____

_____

2. Some psychologists think there are other differences.
   The differences are inborn.

Developed sentence:

_____

_____

3. For example, girls at birth seem to be sensitive to sounds.
   Girls seem to be sensitive to touch.
   Girls seem to notice faces.
   Girls seem to learn speech.
   The learning is easy.

Developed sentence:

_____

_____

4. Newborn boys seem curious.
   They are curious about their surroundings.
   The surroundings are physical.
   Boys grasp shapes.
   The shapes are geometrical.
   The grasping is easy.

Developed sentence:

_____

_____

5. These differences may have come from prehistoric families.
   In these families work was divided.
   Women watched the children.
   Women prepared the food.
   Men went out to hunt.
   They hunted for animals.

Developed sentence:

_____

_____

6. Some prehistoric groups tended to survive.
   These groups contained women.
   The women talked a lot.
   The women were social.
   The groups contained men.
   The men had good visual sense.
   The men were well coordinated.

Developed sentence:

_____

_____

7. These differences may be inborn.
   This does not mean girls are smarter than boys.
   It does not mean boys are smarter than girls.
   It only means they may have patterns.
   The patterns are different.
   The difference is slight.
   The patterns are of development.

Developed sentence:

_____

_____

Now write your developed sentences in order as one paragraph.

EXTRA PRACTICE I: COMBINING SENTENCES

These sentences are too simple and boring. Combine each pair into a more developed, mature sentence.

1. Darryl waited impatiently for the race to begin. He was clutching the steering wheel and muttering to himself.
2. Yvonne waved to her boyfriend. She noticed he had left his Sony Walkman on the counter.
3. Sally owns an enormous dog. It looks like a monster from outer space and terrorizes her friends.
4. Many teachers thought the students' evaluations of them were fair. Some teachers thought students were unfair to teachers who gave them low grades.
5. As he entered the dugout, the catcher made an obscene remark to a noisy spectator. This noisy spectator had been heckling him for three innings.

EXTRA PRACTICE II: COMBINING SENTENCES

Rewrite each set of kernel sentences as a single developed sentence, eliminating boring repetitions.

1. "User friendly" is a term.
   The term refers to computers.
   The term means that a computer or program is easy.
   The easiness is for the person using it.

   Developed sentence:

   _____

   _____

2. Alan Turing was a genius.
   He broke a code.
   The code was used by the Germans.
   It was used during World War II.

   Developed sentence:

   _____

   _____

3. Absentee landlords own buildings.
   They live somewhere else.
   They do not have to live with problems.
   The problems come from poor maintenance.
   The maintenance is of the buildings they own.

   Developed sentence:

   _____

   _____

4. A pecking order is a system.
   The system is of status levels.
   This term comes from hens.
   Hens show dominance over other hens.
   They show dominance by pecking them.

   Developed sentence:

   _____

   _____

5. Subsidies are grants.
   They are given by the government.
   They are given by private organizations.
   These organizations want to foster improvement.
   The improvement is cultural or social.

Developed sentence:

_____

_____

OTHER WAYS TO IMPROVE SENTENCES

Sentence combining, which improves a choppy, oversimplified style, is only one kind of improvement you should learn. Another kind of improvement is avoidance of repetition by substitution of different words for words that are repeated too often. What is wrong with this passage?

> Yvette is my next-door neighbor. Yvette has three children, ages six, eight, and twelve. I first met Yvette three years ago when I moved into the apartment house where Yvette lived. Yvette didn't wait for me to come over to introduce myself; instead Yvette showed up right there at my door with a present to welcome me to the new building. That's what I like about Yvette—Yvette always thinks of others first.

Using Pronouns to Avoid Repeating Nouns*

In the passage you just read, the writer always referred to her neighbor with one word, Yvette. She never used the pronouns *she* or *her* instead. Read the passage again and say *she* or *her* in place of *Yvette* wherever you think it would break up the repetition effectively. (Note: it is not a good idea to use *only she* or *he* instead of a person's name; pronouns can become boring, too.)

Read the following passage, with *she* substituted to avoid repeating *Yvette* too often.

> Yvette, my next-door neighbor, has three children, ages six, eight, and twelve. I first met her three years ago when I moved into the apartment house where she lived. Yvette didn't wait for me to come over to introduce myself; instead she showed up right there at my door with a present to welcome me to the new building. That's what I like about her—she always thinks of others first.

The original passage contained eight references to the name *Yvette*. How many does the revised passage contain? _____

---

*You may at this point want to review the use of pronouns in Unit 5.

EXERCISE: USING PRONOUNS

Read the following passage and underline references to *George*. Rewrite the passage, eliminating too much repetition by substituting *he*, *him*, or *his* in place of the name.

> George is a student in my sociology class. No one would say that George is a model student. Whenever George arrives, the class winces as if expecting a scene. George always enters late, and George usually drops a pencil or book before flopping loudly into George's seat. George never expresses George's opinion during class discussion or answers a question when the teacher calls on George, but as soon as the teacher starts to lecture, George is sure to make a loud remark or ask an irrelevant question.

Varying Your Sentence Beginnings*

One of the most common faults of beginning writers is to begin nearly all sentences the same way. Look over some of your previous writing—your paragraphs and essay exercises. Did you begin most of your sentences with the subject followed by the verb?

Sentences can begin many ways, not always with the main subject and verb. One of the most familiar patterns is the monotonous repetition of "I did," "I saw," "I went," and so on, in essays about a personal experience. Read this sample passage.

> I used to live in a neighborhood where many of the kids committed minor crimes. I thought stealing fruit from an open stand or jumping turnstiles in the subway was a sign of courage and intelligence. I never worried much about what would happen if I got caught doing these things. I wanted to learn from the older kids how to get away fast and how to fool the police. I thought I was leading the life of a legendary outlaw until my cousin was arrested.

It is easy to fall into this "I, I, I" pattern without noticing it. Remember that there are many other ways to begin a sentence.

---

*You may at this point want to review the use of commas after introductory parts in Unit 5.

Ways to Begin Sentences Other than with the Main Subject and Verb

1. Begin with an introductory phrase or clause:

   In my neighborhood, there were many kids who committed minor crimes.

   When my family moved to St. Louis, there were many kids in my neighborhood who committed minor crimes.

2. Begin with a participle (-ing or -ed verb form):

   Influenced by the example of my friends, I began to commit minor robberies.

   Ignoring the possible consequences, I ventured into a life of minor robberies.

3. Begin with an appositive (a short identifying word or group):

   A *skilled thief at the age of ten*, I took pride in my daring and expertise.

Learn to use these sentence beginnings to break up monotonous patterns. Many of your sentences will begin with the ordinary subject/verb combination, but some variety will make your writing more lively and readable. Read the revised version of the original passage.

> In my old neighborhood there were many kids who committed minor crimes. Influenced by their example, I ventured into an early career of robbery. I ignored the possible consequences of stealing fruit from open stands or jumping subway turnstiles. A skilled thief at the age of ten, I took pride in my daring and expertise. From older kids I learned how to get away fast and fool the police. Not until my cousin was arrested did I begin to question the wisdom of trying to become a legendary outlaw.

EXERCISE I: SENTENCE BEGINNINGS

Rewrite the following sentences so that they begin with an introductory phrase or clause, a participle, or an appositive.

Group I: Introductory phrases and clauses

Example: I found a wonderful Mexican restaurant two blocks away.
Rewrite: Two blocks away I found a wonderful Mexican restaurant.

1. Stephanie was lucky to find an apartment with two bathrooms near 94th Street.

Rewrite: _____

2. Most of the jobs had already been filled by the time Steven applied.

Rewrite: _____

3. The old grocery store began to lose business when a new supermarket opened across the street.

Rewrite: _____

4. The price of gasoline is no longer exorbitant because the worldwide prices for oil have declined.

Rewrite: _____

5. We will take a taxi home after the party.

Rewrite: _____

Group II: Participles

Example: The driver noticed a problem with the engine while turning the corner.

Rewrite: While turning the corner, the driver noticed a problem with the engine.

1. Jennifer did her math and Spanish homework after taking a shower.

Rewrite: _____

2. Jerry, knowing that he had a good chance to win, pulled into the lead.

Rewrite: _____

3. The boat, abandoned a year ago by its owner, was now half submerged.

Rewrite: _____

4. Kimberly hurried home to her stepmother, elated by her test score.

Rewrite: _____

5. Some of the patients, committed to the mental ward for false reasons, were eventually released.

Rewrite: _____

Group III: Appositives*

Example: Mr. Rogers, who has been a popular television figure for many years, criticized some of the new commercials.
Rewrite: A popular television figure for many years, Mr. Rogers criticized some of the new commercials.

1. The candidate, a former member of the CIA, insisted on the importance of classified information.

Rewrite: _____

2. My sister, who is an ardent supporter of children's rights, joined a new lobbying group.

Rewrite: _____

3. The professor, a graduate of Purdue University, was an expert on agricultural technology.

Rewrite: _____

4. Most of the actors, who were experienced professionals used to the unexpected, had no trouble coping with the emergency.

Rewrite: _____

5. The Great Lakes, a gigantic creation of the glaciers during the Ice Age, are a source of fresh water for the Midwest.

Rewrite: _____

EXERCISE II: SENTENCE BEGINNINGS

Rewrite the paragraph below, eliminating boring repetition by varying the beginnings of sentences.

Herbert is a totally independent person. He refuses to take advice from anyone, even when he is wrong. He was an only child, and his parents let him do whatever he wanted. He learned to have his own way as a result. He goes his own

*See the use of commas with appositives in Unit 5.

way around his friends, and he expects them to do whatever he wants. He sometimes likes to look at pretty girls with his friends, and he always decides which ones they will try to pick up and where they will go. He once ignored his girlfriend's advice that he should stop hanging out on weekends until exams were over, and he was put on probation. He likes to give advice to other people and criticize them, but he is hypersensitive toward criticism himself. He will get into big trouble someday if he doesn't stop being such a know-it-all.

Diction: Improving Your Choice of Words

In the process of creating paragraphs and essays, you have not concentrated much on word choice. Content, development, and organization have occupied most of your attention. In editing your essays once they are adequately developed and organized, however, **diction**, or choice of words, becomes your most important means of improving your writing. The most noticeable difference between a merely acceptable essay and one that leaves your reader wanting to read it again and again lies in an effective choice of words. Choose words that are precise, idiomatic, appropriate in connotation, and specific.

Being Precise. Legal, scientific, and medical writing must be precise for professional reasons, but all writing is more effective when the words convey exactly the right meaning. You know how infuriating it is when you ask for directions and someone tells you your destination is "down the road a piece" or "a few miles from here." You need more precise directions. Similarly, in writing, make careful statements. Be especially careful with words like *all*, *everybody*, *nobody*, *most*, *many*, *some*, and *a few*. In conversation we casually throw around remarks like "Everybody knows that song." We don't take such remarks literally. But you should not write casual statements about serious issues. "Everybody wants stricter enforcement of drug laws" is not a careful statement. "Most people" would probably be a safe phrase in this statement; "many people" or "some people" would be too weak.

Be careful also to choose the correct transitional expressions and connective words. Don't use *and* as a catchall connective instead of *but*, *therefore*, or some other connective. "Police sometimes react too quickly, *and* they don't have enough training" is less precise than "Police sometimes react too quickly *because* they don't have enough training." Avoid using *which* or *in which* vaguely in place of *and* or other connectives. "Teenagers face many temptations today, *in which* they often get into trouble" is awkward and imprecise. A better statement might be "Teenagers are often in difficult situations *in which* they suddenly need help." Some writers often misuse *whereas*, treating it as an all-purpose transitional word. The correct use of *whereas* is to show a contrast, as in the statement "The state law permits turning right on a red light, *whereas* the city ordinance prohibits it." Do not use it carelessly, as in "The government should do something about the homeless, *whereas* inexpensive public housing should be built and counseling should be provided."

As you learn new vocabulary, do not be afraid to use it in your writing. Just be sure to check the meaning in a dictionary first. When you begin noticing a particular new word in your reading, you may guess at the meaning—and guess wrong. "This will *exacerbate* the condition"; "This will *alleviate* the condition." Which word do you want? What is the difference between *uninterested* and *disinterested*? between *discreet* and *discrete*? What does it mean to *defer* payment? What exactly do we refer to as a *story*, a *novel*, a *poem*, or a work of *prose*? What does it mean to *rationalize*? Is that different from *being rational*? When should you write *infer* and when should you write *imply*? What is the difference between *compose* and *comprise*? These are just some of the hundreds of fine distinctions made by careful writers. If you hope to be a careful writer, you must always have a dictionary at hand, especially when you edit.

EXERCISE: CHOOSING PRECISE WORDS

The underlined words or phrases are imprecise or incorrect as used. Use common sense and a dictionary to help you determine more precise equivalents. Write them in the blanks.

Example:

*consists of*   The kit is comprised of three blank tapes, a film on video, and a head-cleaner tape.

_____ 1. The presence of heavily armed police only alleviated the crowd's anger.

_____ 2. Food served in fast-food restaurants is more nutritious than most people think, and the problem is that it is highly caloric.

_____ 3. Most people believe in astrology and witchcraft.

_____ 4. Both parties in the labor dispute agreed to submit the decision to an uninterested third party.

_____ 5. All of the members of Congress put their constituents' wishes before the needs of the nation.

_____ 6. Biology majors must take at least three courses in subjects not related to science, whereas two must be in the humanities.

_____ 7. Lucile rationalized that she could afford to pay no more than $700 for rent.

_____ 8. The writer is inferring that she really does not believe the government's statistics.

_____ 9. When Donna pointed out his mistake, Frank extracted his statement.

_____ 10. The patient's stomach was badly extended from the internal pressure.

Using Idioms Correctly.   **Idioms** are fixed phrases or combinations like "out of order," "keep an eye on," "take your time," or "out of the question." These phrases often do not make sense if you analyze them word by word, but people who grow up speaking English (all other languages have idioms too) learn the meanings of idioms by habit. Careless writers may, however, occasionally write phrases that are not idiomatic, and students who have learned English as a second language or as a foreign language often have some difficulties with idioms. When you edit your writing, check to see that your phrasing matches the natural phrasing of American speech. If you learned English as a second or foreign language, you may need extra practice with spoken English to become more secure in your grasp of idioms. A dictionary of American idioms may speed the process. All students, however, are likely to have a little trouble with idiomatic word combinations that involve advanced vocabulary. The most common problems occur in matching verbs with prepositions. For instance, we say that a person is accused *of* a crime, charged *with* a crime, convicted *of* a crime, and sentenced *to* ten years in jail. Here is a list of some common errors in idiom:

Not Idiomatic	*Idiomatic*
He was angry at his boss.	He was angry with his boss.
I bought the car off Paul.	I bought the car from Paul.
The horse is not capable to run.	The horse is not capable of running.
She was bored of the party.	She was bored with the party.
The discussion centered around politics.	The discussion centered on politics.
I am concerned for your grades.	I am concerned about your grades.
We went in search for the cat.	We went in search of the cat.
I differ from you on that subject.	I differ with you on that subject.
She was born at Denver.	She was born in Denver.
A cassette deck is preferable than a radio.	A cassette deck is preferable to a radio.
Fish is superior than red meat.	Fish is superior to red meat.
A cheetah has twice the speed as a dog.	A cheetah has twice the speed of a dog.
Sandra was not interested to go along.	Sandra was not interested in going along.
Poor health prevented him to do it.	Poor health prevented him from doing it.

EXERCISE: IDIOMATIC USAGE

One of the following sentences is correct; write C in the blank next to it. In the other blanks, write the word that will correct the unidiomatic expression in the sentence.

_____ 1. Vodka has twice the alcohol content as beer.

_____ 2. You may become bored of going to the library every day.

_____ 3. The president is not interested in holding a press conference.

_____ 4. The Democrats differed from the Republicans about the budget appropriations for child care.

_____ 5. The singer is healthy and capable to give a great concert.

_____ 6. The weather forecast should not prevent farmers to plant early this year.

_____ 7. Far superior than a new law would be a public relations campaign.

Using Correct Connotation.   **Connotation** is what a word suggests; **denotation** is what it means literally. Blue, red, green, and gray denote certain colors, but they all connote something else—blue, sadness; red, radicalism or anger; green, envy or illness; and gray, indistinctness (a gray area). In effective writing one chooses words for their implied meanings and associations as well as for their factual meanings. *Love, adoration, affection, devotion, liking,* and *friendship* all mean about the same thing, but each word suggests a different emotional quality. *Debate, argue, quarrel,* and *clash* all refer to differences of opinion but suggest different degrees of feeling. Some words are more formal than others: *before, previously,* and *hitherto* all refer to the past, but each one is more formal than the one before. Most of us would never use *hitherto* in conversation.

In college writing, faulty connotation may result from not finding the right voice and tone. If your writing shuttles between casual street remarks and formal discussions, your word choice will be erratic. An essay that contains words such as *hitherto, reciprocal, charismatic,* and *extraneous* will sound funny if it also contains expressions like *cop out, cool, booze,* and *dude.* Some words may also have offensive connotations; *gal,* for instance, has a sexist connotation that *woman* does not. *Spinster* used for a single woman has both sexist and old-fashioned connotations that *bachelor* used for a single man does not. Words may also have favorable or negative connotations. *Bureaucrat,* for example, may refer to an office worker in a large organization, but it can suggest a person who merely follows orders without being humanly involved in his or her work. *Government employee* does not have a negative connotation of this kind. Be sure that the words you choose have the connotations appropriate to your intention and tone.

EXERCISE: CONNOTATION

Explain why each of the words in italics has the wrong connotation for its use in the sentence. Write a more appropriate word in the blank.

Example:

assistants _____   I admire the mayor for appointing high-quality *inferiors*.

_____ 1. After the refreshments were served, half of the executives decided to *split*.

_____ 2. The police commissioner told the officers to stop *griping* about the regulations.

_____ 3. The Senate *quarreled about* the bill for two hours.

_____ 4. The SWAT team approached with extreme caution so that the sniper would not suddenly go *wacko*.

_____ 5. Two female attorneys encouraged all the *ladies* in the audience to consider law as a profession.

_____ 6. Eddie Murphy starred in a *mirthful* film.

_____ 7. Martin Luther King, Jr., was America's most *notorious* civil rights hero.

_____ 8. Cooking a pot roast dinner made Stanley feel *homely*.

_____ 9. After the long wait, the diner *leered* at his salad angrily.

_____ 10. The ball-carrier *sidled* head-on into the pack of defensive linemen.

Using Specific Language.   Whenever possible, use specific words instead of general ones. Write "six feet four" instead of "tall," "three hundred pounds" instead of "heavy," "blue spruce" instead of "fir tree," and "1989 BMW" instead of "car." Specific, concrete words communicate more information than vague, general ones. They create a more distinct picture in the reader's mind. They are easier to understand. Acquire the habit of concentrating on specifics and using general statements only when needed. You may be surprised how seldom you need abstract, general terms. When you find yourself about to write, "The American family is less cohesive than it used to be," write instead "Most children are lucky to see their parents more than one hour a day."

Compare the two paragraphs below. The first is written in vague, general vocabulary, the second by the well-known author Maya Angelou in vivid, concrete vocabulary.

Vague:

We lived in a big house. We had a lot of people renting rooms from us; they were all different from one another. Some were workers, and others were prostitutes. One couple talked with me until the husband went away. Then the wife became shy. There was also an older couple who were boring.

Specific:

Our house was a fourteen-room typical San Franciscan postearthquake affair. We had a succession of roomers, bringing and taking their different accents, and personalities and foods. Shipyard workers clanked up the stairs (we all slept on the second floor except Mother and Daddy Clidell) in their steel-tipped boots and metal hats, and gave way to much-powdered prostitutes, who giggled through their makeup and hung their wigs on the door-knobs. One couple (they were college graduates) held long adult conversations with me in the big kitchen downstairs, until the husband went off to war. Then the wife who had been so charming and ready to smile changed into a silent shadow that played infrequently along the walls. An older couple lived with us for a year or so. They owned a restaurant and had no personality to enchant or interest a teenager, except that the husband was called Uncle Jim, and the wife Aunt Boy. I never figured that out.*

Recognize the difference between general, somewhat specific, and highly specific language:

General	Somewhat Specific	Highly Specific
vehicle	car	Porsche
animal	dog	bull terrier
medical worker	nurse	geriatric nurse
sports	track and field	400-meter hurdles

EXERCISE I: GENERAL AND SPECIFIC LANGUAGE

Fill in the blanks with general, somewhat specific, and highly specific terms:

General	Somewhat Specific	Highly Specific
1. educational institution	_____	Georgia State University
2. food	dessert	_____
3. _____	planet	Mars
4. news medium	news magazine	_____
5. celebrity	_____	Michael Jackson
6. _____	soft drink	Pepsi-Cola
7. state	_____	Indiana
8. country	African country	_____
9. book	_____	Webster's Dictionary
10. _____	skyscraper	Sears Tower

*From Maya Angelou, *I Know Why the Caged Bird Sings*. New York: Random House, 1969.

EXERCISE 11: GENERAL AND SPECIFIC LANGUAGE

Revise these sentences using specific, concrete words in place of general, abstract words:

1. Jennifer lived in a large building and worked in a small business not far away. She took public transportation to work.

   _____

   _____

2. Ernie participated frequently in sports. He liked several of them, but was outstanding in one. He won awards in that sport.

   _____

   _____

3. People who are addicted to various substances can do a number of things to get over their addictions.

   _____

   _____

4. Inez took a rather long vacation to several islands; she enjoyed a number of activities while she was there.

   _____

   _____

5. When you live in a big city, you get used to a number of scary sights, loud noises, and unpleasant encounters.

   _____

   _____

Reducing Wordiness

In your prewriting and composing, you have worked hard to develop **fluency**, which means to be able to write many words without too much hesitation and awkwardness. Now it may seem like a step backward to try to *reduce* the number of words in your final drafts. Here we want to distinguish between effective words and wasted words. Well-chosen words add to the meaning and power of your essays; deadwood or clutter, as some editors call wasted words, gets in the way. Expert writers make words count more than beginners do; they improve their rough drafts by shortening them without changing the meaning or reducing the coverage. This is what you will do as your final step in learning to be a good editor of your own writing. If the instructor assigns a 500-word essay, aim for about 700 words first. In your prewriting and writing of a rough draft, you should not be concerned about wordiness; it will hamper your flow of words and ideas. When the time comes to edit, however, your essay should be long enough that you can pare down the excess words and still fulfill the assignment.

Wordiness is a loose, repetitious way of writing. It can have several causes. Carelessness may cause a writer to overlook repetitions and wasted phrases. Or trying too hard to sound impressive can lead to use of formulated, wasted phrases. Quite often, wordiness comes from not recognizing effective writing through lack of experience in reading good writers. Most writing students, in fact, do not realize that good writing is *concise*. Just as an expert swimmer or runner knows how to get the most speed and distance with the least effort, an expert writer learns to get the most mileage out of each word and sentence.

Here is an example of wordy writing:

> In modern times of today, the majority of Americans in our society, by and large, have come to recognize that our senior citizens are in need of quite a number of kinds of help and assistance that they are not receiving as of yet.

The following would do much better:

> Most Americans now realize that the elderly need many kinds of help that they are not receiving.

This sentence has only seventeen words, in contrast to the forty-four words of the first sentence, and it makes the point much more clearly. If you look back at the wordy statement, you will find that none of the extra twenty-seven words adds anything to the meaning. These words are like wood chips to be cut away from the block by the carver. You are the carver.

You will be a more concise writer and better editor if you learn to spot the common patterns of wordiness. Although editing, unlike grammar, cannot be reduced to rules to be learned and errors to be corrected, conciseness (the opposite of wordiness) can be learned through practice. Here are some of the common faults of wordiness:

- Useless repetitions, called **redundancies**. "Modern times of today" is a wordy way of saying "now." "Help and assistance" is saying "help" twice.
- Vague phrases and false connectors. "By and large" sounds like a transitional phrase but really serves no purpose.
- Roundabout substitutes for simple words. "As of yet" means "yet"; "on the basis of the fact that" means "because."

Writing clean, direct sentences does not necessarily mean writing short sentences or using short words. Sometimes using complicated sentences and long words is the best way, even the only way, to express particular ideas. But use these *only* if they are the best; otherwise, keep your sentences simple and straightforward.

Here is a list of wordy phrases commonly used by careless writers; more concise equivalents are on the right.

Wordy Phrase	*Concise Word or Phrase*
due to the fact that	because
with respect to	about
in terms of	about
in this day and age	nowadays
hurried quickly	hurried
in all probability	probably
at that point in time	then
conduct an investigation	investigate
blue in color	blue
circular in shape	circular
there are many students who join	many students join
it is my belief that	I believe that
inside of the house	inside the house
has a preference for	prefers
in my opinion I feel that	I think that
In Alice Walker's story, "Everyday Use," she writes	In "Everyday Use," Alice Walker writes
he is the kind of person who likes to play chess	he likes to play chess

REVISION EXERCISE I: WORDINESS

Rewrite the sentences below to remove wordiness:

1. It was inside of the house that I was frightened on account of the fact that it was my belief that someone was there.

   _____

   _____

2. Susan's joy and happiness with respect to her mother's arrival was due to the fact that they had not been able to see each other for months.

   _____

   _____

3. Leonard made up his mind to conduct a survey that would include many first year students as to their opinions with regard to drugs.

_____

_____

4. In the short story by Shirley Jackson entitled "The Lottery," the author tells a story about a small rural town somewhere in the country.

_____

_____

5. It is my intention in this essay to give an analysis of a number of the ways many people often use in the effort to cover up their true hidden motives.

_____

_____

EXERCISE 11: WORDINESS

Look over your previous paragraph and essay assignments. Make a list of the ten most frequent wordy phrases you have used, and write next to them more concise equivalents. Then choose the assignment that seems wordiest and rewrite it. Try to reduce it by at least twenty percent.

Using the Active Voice for Strength

Difference Between Active Voice and Passive Voice

In the **active voice**, the subject *does* the acting:

    s   *v*

The radio blasted hard rock music on the bus.

In the **passive voice**, the subject *receives* the action:

      s   *v*

Loud rock music was heard by everyone on the bus.

Both active and passive voice are correct English, but too-frequent use of the passive voice weakens writing. Sometimes in news reports and business writing, the passive voice may be best because who is doing the action is not important:

1. Three more <u>suspects</u> <u>were taken</u> into police headquarters for questioning in the continuing search for the mass murderer.
2. The <u>machines</u> <u>were shipped</u> to the Denver branch on Monday.

We do not need to know who took the suspects into custody or who shipped the machines. However, use of the passive is *not* effective in most writing.

Weak Writing	*Strong Writing*
Kim <u>was invited</u> by Raymond to model for him.	<u>Raymond</u> <u>invited</u> Kim to model for him.
The <u>truth</u> <u>was</u> suddenly <u>realized</u> by both contestants at once.	Both <u>contestants</u> suddenly <u>realized</u> the truth at once.

EXERCISE I: USING THE ACTIVE VOICE

Convert these sentences from passive voice to active voice.

Example: The turnoff for Route 287 was finally reached by Carla.

Active voice: *Carla finally reached the turnoff for Route 287.*

1. The poem was read aloud in class by Margaret.

   Active voice: _____

2. The Yankees were beaten by the Tigers in the playoffs.

   Active voice: _____

3. The moon was landed on by the Apollo 11 crew in 1969.

   Active voice: _____

4. Her personal computer was given to Edith by her parents.

   Active voice: _____

5. Many letters have been sent by me to your office.

   Active voice: _____

The following paragraph is in the passive voice. Read it, and then read the revised version in the active voice. Notice how the active voice gives the paragraph strength.

Passive voice:

   Instructions were given to the class by the teacher in how to use the computer keyboard for word processing. The keyboard was unknown to Doris, and she was bewildered by all the symbols. She was assured by Sue, who sat next to her, that her fears would be overcome when the meaning of the symbols had been explained by the teacher to her. The lecture was listened to carefully by her, and notes were taken. Soon the class was told by the instructor to copy and edit a piece of writing on the computer. Everyone in the class was helped by an assistant, and a grasp of the editing techniques was quickly had by all. When the editing was finished by everyone, the results were fed into the printer, and a copy of the work was received by every student.

Revised paragraph in active voice:

The teacher gave instructions to the class in how to use the computer keyboard for word processing. Doris did not know the keyboard, and the symbols bewildered her. Sue, who sat next to her, assured her that she would overcome her fears when the teacher had explained the symbols to her. She carefully listened to the lecture and took notes. Soon the instructor told the class to copy and edit a piece of writing on the computer. An assistant helped everyone in the class, and all quickly had a grasp of the editing techniques. When everyone had finished the editing, the teacher fed the results into the printer, and every student received a copy of the work.

EXERCISE II: USING THE ACTIVE VOICE

Read the paragraph below, noticing that it is entirely in the passive voice. Rewrite the whole paragraph in the active voice.

Joan was called by her new boyfriend, Steve, on Monday night. She was asked by him to go with him to a dance on Wednesday, but she had been told by her mother that she could not go out during the week until her grade point average had been raised to a B. Steve was told by her that he was liked by her but that she couldn't be taken out by him until Friday night. He was annoyed slightly by her answer, and it was said by him that the dance would be attended by him anyway. Joan's mother and Steve were both resented by her when the phone was hung up by her.

Using Strong, Vivid Verbs*

One key to forceful writing is selecting verbs that do heavy work for you. All words count, but verbs are especially important. Pick your verbs as you would pick a pair of designer jeans. A flat, boring, vague verb can numb the reader. A vital, specific verb can make a sentence crackle, sing, or snarl. Be on the lookout for the flat, catchall verbs that do not create pictures—words like *move*, *look*, *go*, and of course *is*. Read some of your previous writing, circling the verbs. Do you come up with nothing but *has*, *have*, *is*, *are*, *does*, *do*, and *looks*? If so, you are still singing on one or two notes. Use the whole scale. Instead of *looks*, try *stares*, *gazes*, *gapes*, *ponders*, *peers*, *surveys*, *contemplates*, or *leers*. Notice the difference between flat, vague verbs and vivid ones in these examples:

---

*You may want to review the section on finding verbs in Unit 5.

1. The runner *moved* to the left, *went* to the right, and *went* through three tacklers for a first down.
2. The runner *feinted* to the left, *veered* to the right, and *ploughed* through three tacklers for a first down.

1. Eleanor *looked* at the photograph for five minutes, *looked* out the window, and then *watched* the other students writing.
2. Eleanor *studied* the photograph for five minutes, *glanced* out the window, and then *glared* at the other students writing.

1. Norman *said* hello to the new vendor, *said* good morning to the bus driver, and *said* a few words to the attractive girl sitting next to him on the bus.
2. Norman *greeted* the news vendor, *tossed* a "good morning" to the bus driver, and began *flirting* with the attractive girl sitting next to him on the bus.

Underline the verbs in the following passage. Notice how the writer has chosen specific verbs instead of repeating *is*, *does*, or *goes*.

Teenagers need privacy; it allows them to have a life of their own. By providing privacy, we demonstrate respect. We help them disengage themselves from us and grow up. Some parents pry too much. They read their teenagers' mail and listen in on their telephone calls. Such violations may cause permanent resentment. Teenagers feel cheated and enraged. In their eyes, invasion of privacy is a dishonorable offense. As one girl said: "I am going to sue my mother for malpractice of parenthood. She unlocked my desk and read my diary."*

EXERCISE: USING EFFECTIVE VERBS

Rewrite these sentences, substituting vivid, precise verbs for vague, flat ones.

Example: Sandra *looked* at the dress with disgust.

Rewrite: _Sandra glowered at the dress with disgust._

1. Robert *went* to the police station for help.
2. The students *were* in the lounge.
3. The van *moved slowly* through heavy traffic.
4. The announcer *said* that the prime minister of India had been killed.
5. A geriatric nurse *has* many responsibilities.
6. The dancers *moved* to the loud music.
7. One driver *said* that he would sue the cab driver who ran into his Porsche.
8. The half-conscious patient *looked* at the ceiling.
9. The ice hockey players *moved* across the ice.
10. Misty blue-green mountains *were* in front of them.

*From *Between Parent and Teenager* by Haim G. Ginott. Copyright © 1965 by Dr. Haim G. Ginott. Reprinted with the permission of Macmillan Publishing Company.

REVISING WITH A WORD PROCESSOR

Word processing is the biggest innovation in writing since the invention of ink and paper. Even the typewriter does not free us to make revisions or speed up the work of producing a neat, error-free copy as much as the computer does. For editing especially, the computer is, or can be, a great asset. This might not be apparent to someone who has used a typewriter for years. The difference between typewriter and computer lies, of course, in the vastly greater freedom to revise and edit that a computer provides. Most of us, no matter how often we are told that neatness is not the substance of writing, find it nearly impossible to hand in a paper that has visible corrections. This results in crippling us at the revision stage. Whether writing by hand or typing, we want *this* to be the final draft. If we realize too late that the sentence just written could have been worded better, we probably settle for it the way it is. Not so when we use a word processor: now we can try a sentence three or four ways and look at all the options before we decide which is best, and we don't have to rewrite the entire page to change a single line. As all writers who use word processing know, we can also shift sentences or paragraphs around—insert, delete, change, and correct without limit—before we put the document on paper.

All this, then, *is* an asset—but only for the person who knows how to revise. The computer only follows orders. You still have to decide which verb is more emphatic, which version of a sentence is more effective. Many people mistakenly think that the only skill needed for word processing is mastery of the commands. You do have to know how to delete, insert, move, and correct words and phrases before word processing can do you any good. The more important skill, however, is that of exploring options, especially word choice, sentence arrangement, and choice of content. Do not imagine that word processing will make you a better writer: word processing will help you learn the craft of revising. For the rare writer who can write one draft quickly and not need to change it significantly, a good typewriter is all the equipment needed.

To put it another way, word processing eliminates our main excuse for not revising—not wanting to retype the page. Therefore, if you are fortunate to have your own personal computer with a word processing program, or if your college enables you to use computers in the classroom, remember that extensive revision is the key to effective writing. Word processing will enable you to do the following with less frustration:

- Revise your overall plan, adding content to develop paragraphs more fully, eliminating material that seems irrelevant, and changing the sequence of sentences and paragraphs. If you want to arrange your body paragraphs in climactic sequence, for instance, you can actually rearrange them without having to retype them.
- Explore sentence options, using the skills practiced in sentence combining to try out several patterns based on the same kernel sentences. You can write three or four versions of a sentence, choose one, and delete the rest.

- *Really* consider your diction, looking at each verb, noun, adjective, and adverb to consider whether another might be more precise, concrete, vivid, or accurate in connotation. Use the skills you have practiced in this unit regarding word choice.
- Eliminate wordiness. Learn the pleasure of deleting wasted words and condensing wordy phrases to create a cleaner, more readable copy; it is one of the joys of writing.

In addition, it is now possible to get help with editing from word processing programs. Be cautious about what you expect, however. The state of the art in style checks is still not advanced enough for you to gain much from such checks unless you already have a strong command of grammar and have revision skills. Most style checks will give you information only about the average length of your sentences and items like the frequency with which you use the passive voice. More sophisticated style checks will question your use of particular phrases, but you are the final authority. The computer will not improve your style; it will only help make you more conscious of your stylistic habits.

As programs become more sophisticated, however, these aids will become more and more useful as learning tools. If you have done any word processing, you probably know how to use a spelling check, and you probably also realize that, instead of making you a lazy speller, it forces you to notice the words that you habitually misspell, thus making you a better speller. So will it eventually be with style checks—they will give you some of the feedback that a good writing instructor might give you. At present, however, they fall far short of the kind of human response listeners and readers can give you about your ideas and attitudes and of the stylistic comments a good teacher will give you on your effectiveness.

5

PROOFREADING YOUR WRITING AND REVIEWING GRAMMAR

Proofreading and correcting grammatical slips involve the most basic elements of writing as well as the final polishing touches. Basic mistakes can destroy the effectiveness of an essay that has been created carefully through the stages of prewriting, composition, and revision. In this unit, practice until your grammar, proofreading, and spelling reach the same high level as the other writing skills you developed in the earlier units.

PROOFREADING AND CORRECTING THE REVISED ESSAY

Proofreading for errors in typing, punctuation, spelling, and grammar is most important on the next-to-last draft. The final copy that you turn in should be letter perfect and without correction marks. On the earlier drafts, you need not spend time making minor corrections, since you will probably change or remove many passages later. In fact, proofreading too soon may make you resist making revisions later, because you won't want to "ruin" your handiwork. Save the really detailed corrections for the late stages. Make a final draft as if you were going to hand it in; then proofread this draft and make final corrections for the one you *really* hand in. This way you will have an almost perfect copy of your own for safekeeping.

Proofreading requires extremely close attention, not the careless attention we usually give to television programs and advertisements. As you read your work slowly aloud, you will learn not to *mentally correct* errors—that is, to read the way you meant the passage to be without noticing little words left out, endings omitted, words repeated, apostrophes missing, letters reversed, and so on. As you do the grammatical exercises in this unit, you will become more expert at recognizing errors. However, even a writer whose grammar is flawless must pay close attention when proofreading. Everyone makes careless mistakes.

Try copying the following passage exactly as it is on the page:

> NOW IS THE TIME FOR
> FOR ALL GOOD MEN TO
> TO COME TO THE AID
> THEIR COUNTRY.

Did you notice the two repeated words and the one left out? When you read passages with which you are familiar, you tend to overlook slips like this. When you read your own writing, you are even more likely to overlook errors. In proofreading your own work, remember these pointers:

1. Read aloud slowly. Most writers are tempted to skim over their work silently. Force yourself instead to read carefully, word by word. Some professional writers even read their work backward to avoid rushing over mistakes. Try it.

2. Know yourself. What mistakes do you always make? Do you make certain spelling mistakes? drop *ed* endings? leave out small words? run sentences together? leave fragments? When you know your own habits, you will know the corrections your writing is most likely to need.

3. Proofread several times. When writing at home, proofread once carefully after you have written the essay. Then put the essay away for a day or two and proofread it again later. You will often catch mistakes that you overlooked the first time.

EXERCISE I: PROOFREADING

The passage that follows contains simple writing mistakes: words left out, words accidentally repeated, wrong punctuation, simple misspellings. Rewrite the passage, correcting as many mistakes as you can.

Teenage Pregnancies

In today's society they are many teenager who are sexual active. They get involved in sex because their friends push them into or because they afraid to be consider unpopular. In order to prevent teenage pregnancies parent should talk with their children They can only give advices they cant make their children do do what they want them too. But at least showing concern give the teenagers a sense of responsibility.

Being a teenager isnt easy you are under alot of pressure and when it gets to much you may want to run away with the person you love. You hope you will escape the pressure but having a baby not going to be the answer. When you have a baby to soon, it mean taking on more pressure, not getting away from responsibility. The mature way to deal with the problem of an unwanted pregnancy is to avoid the problem altogether: take responbility for birth control and wait to have child until your older and ready to become parent, or say no to sex.

EXERCISE II: PROOFREADING

Circle the mistakes in this passage. Then write the passage correctly.

Unsafe Sex

Most high school and college students nowadays are worry about sexually transmitted diseases like AIDS and herpes. It use to be alot safer for adolescents to to experiment with sex then it is today. Because of these diseases. The big question now is, what to do about it. one answer is just to say no this works alright for teenagers who accept the idea. For others the problem is, what kind of protection are really safe? Every where you here that condoms is the answer, but is that true. Some people claims that condoms are not foolproof. Other kinds of birth control like the pill and the diaphragm can help prevent you from getting pregnant, but they wont stop the spread of disease. Is it safe to trust your partner to tell you wether he or she may have a disease. Statistics show that it probably isn't, maybe the only way to be safe is to be *very* careful.

REVIEWING BASICS

Correcting your writing does require knowledge of grammar. When many college students say they "are terrible with grammar," however, they are usually exaggerating. When you speak English correctly, you are following most of the important grammatical rules. Correcting your writing simply requires a keen sense of the occasional mistakes that can show up even in the writing of people who speak mostly correct English. Producing error-free writing is a goal that college students should expect to attain.

You do not have to re-learn grammar from the ground up. Some review of basics, however, will probably help you recognize and correct errors that fall into familiar patterns. In this unit you will review the major kinds of writing errors and concentrate on learning how to correct them, especially the ones that give you the most trouble.

DIAGNOSTIC TEST

The following test will give you an idea of your strengths and weaknesses. You can then use Unit 5 for practice in the areas in which you require the most improvement. Bear in mind, however, that correcting grammatical mistakes on a short-answer test is not the same as correcting mistakes in your own writing. While a test can help you diagnose weak areas in your grasp of grammar, it cannot give you a complete idea of your writing habits. Correct grammar has to be learned as part of writing skills, not separate from them. In learning, students need their instructor's help and also feedback from other students.

Part 1. Sentence Divisions

In each group of sentences, only *one* is correct—A, B, or C. Circle the letter of the correct one.

1. A. Four students left early. Because they had completed the test.
   B. Four students left early because they had completed the test.
   C. Four students left early, they had completed the test.
2. A. Although Barbara was inexperienced, she still got the job.
   B. Although Barbara was inexperienced. She still got the job.
   C. Barbara was inexperienced, she still got the job.
3. A. After the votes were counted; everyone realized that Tracy had won.
   B. The votes were counted, everyone realized that Tracy had won.
   C. After the votes were counted, everyone realized that Tracy had won.
4. A. Insert your bank card in the slot, then pull it out.
   B. Insert your bank card in the slot then pull it out.
   C. Insert your bank card in the slot. Then pull it out.
5. A. Rap music is very popular it combines rhythm, rhyme, and a message.
   B. Rap music is very popular. Because it combines rhythm, rhyme, and a message.
   C. Rap music is very popular. It combines rhythm, rhyme, and a message.

6. A. Steve is the best candidate; he has experience and charisma.
   B. Steve is the best candidate, he has experience and charisma.
   C. Steve is the best candidate. Having both experience and charisma.
7. A. Quiz show winners have to report their earnings. And pay taxes on them.
   B. Quiz show winners have to report their earnings and pay taxes on them.
   C. Quiz show winners have to report their earnings they have to pay taxes on them.
8. A. Writing was easy for Cynthia when she used a word processor.
   B. Writing was easy for Cynthia; when she used a word processor.
   C. Writing was easy for Cynthia, she used a word processor.
9. A. Jerry looked everywhere in the store. To find a tie to match his jacket.
   B. Jerry looked everywhere in the store. Hoping to find a tie to match his jacket.
   C. Jerry looked everywhere in the store to find a tie to match his jacket.
10. A. Running is good for your health it improves your heart and lungs.
    B. Running is good for your health, it improves your heart and lungs.
    C. Running is good for your health. It improves your heart and lungs.

Part 2. Verb Forms, Endings, and Agreement

Circle the correct form in parentheses.

11. People who (insist, insists) on taking risks often have accidents.
12. One of the students (hasn't, haven't) submitted a term report.
13. You shouldn't cry about something that (happen, happened, happens) three years ago.
14. Either the *Los Angeles Times* or the *Washington Post* (is, are) going to make an offer.
15. Anyone who has (drank, drunk, drunken) more than two beers should not even think of driving.
16. An expert sits behind the wheel and (listen, listens, listened) before he decides what's wrong with the engine.
17. Today an apartment in Tokyo (cost, costs, costed) much more than you would expect.
18. On equipment alone the company (spend, spent) over a million dollars.
19. Hector watched the light change, then (walks, walk, walked) across the street.
20. After thinking about the proposal, Dwight wrote a letter in which he (explain, explains, explained) his objections.
21. There (was, were) probably many investors wanting to buy high-risk stocks.

22. Rita had a friend who was (suppose, supposed) to be a famous model.
23. At both sides of the staircase (stand, stands) two sentries.
24. Sri Lanka (use, used) to be called Ceylon.
25. Students who are just entering college often (need, needs) counseling.

Part 3. Spelling

If the word or phrase is correct, write *C* in the blank; if not, write the misspelled word in the blank.

_____	26. at there house	_____	36. decided
_____	27. jewlery	_____	37. fullfil
_____	28. similiar	_____	38. begining
_____	29. believing	_____	39. Your the best.
_____	30. occured	_____	40. to give advise
_____	31. separate	_____	41. convenience
_____	32. alot of money	_____	42. more then enough
_____	33. necessary	_____	43. a losing battle
_____	34. its going to rain	_____	44. height
_____	35. occasionally	_____	45. definitely

Part 4. Punctuation

If the sentence is punctuated correctly, write *C* in the blank. If not, insert the needed punctuation mark in the correct spot. No sentence has more than one punctuation error.

_____ 46. The waiter brought drinks, napkins silverware, and menus.

_____ 47. Exhausted by the heat and humidity the runner stopped and rested.

_____ 48. Nancy registered for the following courses French, mathematics, sociology, and data processing.

_____ 49. Both conventions were held in Denver Colorado, in May 1989.

_____ 50. William Blake wrote "The road of excess leads to the palace of wisdom."

_____ 51. The store sold discount items such as laundry detergent, underwear, pharmaceuticals, and candy.

_____ 52. Stanley knew that he could pass the qualifying examination but he was doubtful about the interview.

_____ 53. Ansel Adams, a great photographer of landscape was especially fond of the Far West.

_____ 54. Babe Ruth was a hard-drinking loud-talking, publicity-seeking superstar.

_____ 55. Wages are going up prices are going down.

_____ 56. Yes, Virginia there is a Santa Claus.

_____ 57. The books that you ordered have been sent; however, there may have been a delay in postal delivery.

_____ 58. Her letter beautifully written and full of compassion, touched the congressman deeply.

_____ 59. This discussion, in my opinion, will lead nowhere unless we can gather some facts.

_____ 60. Ruth, who knew where to buy video equipment recommended a store near the campus.

Possible score: 60   Your score: _____

SUBJECTS AND VERBS

To understand sentences, learn to spot subjects and verbs.

The Subject

The subject names the person or thing the sentence is about:
The whole *family* uses the new personal computer.
The *record* revolved silently on the turntable.
The *waiter* arrived with an order of ravioli.

The Verb

The verb is the word that shows action or being:
The whole family *uses* the new personal computer.
The record *revolved* silently on the turntable.
The waiter *arrived* with an order of ravioli.

Every sentence must have a subject and verb that go together. A sentence states that someone or something does or is something. Underline the subjects and circle the verbs in these sentences:

1. The excited crowd waited for the singers to appear.
2. Seventeen students with high grades received awards.
3. The speed limit is fifty-five miles per hour.

Finding Subjects

In most sentences, subjects appear at or near the beginning. Subjects can be nouns (words that name persons, places, or things):

the *car*   *Chicago*   four *women*   my *book*   college *courses*

Subjects can also be pronouns (words that stand for nouns):

I   you   she   he   it   we   they

Sentences with Noun Subjects

1. The *space shuttle* orbited the earth before descending.
2. A *degree* in hotel management makes you eligible for the job.
3. *Sex education* in schools raises heated controversies.

Sentences with Pronoun Subjects

1. *We* discovered a new way to drive to New Orleans.
2. *She* entered a bicycle race.
3. *You* know the difference between discipline and child abuse.

EXERCISE I: FINDING SUBJECTS

Underline the subjects in these sentences. Two of the sentences have no subjects and are therefore incomplete; write *F* in the margin next to these two fragments.

1. The first book on the list was about Latin America.
2. I know four people who have made their own films.
3. A few retired members contributed large sums of money.
4. Specially trained experts defused the incendiary bomb.
5. Reaching the warning track near the left field wall.
6. Next Monday you will have to pay $8.95 for the album.
7. Science fiction movies have set box office records this year.
8. We have introduced new pension regulations.
9. Latecomers to the theater will not be seated until the end of the first act.
10. During the search for a new university president.

EXERCISE II: FINDING SUBJECTS

Underline the subject of each sentence in the following paragraph. One sentence is incomplete because it lacks a subject; circle the number next to that fragment.

(1) We no longer stereotype people because of their sex. (2) Little girls do not have to limit their interests to paper dolls and toy sewing machines. (3) Little boys are not confined to toy guns, trucks, and erector sets. (4) Today's parents have become more concerned about the individuality of their children than about their children's conformity to stereotypes. (5) Teenagers, too, are less rigid in adopting "feminine" or "masculine" roles than in the past. (6) In most high schools, you will now find a large number of girls majoring in chemistry or mathematics. (7) And

even playing aggressive sports, like lacrosse and basketball. (8) Furthermore, in most families, both parents share in wage earning as well as housework and caring for children. (9) In fact, few adult activities can be labeled "men's work" or "women's work" nowadays. (10) In the place of stereotyped roles, people are now adopting living patterns suited to their individual abilities and needs.

EXERCISE III: FINDING SUBJECTS

Underline the subjects of the sentences in this paragraph. Again, one sentence is incomplete because it lacks a subject; circle the number next to that fragment.

(1) I found working as a camp counselor to be a demanding experience. (2) The job required resourcefulness, patience, energy, and understanding. (3) For eight weeks, I had to supervise the activities of twenty-seven gifted adolescents. (4) My duties cast me in the roles of teacher, parent, and therapist. (5) And often demanded new skills and knowledge. (6) However, the wish to excel brought out the best in me. (7) Every day my routine included improvising musical activities or artistic projects as well as coaching volleyball and water polo. (8) Sometimes, about twice a week on the average, I had to serve as police officer during the noon meal. (9) Another frequent responsibility was giving personal advice to campers with problems. (10) The eight weeks' experience gave me memories and wisdom for a lifetime.

Difficult Subjects

Sentences with Two or More Subjects.   Sentences may contain two subjects connected by *and* or *or*, or three or more subjects that form a list, or series. Writers often make mistakes in grammar if they fail to recognize these multiple subjects.

Sentences with Two Subjects:

Betty and *David* went to see a horror film.
My *brother* and *I* bought tickets in the lottery.
You and *we* disagree about methadone treatment.

Sentences with Three or More Subjects:

1. The *heart*, the *lungs*, and the *reproductive system* may be affected by the use of marijuana.
2. *Buddhism*, *Christianity*, and *Judaism* have much in common.
3. *Cecil*, *Marylou*, *Rachel*, and *I* eat lunch together.

Notice that one or more of the subjects can be pronouns. As subjects, these pronouns must be in the **subjective form** (I, we, he, she, they), not the **objective form** (me, us, him, her, them). If you aren't sure which form to use, try the pronoun by itself in the sentence:

Wrong:	*Me* and *my brother* went to see the Lakers play.
Try the pronoun alone:	*Me* went to see the Lakers play.
Correct:	*My brother* and *I* went to see the Lakers play.

Hard-to-Find Subjects.   Certain types of subjects are hard to identify:

- Subjects not located near the beginning of the sentence.
- Verbal subjects: subjects not really nouns or pronouns but other words used as nouns
- Whole-clause subjects
- You-understood subjects

Subjects that are not located near the beginning:

> Across from the diner was Sam's auto parts *store*.

The sentence begins with a descriptive phrase; *store* turns out to be the *what* word that the sentence is about.

> There are probably many *reasons* why you married Susan.

There is only a position word, never a subject; in sentences beginning with *there*, the subject usually follows the verb.

> When the package arrives, here are the *steps* you should follow.

A very tricky one: *here* is like *there*, only a position word; *steps* comes after the verb *are*.
Subjects that are verbals instead of nouns or pronouns:

> *Moving* away from the city would be difficult for me.

Moving is an -ing word, or gerund, that serves as subject.

> *To find* your sister in this crowd is going to be impossible.

To find is another verbal, an infinitive, that serves as subject.
Subjects that are whole clauses:

> *What I would prefer* is a high-paying job with no responsibilities.

The subject is the noun clause in italics.

> *That you like rock music* is obvious to all your friends.

The subject is the noun clause in italics.

Sentences with *you* as the understood subject:

Give me the rest of the sports section.

Turn left at the second light and follow Route 84.

EXERCISE I: FINDING SUBJECTS

Underline the subjects in the following sentences. If the subject is a command, write *you* in the margin. Two of the sentences are incomplete because they lack subjects. Write *F* in the margin next to these fragments.

1. There is a breakdancing contest this afternoon.
2. Television, newspapers, and magazines compete for money from sponsors and advertising clients.
3. Invest in the stock market before the current boom ends.
4. A series that included documentaries on World War I, the Great Depression, and the rise of fascism.
5. Situated beside the subway entrance was a cluttered newsstand.
6. Later in the afternoon a wedding and reception are scheduled.
7. Sharon, Stanley, and I belong to the same therapy group.
8. Separated from their guide, Shirley and Dumont discovered a new path down the mountain.
9. Abused children, battered wives, and mistreated elderly people cause growing concern.
10. Having good working conditions, high pay, and congenial co-workers.

EXERCISE II: FINDING SUBJECTS

Underline the subjects of the sentences in the following paragraph. One sentence is incomplete; circle the number next to it.

(1) Having a credit card has its advantages and disadvantages. (2) In the first place, using the card for purchases is obviously quick and convenient. (3) Clothes, cosmetics, airline tickets, and liquor can be bought speedily with a credit card. (4) Another benefit is the use of a major credit card for personal identification. (5) Giving the credit card bearer confidence when traveling or working. (6) We all, however, are tempted to abuse the privilege of buying on credit. (7) What causes the biggest problem is that we ignore our financial situation when making purchases. (8) As a result, what was a small convenience can lead to a troublesome debt. (9) Don't get a credit card unless you are sure you can keep your expenditures under reasonable control. (10) Then the advantages of having a credit card will outweigh the disadvantages.

EXERCISE III: FINDING SUBJECTS

Compose a paragraph of seven to twelve sentences, keeping in mind what you have learned about topic sentences, development, and unity. In this paragraph tell about your buying habits. Explain what kind of shopper you are, using a key word to describe your style. Tell where you shop, how you decide on purchases, and what you feel about shopping. After composing the paragraph, underline the subject or subjects of every sentence, being sure that no sentences are incomplete because they lack subjects.

Finding Verbs

Action and Being Verbs.   **Verbs** are the words that tell about action or being. In many sentences they come directly after the subject:

>   *s*   *v*
> The tenth round <u>began</u> violently. (action verb)

>   *s*   *v*
> Both fighters <u>were</u> exhausted. (verb of being)

Sometimes, however, verbs come before subjects (they can appear in almost any position in the sentence):

>   *v*   *s*
> Nearby <u>was</u> a beach with silky white sand. (verb near the beginning)

>   *s*   *v*
> After the game we <u>stopped</u> at a pizza parlor. (verb in the middle, after the the subject)

>   *s*   *v*
> The audience, bored by the sloppy performance, <u>booed</u> loudly. (verb near the end)

EXERCISE I: FINDING VERBS

Underline the verb in each of the following sentences. It may be an action word (throws, dances, swims, etc.) or a word of being (is, are, was, were). One sentence is incomplete because it lacks a verb. Write *F* in the margin next to it.

1. Horror movies usually make Jennifer sick.
2. However, she likes them so much she can't stop seeing them.
3. What is so appealing to her about violence and terror?
4. Her boyfriend Sylvester prefers science fiction films.
5. A young man with a wide knowledge of space technology.
6. He knows all about rockets, satellites, and astronomy.
7. His favorite film was *The Return of the Jedi*.
8. He saw it seventeen times.
9. Jennifer thinks science fiction is an escape.
10. She always insists on seeing murder mysteries instead.

EXERCISE II: FINDING VERBS

Underline each subject and circle each verb in the following sentences. One sentence in the paragraph lacks a verb; circle the number next to it.

(1) Smoking in public places is a nuisance. (2) Many smokers believe they have the right to fumigate restaurants, bars, trains, and offices. (3) Some even insist on chain-smoking in confined places like elevators. (4) Others smoke in nonsmoking train cars and rooms with no-smoking signs. (5) Some restaurants with special sections for nonsmokers. (6) Prohibiting smoking altogether in public places is unreasonable. (7) However, the nonsmoking public has a right to be free from concentrated fumes in most crowded rooms and waiting areas. (8) People with respiratory problems in particular need unpolluted air to breathe. (9) Infants and the elderly also suffer harmful consequences of cigarette smoke. (10) Those who breathe the air in a smoke-filled room are almost as vulnerable to the damage done by tar and nicotine as the smokers themselves.

Sentences with Two or More Verbs. Many sentences have more than one verb; to avoid errors, you must be able to find all the main verbs. Examples:

Mary *left* early and *took* a cab home.

Oscar *feinted* to the left, *crossed* rapidly to the right, and *fired* a jump shot from the foul line.

EXERCISE III: FINDING VERBS

Underline the verbs in these sentences. One sentence is incomplete because it lacks a verb; write *F* next to it.

1. Cable television provides good reception and offers extra program choices.
2. Hot weather lures many people outdoors but produces sunburn.
3. Along with accounting and marketing, Susan wanted to take a course in word processing but eventually changed her mind.
4. I like foreign films and always see new ones when they open.
5. After the first game of the series but before the playoff.

Sentences with Helping Verbs (Auxiliaries). Verbs often take **helpers** (*is going, should be* working, etc.), or **auxiliaries**, as they are also called. Usually the helping verbs come right before the main verbs, but sometimes there are words separating them.

Be, Have, and Do: The Most Common Helping Verbs. Forms of *be* (is, are, was, were), *have* (have, has, had), and *do* (do, does, did) are the most common helping verbs.

The prices of designer jeans *are going* wild.

Sally *has gone* to five rock concerts this month.

Did you *see* the collections of shells in the science building?

Fixed-Form Helpers.   There are many other helping verbs that do not have changing forms like *is* and *are*. These fixed (unchanging)-form helpers often appear next to or near main verbs:

can	might	should
could	must	will
may	shall	would

Examples:

The prices of personal computers *will drop* soon.

We *could arrange* to meet on Wednesday afternoons.

I *can* always *give* you a call tomorrow.

EXERCISE IV: FINDING VERBS

Underline the complete verbs—both the main verbs and the helpers—in these sentences. Write *F* in the margin next to the incomplete sentence that lacks a verb. (*Not* and *never* are not verbs.)

1. Some people have never seen a live circus.
2. The biggest party I ever attended was given by my boss.
3. After the first day of registration last semester.
4. Have you ever gone swimming in the nude?
5. A private school would cost much more than a public school.
6. On the first page you will find a diagnostic quiz.
7. Licenses will be available only to those over sixteen.
8. All lifeguards must learn cardiopulmonary resuscitation.
9. The space shuttle has already provided scientific benefits.
10. Tourism and sales of handicrafts have made the island popular.
11. Public transportation might seem less expensive than private cars.
12. Becoming a professional boxer has never been easy.

Verbals: The Fake Verbs.   Writers often leave sentences incomplete because they mistake verbals for main verbs.

The man in the back row *wearing* a yellow necktie.

Is this a complete sentence?

If you answered yes, you may need to review the difference between verbs and verbals. **Verbals** are forms made from verbs but used for other purposes. *Wearing* in this sentence is only a descriptive word; "wearing a yellow necktie" describes the man, but it doesn't say what he does.

The man in the back row wearing a yellow necktie *lives* in Utah.

Now we have a complete sentence with a verb telling what the man does.

Verbals can be verb forms ending in *ing* (called **present participles** or **gerunds**), forms ending in *ed* (called **past participles**), or forms with *to* in front of them (called **infinitives**).

Examples:

Fragment: The car *approaching* the intersection.
Sentence: The car approaching the intersection *slowed* down in time to avoid an accident. (verb added)
Fragment: The prices *listed* on the menu.
Sentence: The prices listed on the menu *do not include* dessert.
Fragment: *Pitching* against left-handed batters.
Sentence: Pitching against left-handed batters *is* his specialty.
Fragment: *To express* yourself effectively before an audience.
Sentence: To express yourself effectively before an audience, you *should learn* the techniques of public speaking.

EXERCISE I: FINDING SUBJECTS AND VERBS

Underline the subjects and circle the verbs in the following sentences. Be sure to include helping verbs. Three sentences are incomplete because they contain verbals but no main verbs. Write *F* in the margin next to each of these.

1. A good reason to visit Jamaica during the Easter vacation.
2. The cheerleaders formed a pyramid and waited to be photographed.
3. We have collected fifteen articles on alcoholism for the file.
4. Investigating crimes committed with stolen handguns.
5. The unemployment rate has risen and fallen unpredictably.
6. The distance measured by telescopes in orbit.
7. Does Mara know anything about Japan?
8. Stretching exercises are helpful before distance running.
9. Parents of troubled teenagers should be expert listeners.
10. Lost articles at the airport are kept in the security office.

EXERCISE II: FINDING SUBJECTS AND VERBS

Underline the subjects and circle the verbs in the following paragraph. One sentence has deliberately been left incomplete; circle the number next to it.

(1) There is no question about it. (2) Being a member of a successful New York basketball team is a mixed blessing. (3) The notoriety* forces one to look at the

---

*Notoriety: public attention.

world differently from other people. (4) It provides money and access. (5) At the same time, it sets one apart from the rest of society and denies one the privilege of being an equal member of a crowd. (6) There is little chance, for example, for a public figure to fail without people knowing it, and no one grows without failing. (7) Many avoid the embarrassment of public failure. (8) By never placing themselves in positions where they might fail. (9) Therefore, they never grow. (10) My constant problem is to find places where I am allowed to fail in private. (11) Everyone does not thirst for fame. (12) For me, fame holds as much danger as it does benefit.*

FRAGMENTS

You have already been identifying some fragments, or incomplete sentences, in the previous exercises. Fragments are fake sentences; they begin with capital letters and end with periods, but lack some necessary part.

Telling the Difference Between Fragments and Sentences

In the previous exercises, either the subject or the verb was missing from the fragments. Some fragments, however, are incomplete because a word at the beginning turns them into subordinate clauses.

A whole sentence can be called a **main clause**:

s   v
The <u>siren</u> <u>was making</u> an ear-splitting noise.

A **subordinate**, or **dependent, clause** also has a subject and verb but begins with a word like *because* or *when*, which makes the whole clause incomplete. It becomes a modifying part of a sentence:

> *Because* the siren was making an ear-splitting noise

To make it complete, you must add a main clause:

> Because the siren was making an ear-splitting noise, *the nearby residents evacuated the area.*

Subordinate Clauses and Subordinating Conjunctions

The **subordinating conjunctions** are words that turn main clauses into subordinate clauses. If you begin a sentence with one of these words, you must add a main clause to complete the sentence.

---

*Bill Bradley, *Life on the Run*. New York: *Time* Books, 1976, pp. 120–121.

Subordinating Conjunctions

after	even though	since	whenever
although	ever since	though	where
as	for as long as	unless	whereas
because	if	until	wherever
before	just as	when	while

Remember that clauses beginning with these words are not sentences but fragments.

> Because the bus splashed mud on Tina's jeans.

> Although the three brothers grew up in different families.

To make such fragments complete, add a main clause.

> Because the bus splashed mud on Tina's jeans, *she bought a new pair.*

> Although the three brothers grew up in different families, *they attended the same school.*

EXERCISE I: SUBORDINATE CLAUSE FRAGMENTS

Some of the following sentences are complete; others are fragments. The fragments may have subjects or verbs missing, as in the previous lesson, or they may begin with subordinating conjunctions. Underline the subjects and circle the verbs in the complete sentences. Write F next to the fragments.

1. The yeti in Tibet, the alma in the Soviet Union, Sasquatch (or Bigfoot) in the northwestern United States, and the Chinese Wildman all hairy monsters resembling human beings.
2. The skunk ape, a foul-smelling creature that has surprised trappers and fishermen in Florida since the 1920s.
3. While the Missouri monster, named Mo-Mo, is also an apelike figure that has frightened people since the 1960s.
4. Nessie, or the Loch Ness monster, being the most famous of all monsters and one of the oldest, the first report occurring in the sixth century.
5. The beast of Truro, a large creature resembling a mountain lion, was sighted in Cape Cod, Massachusetts, in 1981 and blamed for the deaths of several cats.
6. The coelacanth, hauled in off the South African coast in 1938, was not really a monster but a species of fish once thought to be extinct for millions of years.
7. A monster in Argentina said to carry people off into the water called the iemisch.

8. The nandi bear, in Africa, a beast that purportedly eats only the brains of its victims.
9. Champ is the name of a long-necked monster seen occasionally in Lake Champlain ever since it was first sighted by the lake's discoverer, Samuel de Champlain, in 1609.
10. Because the kraken, first reported in 1752, was supposed to be large enough to drag whole ships under water.*

EXERCISE II: SUBORDINATE CLAUSE FRAGMENTS

All of the following sentences begin with subordinating conjunctions from the list on p. 197. Five of them are complete sentences because they have main clauses after the fragments. Underline the main clause in the complete sentences. Write *F* next to the fragments.

1. Because the book was difficult to read without a dictionary.
2. Although the assignments were easy, the examination was difficult for most of us.
3. Ever since Henry registered for a course in radiation therapy.
4. Unless new photocopy machines are installed in the library.
5. Whenever Jennifer starts talking, people stop and listen.
6. Whereas some professors arranged to have office conferences with their students.
7. After the audience fell silent, the speaker began discussing a flow chart she had drawn on the chalkboard.
8. As the ratings improved, more sponsors sought advertising time on the program.
9. Until the negatives have been developed, we will not be able to identify the fourth person at the table.
10. If employees will not accept the terms of the new contract.

Added-Phrase Fragments

Another kind of fragment that occurs frequently in student writing is the **added-phrase fragment**. This may be a phrase beginning with a verbal (an -ing word or infinitive such as *to go*, *to read*, etc.), or it may be a prepositional phrase, even a string of prepositional phrases.

-ing Word Fragments.

> The last three miles of the race proved to be hilly and dangerous. *Leaving only the most daring motorcyclists in the race.*

> Sarah decided not to go to the party on Friday night. *Being exhausted by the overtime work she had put in at her job on Thursday.*

---

*Facts from Daniel Cohen, *The Encyclopedia of Monsters*. New York: Dodd, Mead, 1982.

Fragment Beginning with to.

> Christopher knew the one thing he wanted most of all in life. *To establish his own computer retail outlet.*

Prepositional Phrase Fragment.

> Eileen had many happy memories of her summer experiences. *In the Caribbean, in Venezuela, and along the coast of Florida.*

Connecting the Fragment.   In each of these examples, the added-phrase fragment really belongs to the sentence preceding it. Usually such writing can be corrected by connecting the fragment to the preceding sentence:

1. The last three miles of the race proved to be hilly and dangerous, *leaving only the most daring motorcyclists in the race.*
2. *Being exhausted by the overtime work she had put in at her job on Thursday,* Sarah decided not to go to the party on Friday night.*
3. Christopher knew the one thing he wanted most of all in life: *to establish his own computer retail outlet.*
4. Eileen had many happy memories of her summer experiences *in the Caribbean, in Venezuela, and along the coast of Florida.*

Bear in mind that not all word groups beginning with to, with -ing words, or with prepositional phrases have to be fragments. A sentence may begin with one of these phrases and then have a main clause after it, forming a complete statement. We could even use one of the added-phrase fragments from the preceding examples as the beginning of a complete sentence:

> *To establish his own computer retail outlet,* Christopher borrowed money from a commercial bank.

As with dependent-clause fragments, the beginning word or phrase may warn you that you *may* have a fragment, *but you must look at the whole sentence to see if it is complete.*

EXERCISE I: ADDED-PHRASE FRAGMENTS

If the sentence or sentence group is complete, write *S* next to it. If it contains a fragment, write *F.*

1. To dramatize the sufferings of Dust Bowl farmers during the Great Depression, John Steinbeck wrote a novel called *The Grapes of Wrath.*
2. Zora Neale Hurston wrote a novel called *Their Eyes Were Watching God.* To portray a young black woman's search for love in rural Florida.

---

*The order of this sentence had to be reversed to avoid a dangling modifier. See dangling modifiers in Unit 5, p. 260.

3. Mark Twain ends *Huckleberry Finn* with his hero about to "light out for the territory." Leaving the reader to wonder what will become of Huck in later life.

4. In World War I, in the Spanish Civil War, and in World War II, Ernest Hemingway served as a war correspondent. Collecting material for his novels and short stories as well.

5. Observing the wealthy upper-class New Yorkers with a realistic eye, Edith Wharton wrote novels that won acclaim in the early twentieth century.

6. Henry James portrayed the dilemmas of highly sophisticated, educated Americans. Striving to find a cultural identity while living and traveling in England, France, and Italy.

7. In *Invisible Man*, Ralph Ellison depicts the efforts of a young black man to adjust to, as well as to change, American society. With its many forms of obvious and subtle racism.

8. J. D. Salinger, in *The Catcher in the Rye*, portrays the hostilities, resentments, and insecurities of an adolescent in the 1950s.

9. F. Scott Fitzgerald's main character in *The Great Gatsby* embodies the wild life-style of the rich during the Jazz Age. Throwing lavish parties attended by movie stars and riding around in a chauffeur-driven Rolls-Royce.

10. Saul Bellow portrays the humorous but also sad and self-defeating lives of urban people in our time. Focusing especially on middle-class people in Chicago and New York.

EXERCISE II: ADDED-PHRASE FRAGMENTS

Create complete sentences using the phrases given at either the beginning or the end. Be sure every sentence has a main clause.

Example:

Fragment: with both rooms still left unpainted
Sentence: Sam knew he would need the rest of the week to finish decorating his apartment, with both rooms still left unpainted.

1. Fragment: in her courses, her social life, and her music

   Sentence: _____

   _____

2. Fragment: to change careers at the age of thirty-two

   Sentence: _____

   _____

3. Fragment: making the lecture even more difficult to follow

    Sentence: _____

    _____

4. Fragment: for the sake of her two children

    Sentence: _____

    _____

5. Fragment: hoping for a major role but expecting a smaller one

    Sentence: _____

    _____

Added-Verb Fragments

Our last category of fragments is the type created by adding a second or third verb to the same subject in a sentence—but without joining the extra verb or verbs to the sentence. One subject in a sentence can have two or more verbs (we call these **compound** verbs), but all verbs must be in the same sentence with their subject. If you break them off and try to start a new sentence with them, you will automatically create a fragment.

Example:

Fragment: Sharon glanced out the window at the park. *And shrieked as she spotted her boyfriend kissing another woman.*

Fragment corrected: Sharon glanced out the window at the park and shrieked as she spotted her boyfriend kissing another woman.

In this example, *shrieked* is a second verb that matches the subject *Sharon* (*glanced* is the first verb). Both *glanced* and *shrieked* belong in the same sentence with their subject *Sharon*. If a period is placed after *park*, as in the first example, the remaining words create a fragment that has no subject (who shrieked?). Remember that every sentence must have a subject and verb that go together. Therefore, to correct added-verb fragments, you can simply drop the period and join the fragment to the preceding sentence, where it belongs. It is also possible to correct the fragment by adding a subject to match the verb:

Sharon glanced out the window at the park. *She* shrieked as she spotted her boyfriend kissing another woman.

EXERCISE I: ADDED-VERB FRAGMENTS

Some of the passages that follow contain fragments; others are complete. Write *F* next to the fragments, *C* next to those that are correct.

1. Many people nowadays are interested in space exploration. But do not know very much about outer space.
2. Most people cannot tell the difference between a planet and a star by looking at them over a period of time. They do not know that a planet changes its position continually.
3. Some people also underestimate the vastness of space. And imagine that we could travel to other stars in a week or two.
4. Comets and meteors also cause a lot of confusion. And lead people to think of them as the same.
5. Comets may appear small in the night sky. But can be millions of miles long.
6. Meteors are usually about the size of a pea. But they seem large because they burn up in our own atmosphere.
7. Some Americans think we should stop spending money on space exploration entirely. And use the money to improve our standard of living instead.
8. This may be partly because we did not come back with anything particularly valuable from the moon. Or definitely prove that life exists on Mars.
9. Many scientists are at work trying to communicate with extraterrestrial beings by means of radio and other technological devices. And hope to discover that we are not alone in the universe.
10. Telescopes in satellites will also help us learn more about outer space. They can peer at other stars and galaxies more clearly because they do not have to look through earth's atmosphere.

EXERCISE II: ADDED-VERB FRAGMENTS

Correct the following fragments either by attaching them to the preceding sentences or by adding subjects to make them complete.

Example:

Fragment: Barbara waited for her cousin to offer to help with the dishes. And then gave up and did them herself.

Correction: Barbara waited for her cousin to offer to help with the dishes and then gave up and did them herself.

Alternative correction: Barbara waited for her cousin to offer to help with the dishes. Then she gave up and did them herself.

1. Fragment: Fred watched soap operas all afternoon. And went to a movie in the evening.

   Correction: _____

   _____

2. Fragment: Jessica prides herself on being able to predict the Dow Jones average a month in advance. And once impressed her economics professor by getting it exactly right.

   Correction: _____

   _____

3. Fragment: Films and books that attack famous, highly respected people often arouse controversy. But earn fortunes for the people who make or write them.

   Correction: _____

   _____

4. Fragment: Mastery of spelling requires a combination of ear and eye training. And can be acquired by most people only through frequent practice.

   Correction: _____

   _____

5. Fragment: The country singers could drive to Nashville in about six hours. Or spend twice as much and get there in an hour by air.

   Correction: _____

   _____

> ## Review: Three Ways to Correct Fragments
>
> 1. Connect fragments to the sentences that precede or follow them.
> 2. Add subjects or verbs to make fragments complete.
> 3. Add main clauses to make fragments complete.

Connect the fragment to the preceding sentence:

> Fragment: The students sat in small groups. And read their papers aloud to one another.
>
> Correction: The students sat in small groups and read their papers aloud to one another.

Add a subject or verb to make the fragment complete:

> Fragment: The shell of the missile fell to earth. And landed in a woods in Kentucky.
>
> Correction: The shell of the missile fell to earth. *It* landed in a woods in Kentucky.

Add a main clause to make the fragment complete:

> Fragment: After Stanley and Evelyn quarreled about her getting a job.
>
> Correction: After Stanley and Evelyn quarreled about her getting a job, they kissed and made up.

In your own paragraphs and essays, one of the easiest ways to correct fragments is to join them to sentences next to them. Fragments are often pieces of longer sentences that were mistakenly broken off; usually they can be reattached to the sentences in front of them. Just be sure that the resulting sentence is not too long and complicated. To check for fragments, read your essay carefully as if it were a list of sentence exercises, taking each sentence one at a time. Notice especially the *beginning* of each sentence.

REVIEW EXERCISE I: CORRECTING FRAGMENTS

Two of the sentences below are complete; underline the subjects and circle the verbs in these. Rewrite the other eight, making them complete by adding subjects, verbs, or main clauses.

1. Athletes in small groups on the grassy infield near the track.
2. Statues of warriors and kings in the left wing of the museum.
3. Tourists throwing coins into the fountain.
4. Brochures and leaflets were given to pedestrians outside the bank.
5. Sold tickets at high prices after the box office ran out.
6. Referees discussing the play on the forty-yard line.

7. French-speaking instructors taught the Vietnamese children.
8. Learned to improve his writing style.
9. While Roger and Inez were whispering together in the hall.
10. On the low walls near the entrance to the dormitory.

REVIEW EXERCISE II: CORRECTING FRAGMENTS

In each of the following passages, underline the fragment. Then rewrite the passage with the fragment attached to the sentence before or after it, whichever makes sense.

Example:

Courses in technical writing are useful. <u>If you become a skilled technical writer</u>. You will find many job openings, usually at high pay.

Rewrite, with fragment attached to sentence after it:

> Courses in technical writing are useful. If you become a skilled technical writer, you will find many job openings, usually at high pay.

1. Euthanasia, or mercy killing, has become increasingly controversial. Some people believe that it is justified. When a patient is terminally ill and in pain.
2. Some people object that any intentional taking of life is wrong. Because life is sacred even when a person is not happy. Therefore they support laws prohibiting euthanasia.
3. Before taking a simple-minded stand on the issue. We should study the difference between several types of euthanasia. We may then decide that we accept some forms and not others.
4. One type is ending the use of life-support machines. For patients in pain and beyond hope of recovery. Cases of this kind have already been disputed in courts.
5. If a patient's death is possible only through a direct act such as administration of a lethal drug. Euthanasia becomes much more controversial. Some people still will argue that it is morally better to relieve suffering than prolong it.
6. When a patient is not conscious, euthanasia is especially open to dispute. One way to simplify the problem is use of the "living will." Stating that if the person is injured or ill beyond recovery and is unconscious, death would be preferable to remaining in a coma.
7. The big moral question is whether life itself is the highest priority. Or whether life without hope or consciousness should be terminated. Obviously people with different philosophies will continue to disagree on the answer.
8. The issue should be discussed in public. Since families, doctors, and hospitals do face such decisions. New medical technology, in fact, makes it easier to prolong life when the patient is in a coma.

REVIEW EXERCISE III: QUICK DRILL ON FRAGMENTS

Do this drill quickly to review the difference between fragments and complete sentences. Write F next to a fragment and S next to a complete sentence.

1. People who drive large gas-guzzling cars to work.
2. After allowing for inflation and changes in international exchange rates.
3. Along the highway were many annoying billboards.
4. Because Spanish I has no prerequisite.
5. We usually go skiing in Vermont in February.
6. Except for those who travel by bus.
7. The governor and his wife appearing on camera together.
8. When spring comes, the water level rises.
9. During the last episode of a soap opera I saw recently.
10. Having passed the bar, she felt exhilarated.

SIMPLE, COMPOUND, AND COMPLEX SENTENCES

To be able to recognize and correct the next groups of sentence errors, you should review the three main types of sentences. Sentences can be **simple**, **compound**, or **complex**:

Simple sentences have one main clause, with one subject-verb combination:

s v

Tony works after school in a restaurant.

Compound sentences* have two main clauses joined together; each clause has its own subject-verb combination:

s v s v

Stephanie buys lottery tickets every week, but Frank spends his money on compact disc recordings.

Complex sentences have one main clause and one (sometimes more than one) dependent clause. Each clause has its own subject-verb combination. The dependent clause can come before or after the main clause:

Main clause before dependent clause:

s v

Irene usually gives money to the homeless people in her neighborhood

s v

because she feels sorry for them.

---

*See commas before conjunctions in compound sentences later in Unit 5.

Main clause after dependent clause:

$$s \qquad v$$

Because Irene feels sorry for the homeless people in her neighborhood, she

$$v$$

usually gives them money.

EXERCISE: SIMPLE, COMPOUND, AND COMPLEX SENTENCES

Identify each sentence that follows by writing S (simple), CD (compound), or CX (complex) in the blank next to it.

_____   1. The American family has changed in the last twenty years.

_____   2. When our grandparents were growing up, they lived in traditional nuclear families.

_____   3. The nuclear family includes the father, the mother, and their children.

_____   4. There are still many nuclear families, but many other kinds of nontraditional families also exist.

_____   5. Because the divorce rate has increased, many families are headed by one parent.

_____   6. Many families also contain stepchildren; these are often called "blended families," like the Brady Bunch.

_____   7. The Huxtables, on the *Cosby Show*, are a nuclear family, but both parents are wage earners.

_____   8. If current trends continue, most American families will be nontraditional in one way or another.

_____   9. Some people think that nontraditional families are healthy; others believe that traditional families are better for children.

_____   10. Most Americans still believe that their family is the most important element in their lives.

RUN-TOGETHER STATEMENTS

Every sentence should end with a period, exclamation point, or question mark. A **run-together sentence** occurs when a writer goes right through the end of the sentence like a driver going through a red light.

> I watched the man enter the bank suddenly I realized he was planning a hold-up.

In this sentence, "enter the bank suddenly" looks like it goes together as a phrase, and it's easy to miss the cutoff point between sentences. Reading more carefully, we see that we have two sentences, not one:

> I watched the man enter the bank. Suddenly I realized he was planning a hold-up.

If two sentences are closely related, you may want to put them together in a compound sentence instead of separating them. Do not run them together, and *do not put just a comma between them*; use a semicolon, as in this sentence. Use a semicolon also in sentences joined together by long connectives like *however, therefore, meanwhile, consequently,* and *nevertheless.* These are called **conjunctive adverbs**; put semicolons before them when they connect main clauses in compound sentences.

Examples: Run-together sentences corrected two ways:

Run-together Sentence:	A many-colored float rolled slowly toward midfield it was circled by cheerleaders and a marching band.
Corrected as Two Separate Sentences:	A many-colored float rolled slowly toward midfield. It was circled by cheerleaders and a marching band.
Corrected with a Semicolon:	A many-colored float rolled slowly toward midfield; it was circled by cheerleaders and a marching band.
Run-together Sentence:	The tenants sent many letters to the landlord about the lack of heat and electricity however he did not reply for two weeks.
Corrected as Two Separate Sentences:	The tenants sent many letters to the landlord about the lack of heat and electricity. However, he did not reply for two weeks.
Corrected with a Semicolon:	The tenants sent many letters to the landlord about the lack of heat and electricity; however, he did not reply for two weeks.

EXERCISE I: SEPARATING RUN-TOGETHER SENTENCES

Indicate the spot where these run-together sentences should be divided by putting in a period and writing in a capital letter.

1. A beautiful woman walked onto the stage to everyone's surprise she began taking off her clothes.
2. The blind man crossed the street confidently by probing with his cane he was able to sidestep the potholes.
3. Sandra had an argument with her mother about dating then she slammed the door and headed for her boyfriend's apartment.
4. Jake's boa constrictor made an entertaining pet at parties it often came slithering out unexpectedly.
5. Harriet sent out twenty-three invitations to the shower afterward she realized she did not have room for that many guests.

EXERCISE II: SEPARATING RUN-TOGETHER SENTENCES

The following paragraph contains five run-together sentences. Rewrite the paragraph, separating the run-together statements with periods or semicolons, *not with commas.*

(1) Lasers are now being used for many purposes for instance they serve as surgical tools in operations on the skin, eyes, and blood vessels. (2) Lasers also have many military uses they can guide bombs to their targets or pierce metal surfaces. (3) In communications, lasers are used in new types of photographic systems some sound devices, such as walkie-talkies, employ lasers. (4) Both art and industry now make extensive use of laser beams, and corporations have discovered countless industrial uses. (5) For instance, lasers have dramatically improved welding techniques, drilling and cutting everything from gems and metals to fabric and paper can be cut with laser devices. (6) Lasers once seemed a remote form of new technology soon, however, we may have lasers in our appliances at home. (7) Yesterday's miracle may become tomorrow's commonplace.

EXERCISE III: SEPARATING RUN-TOGETHER SENTENCES

Separate the following run-together sentences by inserting periods or semicolons (*not commas*) between the main clauses. Two sentences are not run together; do not change them.

1. I have a friend named Patrick he works for the city government.
2. The World Trade Center has increased the amount of business in Tribeca, which is the area in lower Manhattan called Triangle Below Canal Street.
3. Some parents objected to sex education in the schools they thought it would increase the number of teenage pregnancies.
4. The battery in this watch will last for two years or longer it was manufactured in Taiwan.
5. Both women were relieved to hear that they did not need surgery the doctors had told them they had small tumors.
6. The play was about a young black police officer who shot a suspect he caught trying to steal a car.
7. Some animals do not have good eyesight they rely instead on other senses.
8. We met a D.J. named Franklin he had been doing a radio show for two years.
9. Summer jobs are usually hard to find most companies are more interested in permanent staff than in temporary help.
10. Gymnastic routines took up the first third of the program ice skating and track and field events took up the rest.

EXERCISE IV: SEPARATING RUN-TOGETHER SENTENCES

The following sentences were written by students. Two of them are correct; the others are run together. Separate the run-together sentences by periods or semicolons.

1. Minicomputers, the size of a suitcase, are ideal for instructional use they can be moved from one classroom to another.
2. Many college athletes do not become professional stars they need to plan for other careers.
3. Most banks now belong to the Federal Reserve System, which decides the amount of currency to hold against each deposit.
4. Cancer is a disease that can cause severe harm it hurts you both psychologically and physically.
5. This story reveals that money is important to most Americans because it distinguishes one social class from another.
6. The raid on Combahee was Harriet Tubman's idea it was a way of penetrating enemy lines and freeing hundreds of slaves.
7. Nutritional care for the older patient deserves considerable attention the well-nourished patient not only will be more energetic but will be better able to take medical treatment.
8. After a child has been battered, social agencies always try to help the child it may be too late to help the parent.
9. As more and more parents join the work force, their kids are left with little supervision these kids are vulnerable to sexually provocative programs on television.
10. Alcoholics Anonymous was established in 1935 by two alcoholics who had stopped drinking today more alcoholics are treated by A.A. than by any other method.

COMMA SPLICES

In previous exercises you have been warned not to put a comma between the two statements in a run-together sentence. This common mistake is called the **comma splice**.

Example:

Comma splice: We arrived at Danceteria before the main crowd, then we decided to look for a good film near Times Square.

Correct: We arrived at Danceteria before the main crowd. Then we decided to look for a good film near Times Square.

Correcting Comma Splices

Correct comma splices the same way you would correct run-together sentences. Separate the main clauses with a semicolon, or divide them into two separate sentences with a period.

Correcting by Coordinating.   A third way to correct either run-together sentences or comma-spliced sentences is by joining the main clauses with a connecting word and a comma. The connecting words to remember are called **coordinating conjunctions**.

Coordinating Conjunctions:

Use these short connecting words, with commas before them, to join main clauses:

, and
, but
, or
, yet
, so
, for

Example: Compare this comma-spliced sentence with the correct one using a comma with a conjunction.

Comma splice: The retail price of the dress is $41.95, the wholesale price is $25.

Correction: The retail price of the dress is $41.95, *but* the wholesale price is $25.

Ways to Correct Comma-spliced and Run-together Sentences

• Divide the two statements into separate sentences.
• Use a semicolon between the statements.
• Join the statements with a comma and connecting word.

Here is an example of the same comma-spliced sentence corrected all three ways.

> Comma splice: Sandra enjoys soap operas, she never misses an episode of *General Hospital*.
>
> Correction: Sandra enjoys soap operas. She never misses an episode of *General Hospital*.
>
> Sandra enjoys soap operas; she never misses an episode of *General Hospital*.
>
> Sandra enjoys soap operas, and she never misses an episode of *General Hospital*.

EXERCISE I: COMMA SPLICES

Correct the following sentence in three ways.

> Emil attends the University of Texas, he is finding the work difficult but interesting.

1. Separate sentences: _____

_____

2. With semicolon: _____

_____

3. With connecting word and comma: _____

_____

EXERCISE II: COMMA SPLICES

In each pair, one sentence is correct and one is a comma splice. Write C next to the correct one.

_____ 1. A. The first examples of modern skyscrapers were designed by Louis Sullivan, the Wainwright Building in St. Louis was one of his most famous structures.

_____   B. Louis Sullivan designed the first examples of modern skyscrapers, among which was the Wainwright Building in St. Louis.

_____ 2. A. Soon Chicago became a leading center for tall buildings, the Reliance Building started the trend in the 1890s.

_____   B. With its Reliance Building starting the trend in the 1890s, Chicago became a leading center for tall buildings.

_____ 3. A. The Woolworth Building in New York was completed in 1913, defying Chicago's challenge in the skyscraper competition.

_____ B. The Woolworth Building in New York was completed in 1913, it defied Chicago's challenge in the skyscraper competition.

_____ 4. A. Chicago answered with the Tribune Building in the 1920s, this skyscraper added many decorative flourishes.

_____ B. Chicago answered with the Tribune Building in the 1920s, adding decorative flourishes to the style of tall buildings.

_____ 5. A. In the 1930s New York appeared to have won the race for good, both the Empire State Building and Rockefeller Center being built then.

_____ B. In the 1930s New York appeared to have won the race for good, both the Empire State Building and Rockefeller Center were built then.

_____ 6. A. Although many interesting skyscrapers appeared during the 1940s and 1950s, none challenged the Empire State Building.

_____ B. Many interesting skyscrapers were built during the 1940s and 1950s, none challenged the Empire State Building.

_____ 7. A. Then, in 1973, New York strode further ahead with the World Trade Center buildings, these twin towers were 100 feet taller than the Empire State Building.

_____ B. Then, in 1973, New York strode further ahead with the World Trade Center Buildings, whose twin towers were 100 feet taller than the Empire State Building.

_____ 8. A. But in the same year Chicago regained the world title with the Sears Tower, purposely planned to outreach the World Trade towers by another 100 feet.

_____ B. But in the same year Chicago regained the world title with the Sears Tower, it was purposely planned to outreach the World Trade towers by another 100 feet.

EXERCISE III: COMMA SPLICES

Each of the following sentences has a comma in the middle. If the sentence is correct, write *C* in the blank; if it contains a comma splice, rewrite the sentence using a semicolon or divide it into two sentences.

1. Most Latin American countries became independent early in the nineteenth century, at that time the Spanish Empire had become weakened.

_____

_____

2. Because many Latin American cities refused to recognize Napoleon's brother Joseph as their leader, the control that Spain once held over the New World began to slip.

_____

_____

3. In 1817 Jose de San Martin helped Chile gain independence, he led his army in a heroic climb over the Andes.

_____

_____

4. Brazil became independent in 1828, it was still called an "empire" until 1889.

_____

_____

5. When Simon Bolivar defeated the Spanish at Boyaca in 1819, Colombia also joined the emerging group of independent nations.

_____

_____

6. In 1823 the United States proclaimed the Monroe Doctrine, this declaration warned European powers against further colonization in the Americas.

_____

_____

7. The United States, however, was not yet a great world power, the British navy actually did more than the United States to keep other countries out of Latin America.

_____

_____

_____

8. Although the Monroe Doctrine became a permanent policy, some opponents have claimed that it should also have guaranteed nonintervention by the United States in Latin America.

_____

_____

9. In fact, the United States did capture land from Mexico, in 1845 Mexico lost Texas and all the land westward to California.

_____

_____

10. Today the relations between the United States and Latin America remain friendly but tense, the United States continues to stand opposed to intervention by other world powers in Latin America.

_____

_____

_____

EXERCISE IV: COMMA SPLICES

Correct each comma splice by one of three methods: (1) Use a semicolon, (2) divide into two sentences, or (3) add a short connective word. One sentence is correct; leave it as it is.

1. Elvis Presley was born in Tupelo, Mississippi, in 1935, his recording career began in 1953 and continued for the rest of his life.
2. His singing attracted lovers of country music, blues, and rock and roll, he was nicknamed "Elvis the Pelvis" because of his gyrating hip motions.
3. After he became famous as a singer, he tried to achieve equal success as a movie actor, his films, however, were of uneven quality.
4. When Elvis died in 1977 of a drug overdose, he was acclaimed King of Entertainment, his drug problems focused media attention on the growing menace of drugs among celebrities.
5. Another "king" of show business was Nat "King" Cole, who was born Nathaniel Adams Cole in Montgomery, Alabama.

6. Cole began as a pianist rather than a singer, his King Cole Trio played jazz in the 1940s, but he gained real popularity when he became a crooner in the 1950s.
7. His slow, sentimental style now sounds old-fashioned, most people still enjoy his recordings of "Mona Lisa" and "Route 66."
8. Like Elvis, he sometimes attracted huge live audiences, he appeared in several films and achieved modest success as an actor.
9. Nat "King" Cole performed on numerous tours, singing in American cities and foreign countries, he was popular everywhere.
10. Cole died at the age of 46 in 1965, by then he had exerted a big influence on other performers.

REVIEW EXERCISE: COMMA SPLICES AND RUN-TOGETHER SENTENCES

Rewrite these sentences, separating the main clauses in one of these ways: (1) into two sentences, (2) with semicolons, or (3) with commas and short connectives. If a sentence is correct, write *C* next to it.

1. Most people have heard of the main laws of science and the social sciences, they should recognize, however, that the laws of nature are usually more precise than those of human behavior.
2. Kepler's law explains the motion of the planets around the sun, most students of astronomy master it early in their studies.
3. Darwin proposed the theory of evolution in 1859, then he explained its meaning for mankind in *The Descent of Man* in 1871.
4. Einstein's theory of relativity is generally known to be the basis for atomic energy, however, not many people understand it.
5. The English economist Thomas Malthus proposed a theory of population in 1798, he argued that population would increase geometrically (2,4,8,16, etc.), while food supply would increase arithmetically (1,2,3,4, etc.).
6. Another well-known theory in the social sciences is Gresham's law this law states that currency of low value drives currency of high value out of circulation.
7. There are also theories of linguistics Grimm's law and Verner's law, for instance, explain patterns of change in spoken language.
8. Some amusing "laws" have been concocted to explain social phenomena; Parkinson's law, for example, states that work expands to fit the manpower available.
9. The Peter Principle describes the workings of status levels, or hierarchies, it states that workers are promoted until they reach their "level of incompetence," where they remain in jobs they perform poorly.
10. Perhaps the most reliable principle describing modern society is Murphy's law, which states that whatever can go wrong will go wrong.

CORRECTING BY SUBORDINATING

A fourth way to correct run-together sentences and comma splices is to subordinate one statement to another. This means to turn one of the main clauses into a subordinate clause. Do this by adding one of the subordinate conjunctions like *because* or *when* to one of the main clauses or by beginning one of the main clauses with *who, which,* or *that* (making that clause a **relative** subordinate clause).

Run-together sentence:

The students felt nervous they had an examination that morning.

Correction by subordinating one clause:

The students felt nervous *because* they had an examination that morning.

The students, *who* had an examination that morning, felt nervous.

EXERCISE 1: SUBORDINATION

Correct the sentences that follow by making one main clause a subordinate clause. Use *although, because, if,* or *when* to subordinate one clause; or use *who, which,* or *that* to make it a relative clause.

1. Some experts once predicted that computers would make books obsolete, this has not happened so far.

   _____

   _____

2. The computer age began in the 1960s, this age has brought an increase in book publication.

   _____

   _____

3. The use of computers has actually increased the number of books many of them have been written about computers.

   _____

   _____

4. Books on word processing appear every month they have become too numerous to count.

   _____

   _____

5. Other areas of activity besides publishing expand as well, computer technology has an impact on them.

_____

_____

6. Teachers once feared they would be replaced by computers, they have discovered that their role is even more important than before.

_____

_____

7. Computers have enhanced rather than eliminated the teacher's job, teachers now can use computers to relieve them of meaningless drills.

_____

_____

8. A person doesn't know vocabulary like *software* and *spreadsheet programs* he or she is behind the times.

_____

_____

9. It may not be necessary to become a computer programmer, in tomorrow's world, all educated people will be familiar with computer language.

_____

_____

10. Home computers become as common as television sets the effect on our lives will be no less than a computer revolution.

_____

_____

EXERCISE II: SUBORDINATION

Five of the sentences in the paragraph below either are comma splices or are run together. Rewrite the paragraph with these sentences corrected by means of subordination. Refer to the list of subordinating conjunctions on page 197.

(1) Scientists disagree about what caused the dinosaurs to become extinct. (2) One theory is that the dinosaurs vanished about 65 million years ago, an asteroid crashed into the earth. (3) Plants, the dinosaurs' main food supply, may have died out the collision darkened the sky for months. (4) Geologists believe

that such a catastrophe might have eliminated half of all life on earth. (5) They have even found a layer of underground clay containing iridium, an element often present in objects from outer space, matching the period when the dinosaurs disappeared. (6) There is evidence to support the asteroid theory, some scientists think that the dinosaurs died out gradually. (7) Some evidence indicates that the dinosaurs became extinct before the collision supposedly occurred, the asteroid theory cannot be considered proven. (8) It is possible that a change of climate, especially a cooling off, was the cause. (9) An asteroid collision may have been just one of several factors that brought the extinction of many species during that period. (10) More exact methods of dating fossil records can be discovered we may know more certainly just what happened.

SUBJECT-VERB AGREEMENT

In the **present tense**, use the correct form of the verb to match the subject.
Singular subjects take singular verbs:

    s   *v*
Katherine usually arrives on time.

Plural subjects take plural verbs:

    s   *s*   *v*
Katherine and Richard usually arrive on time.

Hint:

Verbs in the singular take the *s* ending in the present, unless *I* or *you* is the subject.

	Singular	*Plural*
First person:	I write	We write
Second person:	You write	You write
Third person:	She, he, it *writes*	They write

Singular and Plural Subjects

Learn to tell the difference between singular and plural nouns. Most nouns form the plural by adding *s* or *es* to the singular:

Singular Nouns	*Plural Nouns*
one ticket	three tickets
a computer	both computers
my shoe	my shoes
Susan's typewriter	Susan's typewriters

Some nouns form their plurals in unusual ways. Some change their spelling instead of adding *s*:

Singular	*Plural*
a woman	four women
the man	those men
one child	all my children
your foot	both your feet
a mouse	two mice

Some stay the same in singular and plural:

one deer	a herd of deer
a big fish	a school of fish
a pet sheep	hundreds of sheep

Words ending in *f* or *fe* may change the *f* to *v* before adding *es*:

one half	both halves
one life	many lives
his wife	several wives

But in some words the *f* remains:

a steep roof	many roofs
definite proof	a number of proofs

Words ending in *o* sometimes take *s* and sometimes *es*:

hero	ten heroes
this tomato	ten tomatoes
one stereo	several stereos
my radio	our radios

Words ending in *y* usually change the *y* to *i* before *es*:

a large company	many companies
a new secretary	two new secretaries

But those with vowels before the *y* just add *s*:

a good play	three good plays
a new toy	some new toys

Hint:

Use your dictionary to find the plural forms of nouns that you are uncertain about. If no plural is listed, you should add *s* or *es*.

EXERCISE I: SINGULAR AND PLURAL SUBJECTS

Write *singular* or *plural* after each noun:

1. tests _____
2. scientists _____
3. bus_____
4. guitars _____
5. videodisc _____

6. hamburgers _____
7. professor _____
8. section _____
9. experiences _____
10. parent _____

EXERCISE II: SINGULAR SUBJECTS

Write singular nouns as subjects in the following sentences.

1. A_____ always eats a lot.
2. One _____ is not enough.
3. Every _____ knows how to read.
4. Each _____ belongs in the class.
5. This _____ looks like a winner.
6. My _____ works in a large corporation.
7. That _____ matches your shoes.
8. A single _____ ruins a good photograph.
9. An _____ helps relieve pain.
10. Another _____ doesn't cost much.

EXERCISE III: PLURAL SUBJECTS

Write plural nouns as subjects in these sentences.

1. Many _____ think they know everything.
2. Some _____ like to cause trouble.
3. Three _____ have new cars.
4. All of the _____ belong in the Hall of Fame.
5. Most _____ have several charge accounts.
6. Very few _____ are open on Sunday.
7. A large number of _____ have gotten loose.
8. Four _____ hire summer employees.
9. Both _____ play on the basketball team.
10. Seven _____ are on stage already.

EXERCISE IV: SINGULAR SUBJECTS

The following list contains *ten* subjects in the third person singular. Circle these ten. Then write ten sentences using them as subjects, remembering to use the *s* form of the verb in every sentence.

he	I
the store	your opinion
my shoes	her dress
that dog	our reasons
a test	seven women
two books	this corner
they	it
she	the game

Finding and Correcting Errors in Agreement

Most errors in subject-verb agreement involve missing *s* endings on nouns or verbs. Sometimes writers put *s* endings where they should not be.

Typical errors:

Incorrect singular statement:	My sister Ellen insist on going her best.
Corrected form:	My sister Ellen insist*s* on doing her best.
Incorrect plural statement:	Those people always argues with foreign visitors.
Corrected form:	Those people always *argue* with foreign visitors.

EXERCISE I: CORRECTING ERRORS IN AGREEMENT

Some of the verbs in the following sentences agree with their subjects; some do not. If the verb is correct, write C in the blank; if not, write the correct form.

1. Wise investing depend upon several
   factors.   _____
2. It involves your income, needs, and
   willingness to take risks.   _____
3. Some people invests their money only in
   stocks.   _____
4. Other opportunities also exists.   _____

5. Municipal bonds, mutual funds, and term savings accounts all offer investment advantages. _____

6. The right kind of investment for you mean considering several elements. _____

7. Tax benefits from municipal bonds appeals to some investors. _____

8. Stocks present possibilities for high income but with high risk. _____

9. The investor who wants to avoid risks often choose mutual funds. _____

10. Corporate bonds also offer high income possibilities but also with greater risk than municipal bonds. _____

EXERCISE II: CORRECTING ERRORS IN AGREEMENT

The following paragraph contains errors in subject-verb agreement. Underline the subject of every sentence and circle every verb. Write the correct verbs above the wrong ones.

(1) Stanley arranges his day in three segments. (2) He usually devote the whole morning from 8:00 A.M. to noon to his classes. (3) Most of this time he concentrate very hard on his work. (4) On Mondays, Tuesdays, and Thursdays mathematics and sociology occupy most of his time. (5) On Wednesdays and Fridays his schedule include Spanish and English literature. (6) In the afternoon, from noon until 4:30, his job at the student union take up all his time. (7) He always works at a cash register, where he receive payments for tickets to football and basketball games. (8) In the evening he and his friends often goes to parties, discos, or movies. (9) His life keep him active and socially busy, and he needs the weekend to rest and do his homework.

Special Problems with Agreement

Forms of Be, Have, and Do. The common helping verbs *be, have,* and *do* present special difficulties with agreement because they have more forms than other verbs. Instead of just adding an *s* ending, *be* has these forms:

Singular		*Plural*
First person:	I *am*	We *are*
Second person:	You *are*	You *are*
Third person:	He, she, it *is*	They *are*

Note: In the **past tense**, *be* is the only verb that can cause agreement problems because it has two past forms:

She *was*   They *were*

Have has two forms in the present: *has* for third person singular and *have* for all other subjects.

Do also has two forms: *does* for third person singular and *do* for all the others. Be careful about *don't* and *doesn't* as well.

EXERCISE I: BE, HAVE, AND DO

If the verb is correct, write *C* in the blank; if not, write the correct form.

1. People who doesn't belong to the plan will lose out.　　_____
2. Hector thinks he have the best arm in the league.　　_____
3. One of the new bookcases are going to be painted.　　_____
4. Some of the students does their essays on computers.　　_____
5. The first day of spring has a special meaning.　　_____
6. Barbara and Karen is the most talented women.　　_____
7. Social activities has taken up too much time.　　_____
8. Each film in the series is narrated by a sports announcer.　　_____
9. Several mothers does their shopping together.　　_____
10. Nathan always have his work done before class.　　_____

EXERCISE II: BE, HAVE, AND DO

Underline all incorrect forms of *be*, *have*, and *do* in the following paragraph. Write the correct forms above the wrong ones.

People has to face many pressures on holidays. Those who entertain a lot has to send invitations to friends and relatives, prepare food, and decorate their homes. On some holidays, especially Christmas, giving gifts are in order, so many people does a lot of shopping and has to worry about choosing, wrapping, and mailing presents. On religious holidays, churches, synagogues, and mosques are full of worshippers practicing their religion. Loneliness and depression is widespread during major holidays, especially among the elderly, who is often far away from their relatives. Many families has to plan and pack for vacation trips during the holidays, and the crowded hotels and highways is usually a source of difficulty for them. Patients in hospitals, inmates in penitentiaries, and children in foster homes is likely to feel more isolated during holidays than at other times because they does not share the holiday festivities with their families. The financial and emotional pressures of the holidays has an effect on the rates of suicide, crime, and mental illness. Although most experts is likely to agree that the importance we place on holidays does great harm, few of us is going to stop observing and enjoying our favorite holidays. The pleasures of holiday parties and vacations is too great for us to abandon.

EXERCISE III: BE, HAVE, AND DO

Fill in the correct forms of *be*, *have*, and *do*.

1. One of the students in this class _____ a sushi chef.

2. A school that _____ not give athletic scholarships _____ at a big disadvantage.

3. Connie and Janice, my two cousins, _____ overtime work on Saturday.

4. The supporters of the death penalty _____ a hatred of criminals.

5. Most of the page numbers _____ to be changed.

6. One of the best teachers in the college _____ not have a Ph.D.

7. Where _____ the narcotics agents hiding when passengers got off?

8. Shirley _____ a spiked hair style and now she _____ popular.

9. People at the new dance clubs _____ any steps they feel like doing.

10. The other two cars _____ broken into, but mine _____ only scratched on the front fender.

Subjects that Come after Verbs.   Some of the sentences in the preceding exercises may have made you stop and think. You could not always just choose a verb that "sounds right." Such difficulty is likely to occur in sentences that do *not* follow the ordinary subject-verb-object order. Sometimes the verb comes before the subject, and you can choose the right verb form only by finding the subject and matching the verb with it.

Verbs come before subjects in several kinds of sentences:

1. *Questions* contain reversed word order:

   Are there any new *students* here today?
   Why *have* the *lights* been turned off?

2. Sentences beginning with *there* or *here* place the verb before the subject:

   There *have* to be many *reasons* for her decision.
   Here *is* an exciting *picture* of her as a teenager.

3. Sentences beginning with descriptive phrases sometimes place the verb before the subject:

   Behind the door *were* three armed *men*.
   Sprayed on the walls *was* an angry *message*.

Notice that in such sentences you should not try to match the verb with the word right before it so that the combination sounds right. You must find the subject. In the last sentence, 3, ask yourself: *What* was sprayed on the walls? A *message* was sprayed.

EXERCISE I: SUBJECTS THAT COME AFTER VERBS

Underline the subject (the *who* or *what* word) in each sentence and circle the verb form that matches it.

1. There (has, have) been several excellent films this year.
2. Among the best (was, were) two science fiction movies.
3. Why (is, are) audiences still flocking to see such films?
4. There (has, have) to be several reasons.
5. (Doesn't, Don't) most people enjoy flights of imagination?
6. Among other attractions (is, are) the high degree of violence in fantasy and science fiction films.
7. Where else (do, does) anyone get a chance to learn about the scientific advances that may occur?
8. For children and adolescents, there (is, are) few forms of entertainment equal to top science fiction and fantasy films.
9. How (does, do) rock videos succeed without an appeal to fantasy?
10. There (is, are) always new techniques to startle audiences.

EXERCISE II: SUBJECTS THAT COME AFTER VERBS

Circle the wrong verb forms and supply correct ones. Write *C* if the sentence is correct.

1. What does most people think of subway vigilantes?   _____

2. Is ordinary citizens right when they take the law into their own hands?   _____

3. What have to be done to make the subways safe?   _____

4. There isn't ever going to be enough police officers.   _____

5. Among the crowds is many angry people.   _____

6. There is often a chance of violence breaking out.   _____

7. Don't this problem demand a solution?   _____

8. What are going to prevent more vigilantes from acting?   _____

9. On television news there is many such incidents.   _____

10. Here is a topic for many good term papers.   _____

EXERCISE III: SUBJECTS THAT COME AFTER VERBS

Compose sentences beginning with the phrases below:

1. What is _____ ?

2. There are _____ .

3. How does _____ ?

4. Along the fence are _____ .

5. What have _____ ?

6. On the sidewalk were _____ .

7. Where have _____ ?

8. When were _____ ?

9. Here is _____ .

10. Why were _____ ?

Special Subjects.   Some subjects are hard to match with verbs because they seem to be plural but are singular grammatically or because they are singular when used one way and plural when used another.

Singular Pronouns	Singular/Plural Words
everyone	all
anyone	half
someone	some
everybody	most
anybody	more
somebody	

Write *everyone has* some kind of special talent, not *have*. *Each, either,* and *one* are also singular, even though they are often followed by plural phrases. *Each of the students is* (not *are*). *Either* of the women *has* the right to participate (not *have*).

Some words are singular when they refer to amounts and plural when they refer to numbers.

> All of the money *has* been spent (singular—an amount)
>
> All of the visitors *are* required to wear passes (plural—a number)

EXERCISE: SPECIAL SUBJECTS

Choose the correct form of each verb in parentheses; underline the subject before writing the verb in the blank.

1. Despite the enormous wealth in America, many still _____ (be) unemployed in the big cities.

2. According to federal reports, almost half of working-age residents in the largest cities _____ (be) neither employed nor looking for work.

3. Most of the young people in their late teens _____ (do) not have either part-time or full-time jobs.

4. In some cities only about one out of three men and women between sixteen and nineteen years of age _____ (be) in the labor force.

5. Each of the unemployed _____ (have) a reason for not working; it may be lack of skills, psychological problems, dependence on drugs or alcohol, or unavailability of jobs.

6. Some economists _____ (do) not give us hopeful predictions, because improving economic conditions do not seem to improve these unemployment figures.

7. All of the experts _____ (be) in agreement that the source of the problem is deeply rooted in our changing society.

8. Everyone who lives in or near a large city _____ (have) a stake in this problem.

9. Anyone who has been out of a job _____ (have) to realize what a serious problem unemployment is.

10. All of the money that has been spent on job programs _____ (have) not been able to solve the problem yet.

Group Nouns.   Nouns that refer to groups of people present a special problem. Words like *army, family, team, jury, chorus, union, committee, company,* and *organization* seem to be plural because they refer to many people; however, they have plural forms (armies, families, etc.), so the singular forms should be used with singular verbs: An *army marches* on its stomach, or The *team has* won eleven games this season. When you refer to such words as single units, using the singular form, use singular verbs as well. However, when you use the word to refer to the individual members of the group, it is permissible to use a plural verb. Some writers find it awkward and not strictly correct to write, the team *are* taking their places on the field. It is less objectionable to write, the players *are* taking their places, or the members of the team *are* taking their places. Most experts agree that it is permissible, at least, to use group nouns as plurals in this way. Just be sure to tell the difference between the group as a unit (singular) and as separate individuals (plural).

EXERCISE: GROUP NOUNS

Circle the correct verb form in each sentence.

1. The committee (has, have) reached its decision.
2. Our family (has, have) an unusual kind of annual reunion.
3. The army (has, have) just published a new training manual.
4. The band (don't, doesn't) usually leave their instruments in the rehearsal room.
5. The company (is, are) making its projections for the next year.

6. The union (schedule, schedules) a meeting every Wednesday.
7. The jury sometimes (disagree, disagrees) violently with one another.
8. The police force (include, includes) members of all minority groups.
9. The National Organization for Women (hold, holds) meetings during the summer.
10. The chorus usually (arrive, arrives) at the church around seven o'clock.

Verbs Separated from Subjects.   Quite often a verb will be separated from the subject by a phrase or even several phrases. Be able to find the subject and match the verb form with it. If you merely choose a form that sounds right, you may mistakenly match it with a word next to the verb and not with the subject. Notice the difference:

The *names are* in alphabetical order.

One of the names on the list *is* out of place.

Notice how many words come between the subject *one* and verb *is* in the second sentence. How can you identify the subject in such a sentence? Use common sense: What is out of place? Not the list, not the names; the sentence is stating that only *one* is out of place. In your mind, you must erase the words between the subject and verb and place the two next to each other; otherwise, you may have to make a wild guess at the correct verb form.

EXERCISE: VERBS SEPARATED FROM SUBJECTS

In the following sentences underline the subject, cross out the words between the subject and verb, and circle the verb that matches the subject.

Example: The cars parked in the lot next door (is, are) for sale.

1. Some students in a difficult nursing program (find, finds) the science courses challenging.
2. One of the trails in the western section of the park (has, have) been closed to hikers.
3. Most luxury cars built in the 1950s (was, were) gas guzzlers.
4. Intelligent students who earn low grades in college sometimes (has, have) problems at home.
5. Training for guidance counselors (include, includes) courses in psychology and sociology.
6. Detroit and Chicago, along with five other cities, (has, have) undergone changes in residential patterns.
7. A stimulating environment, including objects and activities that appeal to all five senses, (is, are) crucial to an infant's development.
8. Waiting for others to finish their work always (frustrate, frustrates) Michael.

9. A woman with ambitious career plans (need, needs) a good tax accountant.
10. The money left over from the sales of the films (belong, belongs) to the stockholders.

Compound Subjects: And Versus Either/Or.   Two or more subjects joined by *and* take a plural verb:

> *North Carolina* and *Tennessee have* good teams this year.
>
> *Rhoda* and *Richard are* my best friends.

Joining two subjects with *either . . . or,* however, does not make the subjects plural. A statement with *either . . . or* says that only one person does the action:

> Either *Sandra* or *Ted is* going to drive.

This sentence takes a singular verb because it says that one person *is* going to drive. Notice, however, that *either . . . or* sometimes joins subjects that are already plural; then of course the verb is plural:

> Either *parents* or *teachers have* to be notified.

A rare sentence may contain one singular and one plural subject joined by *either . . . or.* This is awkward, so try to avoid it; if you can't, the rule is to make the verb agree with the subject nearer to it:

> Either *Fred* or his *brothers are* going to inherit a fortune.

EXERCISE: COMPOUND SUBJECTS

Underline the subjects and circle the correct verbs in these sentences.

1. Either Diane or Carla (know, knows) how to do that problem.
2. Either cocaine or heroin (was, were) found in their possession.
3. Either Syria or Jordan (send, sends) diplomats.
4. Coffee, tea, and orange juice (is, are) served during the break.
5. Either sociology or government (is, are) a prerequisite.
6. Accounting and business management (is, are) offered every semester.
7. Either Chinese or Italian food (seem, seems) to suit her taste.
8. Either the president or his advisors (answer, answers) such letters.
9. Payments and receipts (show, shows) up on the same financial statement.
10. Either the A train or the downtown express (stop, stops) at that station.

Compound Verbs.   Many sentences have two or more verbs that go with the same subject. Be sure to make all such verbs agree with the subject; it is easy to slip and not notice that one of them, usually the last one, does not agree with the subject. Notice the error in this sentence:

> Charles always gets up at seven, drives to work, and spend his whole morning at the office.

How many verbs go with the subject *Charles*? Which one does not agree?

EXERCISE: COMPOUND VERBS

Circle the incorrect verbs in these sentences and write the correct forms in the blanks. If the sentence is correct, write C.

1. Violent programs on television frighten, fascinate, and disturbs small children. _____

2. A company without fringe benefits for its employees shortchanges them and put them at a disadvantage. _____

3. Losing weight is usually difficult and require a lot of self-control. _____

4. Earning a pilot's license is demanding but opens up new experiences. _____

5. The room strikes most visitors as well furnished but leave some people with a cold feeling. _____

6. Milan has become a center of fashion and now compete with Paris as the pacesetter. _____

7. Richard Pryor entertains and moves audiences with his humor but shock some conventional people with his language. _____

8. Marijuana has been used for centuries and has appeared under many names throughout history. _____

9. Chemical wastes have been dumped into our rivers and lakes for decades and now threatens to poison our drinking water. _____

10. Swimming long distances requires rhythmic breathing and demand coordination of arm, shoulder, and leg muscles. _____

Verbs in Who, Which, and That Clauses.   Verbs that come after *who, which,* or *that* are usually tricky because *who, which,* and *that* can be either singular or plural. You cannot tell whether a sentence should read "who is" or "who are" without knowing whether the *who* is singular or plural. You must identify the antecedent, or preceding word that *who* represents. *Who, which,* and *that* are relative pronouns; that is, they *relate* to something earlier in the same sentence. The verb depends on the word that *who* relates to. For instance, you would use a singular verb in the phrase "a student who *registers* for Spanish" but a plural verb in the phrase "students who *register* for Spanish." Use a singular verb in the phrase "a course that *requires* a term paper" but a plural verb in the phrase "courses that *require* term papers."

EXERCISE: VERBS IN *WHO*, *WHICH*, AND *THAT* CLAUSES

Underline the antecedent of *who, which,* or *that* in each sentence and circle the verb form that agrees in number with it.

1. Police officers who (carry, carries) guns try to avoid using them.
2. A channel that (show, shows) only sporting events is available on cable television.
3. Newscasters who (attract, attracts) large audiences earn high salaries.
4. The systems that (was, were) still operating were partly damaged.
5. The store is not responsible for items that (is, are) left for more than six months.
6. Changes that (occur, occurs) after the fifteenth of the month are not recorded until the next statement.
7. People who (spend, spends) their money on luxuries may find their incomes inadequate.
8. Immigrants who (go, goes) to colleges in the United States have to adjust to a new kind of curriculum.
9. An article that (appear, appears) weekly in the magazine section discusses issues that interest men.
10. Four new species that (was, were) discovered last year are described in the March issue.

REVIEW EXERCISE I: SUBJECT-VERB AGREEMENT

Underline the subject or subjects and circle the correct form of the verb in each sentence.

1. Half of the people in this experiment (has, have) already stopped smoking.
2. Most of the money allotted for travel expenses (is, are) spent.
3. Drinking and watching television (is, are) both forms of addiction.
4. Beside the abandoned building (stand, stands) four ragged tents.
5. Expecting instant success and wealth (lead, leads) to frustration.
6. People who (work, works) in large corporations sometimes develop an identification with the organization.

7. Either newspapers or other media always (carry, carries) stories about crimes.
8. Sam and his brother both (like, likes) to study with the stereo on.
9. Here (is, are) the separate checks that you asked for.
10. (Do, Does) all of the excuses have to be in writing?

REVIEW EXERCISE II: SUBJECT-VERB AGREEMENT

Underline the subject or subjects and circle the correct verb form in each sentence.

1. Hitchhiking along a throughway (is, are) illegal.
2. Ground-to-air missiles, which are now housed in bombproof underground casing, (present, presents) a powerful form of defense.
3. Experimenting on animals sometimes (has, have) to be done, even though it seems inhumane.
4. Junior high school students who (attend, attends) parochial institutions will visit the hospital on Tuesday.
5. Elbowing noisily through the crowd (come, comes) three burly strangers.
6. Either drugs or psychotherapy (is, are) usually prescribed for the condition.
7. Acting and playwriting by amateurs (has, have) attracted widespread interest.
8. Spelling, grammar, and style are important and (affect, affects) the grade.
9. People who (live, lives) in small towns like to gossip.
10. There (doesn't, don't) seem to be many exits on this floor.

REVIEW EXERCISE III: SUBJECT-VERB AGREEMENT

Rewrite the following paragraph, converting it from plural to singular. Remember to include *s* endings on singular verbs. Instead of beginning with Sonia and Diane, begin with just Sonia. Use *she* instead of *they*.

Sonia and Diane have alcoholic husbands who abuse them frequently. They are afraid for their husbands to come home after they have been drinking because they expect loud, insulting language and physical abuse. Their husbands hold full-time jobs and support them fairly well most of the time, so they are not eager to leave their marriages. They have small children and do not possess advanced job skills that would make it easy for them to support themselves as single mothers. They have tried to get their husbands to go to Alcoholics Anonymous and receive psychological counseling. However, they have not been very successful in getting outside help. Their friends and relatives tell them to leave their husbands before any further harm to them or the children occurs. Although they have rejected this advice so far, they are reaching the point where they will have to take drastic steps. As for many women, there is likely to be a major change in their lives soon.

S ENDINGS: A REVIEW

Many writers have trouble with *s* endings. This happens because *s* endings can be added to words for different reasons. Some words, of course, already end in *s*, like *kiss* or *class*. There are four *s* endings that we *add* to words:

Adding *s* Endings

1. Add *s* or *es* to verbs in the third person singular, present tense: The dancer moves.
2. Add *s* or *es* to plural nouns: The dancers move.
3. Add *'s* to singular possessives: a dancer's movements.*
4. Add *s'* to most plural possessives: four dancers' movements.
(Exception: Add *'s* to plural possessives when the plural does not already end in *s*: women's opinions.)

EXERCISE I: S ENDINGS

Identify which of the *s* endings listed in the box is underlined in each sentence and write the number from the box (1, 2, 3, or 4).

Example: ___1___ The jury wants more evidence.

_____ 1. Most citizens know their constitutional rights.
_____ 2. The public needs to be informed by the media.
_____ 3. Most states' constitutions have similar features.
_____ 4. Changes in constitutions take the form of amendments.
_____ 5. The first ten amendments to the Constitution of the United States are called the Bill of Rights.
_____ 6. Passing an amendment requires a three-fourths majority of the states.
_____ 7. Amendments can also be repealed.
_____ 8. The prohibition amendment's unpopularity caused it to be repealed in the early 1930s.
_____ 9. The most recent amendment to approach a three-fourths vote was the Equal Rights Amendment.
_____ 10. The National Organization for Women still supports this amendment.

---

*See apostrophes later in this unit.

EXERCISE 11: S ENDINGS

Proofread the paragraph that follows. Circle the *ten* errors in the use of *s* endings—either incorrect or missing endings. Write the correct endings above the errors.

Stacy's Pet Peeves

Stacy made a list of her pet peeves. She decided that the list would include only things that could be called annoyance, not serious dangers or threats. The first one that occurred to her was what she calls "fall-outs." These are the subscription cards that fall out every time she pick up a magazine to read. Another one is the ballpoint pen that is supposed to clip into her shirt or blouse pocket but falls on the floor every time she bend down. Outside Stacy building there are some more irritation. She particularly dislikes the scaffolds that are erected to renovate storefronts because they makes it impossible for two people to walk side by side. Many restaurant's noise levels also add to the nuisances in Stacy's life. She finds it hard to talk to friend over the hubbub of voices and pots and pans. Like many people she also object to people smoking in buses, airplanes, and other closed-in places. And she hates to go on very hot days to movie theaters, restaurants, or supermarket where the air-conditioning is so cold that she has to wear a sweater to keep from shivering.

SPECIAL PROBLEMS WITH VERB TENSES

Verb tenses present many special problems. We will consider the following nine.

- Recognizing past, present, and future tenses.
- *d* Endings in the past—regular verbs
- When *not* to use *d* endings
- The past tense of irregular verbs
- Forming past participles
- Past participles with helping verbs
- Past participles as adjectives
- Past participles of irregular verbs
- Avoiding shifts in verb tense

Recognizing Tenses

To use correct verb tenses and avoid awkward shifts in tense, you must know the verb tenses and what they mean. There are three basic verb tenses:

Present: Phyllis *enjoys* racquetball.

Past: Phyllis *enjoyed* racquetball.

Future: Phyllis *will enjoy* racquetball.

Present Tense.   All verbs take *s* endings (singular, third person) or *no endings* (plural and first and second person singular) in the present.

	Singular	*Plural*
First person:	I succeed	We succeed
Second person:	You succeed	You succeed
Third person:	He, she, it succeeds	They succeed

All verbs follow these forms for the present tense.

Past Tense.   In the past tense, verbs fall into two categories: regular verbs, which take *d* endings, and irregular verbs, which change their spelling and do not take *d* endings.

Past Tense for Regular Verbs	*Past Tense for Irregular Verbs*
succeeded	became
walked	bought
kissed	saw
stampeded	drank
murdered	sang
worshipped	took
doubted	drove
discussed	broke
wandered	spent

Future Tense.   All verbs form the future tense by adding the helping verb *will* to the main verb *with no ending.*

will succeed	will study
will deliver	will purchase
will work	will spend
will register	will jog

D Endings in the Past Tense

One of the most common writing errors is dropping or forgetting to add *d* endings on regular verbs.

EXERCISE I: *D* ENDINGS IN THE PAST TENSE

Circle incorrect verb forms and write the correct forms in the blanks.

1. Many natural disasters have occur in the twentieth century. _____
2. Avalanches, floods, earthquakes, hurricanes, and mudslides have happen all over the world. _____

3. The San Francisco earthquake in 1906 was one of the most famous because it demolish hundreds of beautiful buildings.   _____

4. The most lethal earthquake in recent years was the one in Armenia in 1988, in which over 55,000 people perish.   _____

5. The worst flood in modern times and possibly in history occurred when the Hwang-ho River overflow in 1931, killing millions of people.   _____

6. A ferocious hurricane pass through Key West, Florida, in 1919 and raged through Corpus Christi, Texas.   _____

7. In 1959 Typhoon Vera nearly destroy Nagoya, Japan's third largest city.   _____

8. In 1963, when Hurricane Flora almost wiped out the Cuban coffee crop, Fidel Castro apply to the United States for aid.   _____

9. The volcano Pelee erupted in Martinique in 1902; it spew forth lethal gas that killed 36,000 people.   _____

10. The famous Mount Vesuvius in Italy erupt several times in the twentieth century: in 1905, 1929, and 1944.   _____

EXERCISE 11: *D* ENDINGS IN THE PAST TENSE

Rewrite the following paragraph in the past tense. Be sure to include all necessary *d* endings.

Richard visits Tijuana, Mexico, with his girlfriend Pauline. They discover that the gasoline costs very little in that country, so they fill the tank. While browsing in the tourist shops, they listen to other shoppers bargaining with storeowners and realize that the prices seem to be negotiable for most items. Soon they enjoy haggling about the cost of sombreros, jewelry, and dresses. They consider going to a bullfight but decide that they prefer to continue shopping and exploring. Richard stops at a body shop and asks about the cost of repairing the rear fender of his Citation. He learns to his satisfaction that the repair work appears excellent and the prices seem reasonable. Pauline purchases several onyx jewelry boxes and a chess set as presents for relatives. She and Richard agree that it is getting late, but they expect to return the following week for more shopping.

EXERCISE III: *D* ENDINGS IN THE PAST TENSE

Rewrite these sentences in the past tense.

1. The course on human sexuality attracts many students.
2. Michael and Veronica often argue violently over money.
3. Sensible students always finish the reading a week before final examinations.
4. Seeing a videotape of her performance usually improves an actress' delivery.
5. An outbreak of influenza occurs in January.
6. The survey names over one-hundred cities and towns that have black mayors.
7. Spike Lee's film "Do the Right Thing" stirs up controversy.
8. Cocaine sales amount to $30 billion every year.
9. Living in San Francisco costs just about as much as living in Manhattan.
10. A drop in hormone output happens every time Deborah suffers from depression.

When *Not* to Use *d* Endings

If you tend to omit *d* endings in the past tense, remember that there are a few places where *d* endings should *not* be used. No *d* endings:

1. After the helping word *did*. *Did* is already in the past tense and does not need another past tense form to go with it:

   Did you *discuss* (not *discussed*) the salary?

   It really *did happen* (not *happened*) that way.

2. After other helping verbs (except *be* and *have*): *may, might, can, could, will, would, must,* and *should*:

   We *will walk* (not *walked*) there together.

   He *could learn* (not *learned*) a lot from you.

3. After the word *to*. A verb with the word *to* in front of it is called an infinitive; it is not in the past tense and does not take a *d* ending:

   We used *to live* (not *to lived*) in Cincinnati.

   They tried *to reach* (not *to reached*) the turnoff.

EXERCISE IV: *D* ENDINGS

Circle the correct form of the verb in each sentence. Keep in mind that regular verbs in the past tense need *d* endings and that verbs following helping words do not.

1. The money he (earn, earned) last year should (help, helped) him pay this semester's tuition.
2. Did you (reach, reached) any conclusions when you (discuss, discussed) the matter?
3. Tom already (register, registered) to vote; will you (ask, asked) him where we can go to register?
4. Elizabeth and John (arrange, arranged) last week to (prepare, prepared) their own marriage contract.
5. A nurse (inform, informed) me last night that I could (visit, visited) Marie after 11 a.m.
6. Henry (compose, composed) a musical review that (include, included) a jazz band and forty dancers.
7. Predicting the weather (use, used) to be unscientific; it (involve, involved) a lot of guesswork.
8. Exercise and dieting (help, helped) Carlos lose weight; he may even (work, worked) off another twenty pounds.
9. Customers didn't (realize, realized) that the store (open, opened) at 8 a.m.
10. Writing her autobiography (encourage, encouraged) Rita to (explore, explored) the meaning of her experience.

The Past Tense of Irregular Verbs

Irregular verbs never take *d* endings. Instead, they change in different ways— *go* changes to *went*, *think* to *thought*, and so on. Most of these verbs you know by usage, but some do cause frequent mistakes. Look over this list to see if you recognize the past tenses.

Present	Past	Present	Past
be (am, is, are)	was, were	get	got
become	became	give	gave
begin	began	go	went
bring	brought	have	had
buy	bought	hear	heard
choose	chose	keep	kept
cost	cost	know	knew
do	did	lay	laid
cut	cut	lead	led
feel	felt	lie	lay
fly	flew	lose	lost

Present	Past	Present	Past
make	made	spend	spent
meet	met	stand	stood
pay	paid	steal	stole
put	put	swim	swam
quit	quit	take	took
rise	rose	teach	taught
seek	sought	tear	tore
sell	sold	think	thought
send	sent	throw	threw
shine	shone	write	wrote
sing	sang		

EXERCISE I: PAST TENSE OF IRREGULAR VERBS

Without looking at the preceding chart, fill in the past tense of the following verbs. After checking your answers, be sure to memorize any that you found you did not know already.

Present	Past	Present	Past
1. I spend	I _____	19. I buy	I _____
2. I send	I _____	20. I bring	I _____
3. I go	I _____	21. I seek	I _____
4. I meet	I _____	22. I teach	I _____
5. I feel	I _____	23. I hear	I _____
6. I keep	I _____	24. I stand	I _____
7. I lead	I _____	25. I lay	I _____
8. I write	I _____	26. I do	I _____
9. I steal	I _____	27. I begin	I _____
10. I choose	I _____	28. I sing	I _____
11. I rise	I _____	29. I swim	I _____
12. I sell	I _____	30. I know	I _____
13. I become	I _____	31. I fly	I _____
14. I give	I _____	32. I throw	I _____
15. I lie	I _____	33. I quit	I _____
16. I make	I _____	34. I put	I _____
17. I pay	I _____	35. I cut	I _____
18. I think	I _____		

EXERCISE II: PAST TENSE OF IRREGULAR VERBS

Circle any incorrect past verb form and write the correct form in the blank.

1. The meal and hors d'oeuvres probably
   costed them over two hundred dollars.   _____

2. Mona send an express letter to you last
   night.   _____

3. The book laid on the library table for three
   days.   _____

4. The sun shine brightly as we left for the
   islands.   _____

5. The company spend more than a million
   dollars in its advertising campaign last year.   _____

6. Television programs lead her to think that
   her life should be like a soap opera even
   though she was working in a department
   store.   _____

7. My son brought a stereo set at Macy's last
   week.   _____

8. Burglars stold the radio and battery from
   the car.   _____

9. I told them that I had payd the bill over
   three weeks ago.   _____

10. The school choose members of the honor
    society last month.   _____

EXERCISE III: PAST TENSE OF IRREGULAR VERBS

Supply the correct past tense forms for the verbs in parentheses.

Abraham Maslow has done much to change our views of human nature.

He (1) _____ (begin) as an experimenter who (2)

_____ (spend) most of his time studying emotional illness.

He (3) _____ (write) a book on abnormal psychology but

then (4) _____ (become) dissatisfied with approaches that

(5) _____ (seek) only to understand the disturbed person.

Instead, he (6) _____ (choose) to examine the characteristics

of the unusually healthy person. He (7) _____ (make) many

original contributions to modern psychology and (8) _____

(bring) a new emphasis on health and potential rather than sickness. He

(9) _____ (know) that many mysteries still (10) _____

(lie) unsolved in the psychology of the healthy personality. He (11)

_____ (teach) for many years and (12) _____

(be) so popular he was called the Frank Sinatra of Brooklyn College. He later

(13) _____ (go) to Brandeis University and finally to Cali-

fornia. His many articles and influential books (14) _____

(do) much to win fame for him and his theories. Certain of his concepts, such

as self-actualization and the hierarchy of needs, (15) _____

(take) their place among the leading ideas of modern psychology.

Forming Past Participles

Past participles are used with forms of *be* and *have* for special purposes. Past participles of regular verbs are formed by adding *d* endings. Past participles of irregular verbs often differ from the past tense.

Regular Verbs

Present	*Past*	*Past Participle*
I believe	I believed	I have believed
I dance	I danced	I have danced
I study	I studied	I have studied

Irregular Verbs

Present	*Past*	*Past Participle*
I go	I went	I have gone
I sing	I sang	I have sung
I send	I sent	I have sent

Past participles cause some of the same problems in writing as the past tense does. You will need to avoid dropping *d* endings on regular verbs, and you will have to know the correct forms of irregular verbs from memory.

Past Participles with Helping Verbs

Past participles are used with helping verbs in two ways.

1. With *have, has,* and *had* to form the perfect tenses:

Past perfect: I *had* already *given* a brilliant performance.
                    I *had* previously *entered* the competition.
Present perfect: I *have* always *done* my taxes by myself.
                    I *have* never *cheated* on an examination.
Future perfect: I *will have begun* by the time you arrive.
                    I *will have reached* Charleston by noon.

2. With forms of *be* (is, are, was, were) to form the passive voice. The passive voice is not a tense; it is an arrangement of words in which the subject receives the action. In the active voice, the way we usually make statements, the subject does the action.

Active voice: Sharon admired Hector.
Passive voice: Hector was admired by Sharon.

In the active voice, the subject, Sharon, does the admiring; in the passive voice, the subject, Sharon, receives the admiration. Form the passive voice with forms of *be* and the past participle:

Active voice: Sidney threw a party.
Passive voice: A party *was thrown* by Sidney.

Past Participles as Adjectives

Past participles are sometimes used as adjectives, either before or after the nouns they describe:

Participle before noun: I sent a *registered* letter.
Participle after noun: I sent a letter *registered* on March 5th.
Participle before noun: A *frozen* daiquiri is tasty.
Participle after noun: A daiquiri *frozen* properly is tasty.

EXERCISE I: PAST PARTICIPLES

In the following sentences, circle past participles with missing *d* endings. Remember that past participles may appear after *have, has,* or *had*; after *is, are, was,* and *were*; and before and after nouns.

1. A close friend of mine name Henry just won the lottery.
2. Rachel was dress well for the interview.
3. The students were confuse by the examination questions.
4. Old people should not be force to retire.
5. It could have happen to you if you had been there.
6. If the real assailant had not confess, he might have been convicted.
7. The mayor was ask to preside over the ceremony.
8. The manager was face with a crucial decision.

9. Julia was divorce three years ago.
10. A young woman marry to an older man has to make adjustments.

EXERCISE II: PAST PARTICIPLES

Write sentences using the following phrases. Don't forget the *d* endings!

1. got married

_____

2. was named

_____

3. were forced to

_____

4. has happened

_____

5. is finished

_____

6. are convinced

_____

7. is concerned

_____

8. has been canceled

_____

9. have promised

_____

10. was placed

_____

Past Participles of Irregular Verbs

The past participles of irregular verbs are usually different from the past tense. Do not use the past tense in place of the participle with *have* or *be*.

Not: I have drank all the tea you gave me.
Correct: I have drunk all the tea you gave me.
Not: The bicycle was stole while I was shopping.
Correct: The bicycle was stolen while I was shopping.

Here is a list of irregular past participles that often cause mistakes:

Present	*Past*	*Past Participle*
become	became	become
begin	began	begun
bring	brought	brought
choose	chose	chosen
come	came	come
cost	cost	cost
do	did	done
drink	drank	drunk
drive	drove	driven
eat	ate	eaten
fall	fell	fallen
forget	forgot	forgotten
get	got	gotten
give	gave	given
go	went	gone
have	had	had
hide	hid	hidden
hurt	hurt	hurt
keep	kept	kept
know	knew	known
lay	laid	laid
lead	led	led
lie	lay	lain
meet	met	met
pay	paid	paid
quit	quit	quit
ride	rode	ridden
rise	rose	risen
run	ran	run
see	saw	seen
send	sent	sent
shake	shook	shaken
shine	shone	shone
sing	sang	sung
speak	spoke	spoken

Present	*Past*	*Past Participle*
spend	spent	spent
steal	stole	stolen
take	took	taken
throw	threw	thrown
write	wrote	written

EXERCISE III: PAST PARTICIPLES

Write the correct past participles in the blanks.

1. Has he ever _____ (shake) hands with Aresenio Hall?

2. I have _____ (send) a postcard to you.

3. That accident could have _____ (cost) you a fortune.

4. The bill was _____ (pay) by my uncle.

5. The winner was _____ (choose) by three judges.

6. The grant money has been _____ (spend) by now.

7. The prices have _____ (rise) since August.

8. You should have _____ (take) a nap before you came.

9. The message was _____ (write) on yellow paper.

10. She has not _____ (come) here to argue with you.

EXERCISE IV: PAST PARTICIPLES

Use the correct form, either the past tense or the past participle, in each sentence.

1. Sandra has _____ (throw) many parties for her friends.

2. A gallon of punch was _____ (drink) at the reception.

3. The course has _____ (become) more interesting.

4. The spotlight _____ (shine) suddenly on the drummer.

5. The lines were _____ (speak) softly but intensely.

6. Stanley _____ (choose) a pair of argyle socks.

7. The restaurant has _____ (begin) to serve croissants.

8. The words she spoke will never be _____ (forget).

9. Her presence has _____ (bring) hope to the children.

10. I wish we could have _____ (spend) the holidays with you.

REVIEW EXERCISE I: PAST TENSE AND PAST PARTICIPLES

Underline the *ten* incorrect verb forms in this paragraph and write the correct forms above them.

One of the people who have change public life the most is George Gallup. Before he began using scientific methods to sample public opinion, politicians and corporations rely on hunches or inaccurate surveys to determined public opinion. He develop reliable sampling methods that have came to be, with many refinements, the modern device for finding out public opinion and consumer preference. Previously, newspapers and political parties payed huge sums to collect millions of samples and still made big mistakes. Gallup discovered that by using theories of probability researchers could arrived at accurate predictions on the basis of a small number of samples. Soon Gallup's weekly poll of opinion appear in many newspapers, and he published results of his surveys on many questions. For instance, the percentage of Americans who favored a woman president was only 37% in 1937 but has since rose to 80%. On presidential elections, Gallup's results usually ran very close to the actual vote. Once, however, he did made a mistake: he predicted Truman would lose in 1948. Still, his successes far outweighed his failures.

REVIEW EXERCISE II: PAST TENSE AND PAST PARTICIPLES

Write the correct form of the verb in the blank.

1. Many kinds of special words and phrases, which are _____

   (call) figures of speech, are _____ (use) to express ideas vividly.

2. Poets have _____ (invent) thousands of metaphors; Shakespeare, for instance, _____ (write) that "All the world's a stage."

3. Through such imaginative comparisons, writers have _____ (give) us means of perceiving our lives in new ways.

4. Similes, comparisons using *like* or *as*, have also _____ (appear) frequently in literature. When Christina Rossetti wrote, "My heart is like a singing bird," she _____ (choose) a simile to express joy.

5. Synecdoche, referring to something by naming part of it, has also _____ (take) its place in literature.

6. You have probably _____ (hear) someone ask, "Do you have wheels?" He or she really wants to know if a car is available.

7. Metonymy, naming something by referring to an idea or fact associated with it, has also _____ (play) its part in writing.

8. For instance, you may have _____ (notice) the term "grandfather clause" in labor agreements. It refers to rules that apply to people who have _____ (work) for the company a long time, associating time with the age of grandfathers.

9. A euphemism, a mild term used in place of a blunter one, may be _____ (use) to avoid offending readers, but some writers have always _____ (consider) it better to be direct.

10. Prostitutes, for instance, _____ (use) to be _____ (call) "ladies of the evening."

Avoiding Shifts in Verb Tense
Once you can recognize verb tenses and use the correct verb forms, learn to write without shifting awkwardly between tenses.

What's wrong with this passage?

> When I *got* up this morning, I *felt* excited. I *know* I *have* an exam at eleven o'clock, but I *was* ready for it because I *study* hard the night before.

If you are writing in the past, *stay in the past tense*:

> When I *got* up this morning, I *felt* excited. I *knew* I *had* an exam at eleven o'clock, but I *was* ready for it because I *had studied* hard the night before.

What's wrong with this description of a story?

> This story *is* about two girls who *lived* in the South. Although they *are* sisters, one of them *was* bright while the other *is* slow and simple. The mother *tries* to be a good parent to both, but she *couldn't* treat them the same way.

When discussing a story, *stay in the present tense*:

> This story *is* about two girls who *live* in the South. Although they *are* sisters, one of them *is* bright while the other *is* slow and simple. The mother *tries* to be a good parent to both, but she *can't* treat them the same way.

Verb Tenses in Writing: Some Guidelines

1. Stay in the same tense as long as the time you are writing about does not change.

2. If the time changes, the verb tense *should* change, even in the same paragraph or sentence.

> I once *believed* that money *makes* people happy, but now I *realize* that happiness *depends* on your inner self and your relationships.

3. Tell about the plot of a play, novel, or story in the present tense.

4. Statements about eternal truths may be in the present even when you are telling about past events:

> The child *learned* quickly that not all people in this world *can* be trusted.

5. If you are writing about experiences that you remember, statements like "I recall" or "I remember" are in the present. The events happened in the past, but you are recalling them now:

> I *remember* (not remembered) how cold the winters *used* to be in Wisconsin when I *was* a child.

6. Use helping verbs correctly: *may, can,* and *will* in present and future tenses and *might, could,* and *would* in the past.

EXERCISE I: SHIFTS IN VERB TENSE

Rewrite the following paragraph so that it remains entirely in the past tense, with no shifts to the present. Underline the verbs you change from present to past.

David Bowie was born in Brixton, a lower-middle-class section of London, on January 8, 1947. His parents are rather poor; his father did odd jobs, and his mother was an usherette at a movie theater. As a teenager he begins playing the saxophone and joined a band. In his late teens he is managed by Kenn Pitt, who got him numerous record contracts as a singer, none of which produce particularly successful records. Bowie then acquired another manager, Tony Visconti, who helps him produce his first successful album, *Space Oddity*. After making a few more albums in both England and America, Bowie, posing as "Ziggy Stardust" in elaborate stage performances, decides to retire in 1973. But in 1974 he reappeared with yet another character known as "Aladinsane" and retires again in 1976 as "The Thin White Duke." After spending three years in Berlin being rehabilitated from his serious drug problem, Bowie emerges on the scene as the best character of all, himself.

EXERCISE II: SHIFTS IN VERB TENSE

Rewrite the following paragraph so that it remains entirely in the present tense, with no shifts to the past. Underline the verbs you change from past to present.

Shirley Jackson's short story, "The Lottery," shows real human behavior in a fantasy setting. The story takes place in an imaginary village that resembled a New England or midwestern town in modern times. Although the villagers were just like real small town people, with their gossip and chatter about tractors and taxes, the town has an annual custom that was not at all like everyday life. Every June the people held a lottery in which the "winner" was stoned to death by friends, neighbors, and even family members. The lottery itself is a fantasy, but the way people behaved toward it was realistic. They conformed to a tradition without questioning its harmful effect. No one protests even though they knew they were being cruel to someone they loved. "The Lottery" taught a valuable lesson about how people were able to hang onto worn-out customs and conform to the behavior of their peers even when they should have known better.

ADJECTIVES AND ADVERBS

People often confuse adjectives with adverbs, and vice versa.

Telling the Difference Between Adjectives and Adverbs

The most common mistake people make with adjectives and adverbs is to write *good* when they mean *well*.

> *Not*: This car runs good.
> *But*: This car runs well.

Good is an adjective; well is an adverb. What is the difference?

Adjectives tell *which, what kind of,* or *how many*; they modify nouns or pronouns:

a *violent* storm	a *busy* street
the *first* exit	*five* drinks

Adverbs tell *how, when,* and *where*; they modify verbs, adjectives, and other adverbs:

She talks *brilliantly*.	He will write *soon*.
an *extremely* tall man	They played *very* skillfully.
We are parked *nearby*.	

Another common mistake is to omit the *-ly* ending on adverbs. Many adjectives can be converted into adverbs by adding *-ly*.

Adjective	*Adverb*
a *quick* meal	We ate the meal *quickly*.
a *real* diamond	a *really* fine diamond
a *bad* feeling	They arranged it *badly*.
The answer was *correct*.	They answered *correctly*.

Remember to use *adjectives* after forms of *be* (*is, are, was, were*); adjectives modify the subject. Also use adjectives after verbs of the senses such as *feel, smell, sound,* and *taste*.

1. The novel sounds *exciting*. (*Exciting* modifies *novel*.)
2. The quiche smells *delicious*. (*Delicious* modifies *quiche*.)
3. I feel *good* this morning. (*Good* modifies *I*.)
4. The fish tastes *stale*. (*Stale* modifies *fish*.)

Do not confuse these adjectives (called predicate adjectives because they come after the verb, not before the noun) with adverbs that come after verbs.

1. The novel reads *smoothly*. (*Smoothly* modifies *reads*.)
2. The chef makes quiche *expertly*. (*Expertly* modifies *makes*.)
3. I dress *quickly* in the morning. (*Quickly* modifies *dress*.)
4. She catches fish *frequently*. (*Frequently* modifies *catches*.)

Do not confuse *well*, the adverb, with *well*, the adjective:

1. You certainly can swim *well*. (*Well* [adv.] modifies *swim*.)
2. You look *well* now that you've recovered. (*Well*, meaning healthy, is an adjective modifying *you*.)
3. You look *good* in that skirt. (*Good* is an adjective modifying *you*.)

Some Tricky Adverbs

Certain adverbs are often confused with adjectives. Be on the lookout for:

Adjective	*Adverb*
most people	*almost* always
She feels *bad*.	She sings *badly*.
an *easy* job	He does it *easily*.
an *everyday* task	He swims *every day*. (two words)
a *smooth* landing	We landed *smoothly*.
a *slow* pace	Drive *slowly*. (*Slow* is also accepted as an adverb.)

EXERCISE I: ADJECTIVES AND ADVERBS

Circle the correct form in each sentence.

1. Television newscasters have to be (real, really) articulate.
2. Educational programs help children learn (easy, easily).
3. Some people feel (bad, badly) after watching too much television.
4. Soap operas have become an (everyday, every day) activity for many people.
5. Commercials are (most, almost, mostly) always louder than the programs.
6. Some children behave (violent, violently) after watching (violent, violence, violently) programs.
7. To choose programs (careful, carefully), you should read reviews of the programs first.
8. Commercials lead customers to decide too (quick, quickly) about buying products.
9. Some sports fans react (wild, wildly) to athletic events.
10. Most viewers respond (emotional, emotionally) to soap operas.

EXERCISE II: ADJECTIVES AND ADVERBS

Supply the missing forms.

Adjective	*Adverb*
Example:	
She is *stylish*.	She dresses *stylishly*.
1. The child seemed *happy*.	The child lived _____ .
2. The interview was *easy*.	She passed the test _____ .
3. The crowd became _____ .	She approached *quietly*.
4. Their anger was *extreme*.	They were _____ angry.

5. She feels _____ about it.   We performed *badly* yesterday.

6. The food made him *heavy*.   He moved _____ .

7. The apartment looks _____ .   He arranged the chairs *neatly*.

8. The crossing looked *dangerous*.   Let's live _____ .

9. Your statements are _____ .   She predicts *accurately*.

10. His office was *open*.   She talked _____ about it.

EXERCISE III: ADJECTIVES AND ADVERBS

Compose sentences using the following words and phrases.

1. feels good _____

   feels well _____

2. especially _____

   special _____

3. bad _____

   badly _____

4. probable _____

   probably _____

5. everyday _____

   every day _____

6. careful _____

   carefully _____

7. real _____

   really _____

Special Practice with *Good* and *Well*

Write the adjective *good* or the adverb *well* in each blank; remember that *well* may be an adjective meaning healthy.

1. The pilot flew jet planes _____.

2. She had _____ training and understood aircraft _____.

3. After an illness, she had gotten _____ again; she was waiting for a _____ day to resume her flying.

4. It felt _____ to be in the air once again.

5. She remembered all the instruments on the panel _____.

6. As the engines roared, they sounded _____ to her.

7. This was a _____ career, and it paid _____.

8. She made the plane perform as _____ as possible, doing loops and dives.

9. She stayed up as long as she could, then made a _____, smooth landing.

10. People in the airport saw how _____ she flew the plane.

Adjectives in Comparisons

Besides their simple forms, adjectives have two forms that are used in comparisons. The comparative form is used to compare two unequal things, and the superlative form is used to set one thing off from all the others.

Simple Form	*Comparative Form*	*Superlative Form*
good	better	best
young	younger	youngest
strange	stranger	strangest
gentle	gentler	gentlest
happy	happier	happiest

Adjectives with three or more syllables always take *more* and *most* rather than the *er* and *est* endings.

beautiful	more beautiful	most beautiful
exciting	more exciting	most exciting

Your dictionary will show that some two-syllable words take *er* and *est* while others take *more* and *most*.

heavy	heavier	heaviest
friendly	friendlier	friendliest
subtle	subtler	subtlest
cheerful	more cheerful	most cheerful
precise	more precise	most precise

Use the comparative form when comparing two things or people:

She is wealthier than her cousin.

She is the wealthier of the two cousins.

(Remember to use th*a*n, not th*e*n, in making comparisons.)

Use the superlative form to set off one from a whole group:

She is the wealthiest woman in the group.

She is the wealthiest of the three cousins.

Adverbs in Comparisons

Adverbs also have comparative and superlative forms. Nearly all adverbs take *more* and *most*. The only exceptions are the few that serve as both adjectives and adverbs—early, late, hard, fast, low, and straight. These take *er* and *est*: earlier, earliest.

Simple Form	*Comparative Form*	*Superlative Form*
easily	more easily	most easily
violently	more violently	most violently
recently	more recently	most recently
happily	more happily	most happily

We also make negative comparisons, using adjectives and adverbs in combination with *less* or *least*.

expensive	less expensive	least expensive
difficult	less difficult	least difficult
safely	less safely	least safely
forcefully	less forcefully	least forcefully

Do not use both the *er* or *est* ending *and* the helping words *more, most, less,* or *least*.

Wrong: You are *more better* than the last shortstop.
              They are *less healthier* than they should be.
Right: You are *better* than the last shortstop.
              They are *less healthy* than they should be.

Wrong: This was the *most saddest* film I have seen.
This was the *least richest* pastry on the menu.

Right: This was the *saddest* film I have seen.
This was the *least rich* pastry on the menu.

EXERCISE I: ADJECTIVES IN COMPARISONS

Write the correct form of the adjective or adverb in the blank.

1. Most people enjoy films that are _____ (long) than ordinary ones.

2. Being longer, of course, does not make a film _____ (good).

3. Some of the _____ (fine) films ever made have been rather short.

4. Still, audiences often expect a longer film to provide a _____ (rich) experience than a short one.

5. One of the _____ (great) efforts of all time in filmmaking was the Russian version of *War and Peace*.

6. This was the _____ (accurate) of all film adaptations of Tolstoy's novel.

7. The original Russian version runs eight hours, twenty-seven minutes, a _____ (big) block of time than three or four normal films would require.

8. A Japanese film company made a still _____ (ambitious) film called *The Human Condition*, which lasted nine hours and twenty-nine minutes.

9. Much _____ (early), in 1925, a seven-hour, fifty-eight-minute silent film called *Sparks of the Flame* was made in the Soviet Union.

10. Two years _____ (late) a French filmmaker, Abel Gance, created a six-hour, eighteen-minute epic on Napoleon.

EXERCISE 11: ADJECTIVES AND ADVERBS IN COMPARISONS

After each sentence, write a sentence using the same adjective or adverb in comparing two persons or things.

Examples:

Lead is *heavy*.
Lead is heavier than tin.

John ran *fast*.
John ran faster than the moped.

1. This home computer is *easy* to use.

   _____

2. Algebra is *difficult*.

   _____

3. Esther sings *loudly*.

   _____

4. Working in a nuclear power plant is *dangerous*.

   _____

5. Magazine models have to be *slender*.

   _____

6. The Huxtables lived *happily*.

   _____

7. The language in that film was *strange*.

   _____

8. This ice cream tastes *good*.

   _____

9. Sam always walks noisily.

_____

10. The dancer looked *young*.

_____

EXERCISE III: COMPARATIVE AND SUPERLATIVE FORMS

Write a sentence converting each adjective or adverb from comparative to superlative form.

Examples:

Mike is *taller* than the other team's center.
Mike is the tallest center in the league.

This book is *less interesting* than *The Bonfire of the Vanities*.
This book is the least interesting one on the best-seller list.

1. This pattern suits you *better* than the one you used last time.

_____

2. The weather was *worse* this January than it was last year.

_____

3. Karen is *smarter* than most of her teachers.

_____

4. This diamond is *more expensive* than Elizabeth Taylor's.

_____

5. Grammar is *more interesting* than disco dancing.

_____

6. My dentist tells *funnier* stories than Johnny Carson does.

_____

7. Sleeping in class is *more pleasant* than studying.

_____

8. Robert moves *more quickly* than his opponent.

_____

9. This is a *warmer* day than yesterday.

_____

10. This is a *sillier* program than *Saturday Night Live*.

_____

Misplaced and Dangling Modifiers

Modifiers are adjectives, adverbs, or phrases that function as adjectives or adverbs. Modifiers describe or change the meaning of other words in the sentence, so they should be close to the words that they modify. If they are too far away from the words they modify and cause confusion, we call them misplaced modifiers. If the words they modify are not really in the sentence, we call them dangling modifiers.

Misplaced Modifiers.

> *As a child*, my grandmother took me to see a bullfight.
> *Standing on the curb*, a bicyclist whizzed by and almost knocked her over.

The italicized phrases in both sentences are out of place. If we take them to be describing the words next to them, the meaning is confused. It sounds as if grandmother were a child and the bicyclist were standing on the curb. Rearrange sentences like these to say what you mean.

Better:

> When *I* was a child, my grandmother took me to see a bullfight.
> While *she* was standing on the curb, a bicyclist whizzed by and almost knocked her over.

Another way:

> *As a child*, I went to see a bullfight with my grandmother.
> *Standing on the curb*, she was almost knocked over by a bicyclist.

Dangling Modifiers.

> *While drying her hair,* the clock radio suddenly began blasting.
>
> *As a teenager,* school became boring and homework was a drag.

These dangling modifiers are not much different from misplaced modifiers, except that in these sentences there is no word at all that the modifiers describe. Who was drying her hair? Who was a teenager? The reader has to guess. Add the necessary words.

Better:

> While *Karen* was drying her hair, the clock radio suddenly began blasting.
>
> *As a teenager, I* found school boring and homework a drag.

Identifying Misplaced and Dangling Modifers. Many students who have good control of grammar in other areas still have trouble finding and correcting misplaced and dangling modifiers. The meaning may seem clear to them while it is not to the reader. Misplaced and dangling modifiers are often introductory phrases, so watch for them at the beginning of your sentences. However, they can occur in the middle or at the end of sentences:

> Sergio reached for the drawer *filled with anger and resentment*.
>
> A hurricane was moving slowly up the coast *while at Cape Cod*.

In the first sentence, the underlined phrase is misplaced: it should describe Sergio, but appears to describe the drawer.

Better:

> *Filled with anger and resentment*, Sergio reached for the drawer.

In the second sentence, the modifying phrase would be dangling no matter where we put it; the sentence must say *who* was at Cape Cod.

Better:

> A hurricane was moving slowly up the coast *while we were at Cape Cod*.

EXERCISE I: DANGLING AND MISPLACED MODIFIERS

Underline the misplaced word or phrase and rewrite the sentence with the modifier in the right place.

Example: He will pick up the car that was wrecked <u>tomorrow morning</u>.

Tomorrow morning he will pick up the car that was wrecked.

1. She will have to repair the radio that was damaged with a screw-driver.

   _____

   _____

2. Sitting on the top shelf I discovered a copy of *Gone with the Wind*.

   _____

   _____

3. She wanted an apartment that would be large enough for two children with plenty of light.

   _____

   _____

4. Nearly starved, the helicopter pilot spotted her shivering in the snow.

   _____

   _____

5. Decorated with rhinestones, the salesman placed the sweater back in the display case.

   _____

   _____

6. Puffed up with air, the scientist placed the bag over the flame.

   _____

   _____

7. Sketches of the suspect were drawn by an artist that looked like photographs.

   _____

   _____

8. Several people in Arizona reported seeing flying saucers in the newspapers.

_____

_____

9. Scratching his nose against an oak, Robert at last found his pony.

_____

_____

10. Joking with news reporters, we watched the president join his staff.

_____

_____

EXERCISE II: DANGLING AND MISPLACED MODIFIERS

Rewrite each sentence, placing the italicized phrase where it logically belongs.

Example: *with its headlights on*

The crowd watched the limousine roll silently onto the ferryboat.

The crowd watched the limousine, with its headlights on, roll silently onto the ferryboat.

1. *with a view of the river*

They were looking for a colonial house big enough for a growing family.

_____

2. *hoarse from shouting*

Two minutes after the game the coach congratulated the whole team.

_____

3. *in V formation*

We watched the jets flying overhead.

_____

4. *purring with contentment*

The children found the kitten in the back seat of the car.

_____

5. *that included word processing*

She finally found a course in a community college nearby.

_____

6. *that was too salty*

Several customers sent the lamb stew back to the chef.

_____

7. *listed in the telephone directory*

Sally gave the names of three dentists to Tom's cousin.

_____

8. *alarmed by a sudden noise*

We watched the deer start, then leap over a split rail fence and disappear.

_____

9. *next Monday*

Beverly will arrange to deposit the check she received.

_____

10. *that resembled the Goodyear Blimp*

Susan bought a balloon to give to her little brother.

_____

EXERCISE III: DANGLING AND MISPLACED MODIFIERS

Rewrite these sentences, adding or changing words so that the modifying phrases are not dangling.

Example: Living in Chicago, the winters were cold and windy.

Living in Chicago, we found the winters cold and windy.

1. Famous for his stage performance, his first album was a big success.

_____

2. Shouting angrily, the pressure of his new job finally became felt.

_____

3. Working as hard as possible, my term report was finally done.

_____

4. Concentrating on the fine print, the meaning became clear.

_____

5. Riding five hours on a Greyhound bus, the afternoon was boring.

_____

6. Excited by the news, the room began to swim before her eyes.

_____

7. When building a ship model, the parts should be arranged carefully before glueing them together.

_____

8. Adopting a child can be rewarding if prepared for it.

_____

9. Playing an electric guitar, the room vibrated.

_____

10. Having won a scholarship, the future looked bright.

_____

REVIEW EXERCISE: MISPLACED AND DANGLING MODIFIERS

Correct any misplaced or dangling modifiers in these sentences by rewriting the sentences. Write *C* if the sentence is correct.

1. Susan gave Ted a poster for his room in the dormitory that looked like a spring landscape.

_____

_____

2. After buying three tickets, on the way home it became apparent that they would need four.

_____

_____

3. Henry had to drive his old Ford to get to the party on time without a spare tire.

_____

_____

4. Learning how to use their home computer, a surprising number of tasks suddenly became easier.

_____

_____

5. Checked three times by the examiners, his answers nevertheless proved all correct.

_____

_____

6. While using the hair dryer, the doorbell was inaudible.

_____

_____

7. The people usually vote for a candidate they see on television with charm and poise.

_____

_____

8. After being in South America all summer, the neighborhood looked different.

_____

_____

9. The inspector tried to find violations of the building code looking through the furnace room.

_____

_____

10. Statistics were released in March by five government departments that indicated a drop in inflation.

_____

_____

PRONOUNS

Pronouns cause several kinds of writing difficulties.

Types of Pronouns

Pronouns are of several types.

Personal pronouns used as subjects	*Reflexive pronouns*
I	myself
you	yourself
she	yourselves
he	herself
it	himself
we	itself
they	ourselves
	themselves

Personal pronouns used as objects of verbs and prepositions	*Impersonal pronouns*
me	one
you	each
her	either
him	anyone
it	anybody
us	everybody
them	everyone
	somebody
	someone
	none
	no one
	nobody

Pronoun Case

Probably the most frequent difficulty people have with pronouns lies in choosing the correct case for personal pronouns. This means knowing whether to use *I* or *me, we* or *us, she* or *her,* and *he* or *him.* When one of these pronouns occurs by itself, we can usually pick the correct form by the sound. However, when there are two pronouns or a pronoun occurs with a noun, choosing may be more difficult.

Which is correct?

Between you and me, the boss plans to promote Carol.

Between you and I, the boss plans to promote Carol.

Are you surprised to find out that the *first* one is correct? Both *you* and *me* are the objects of *between*.

Which is correct?

> My brother and I tried out for a professional soccer team.
> Me and my brother tried out for a professional soccer team.

The first one is correct again, because both *I* and *brother* are the subjects of the verb *tried*.

How can you tell which is right? The easiest way is not to analyze the grammar but to take out the other word, whether noun or pronoun, and read the sentence without it:

> *I* tried out for a professional soccer team.

EXERCISE I: PRONOUN CASE

Choose the correct pronoun(s) in each sentence (read the sentence in your mind without the other word). Circle the correct form.

1. Send applications to (she and I, her and me).
2. Wait until the neighbors hear about you and (I, me).
3. (Me and my sister, My sister and I) live a block from each other.
4. The proceeds will go to Bob and (he, him).
5. After (she and I, me and her) save enough money, we will visit Cuba.
6. (We, Us) students should organize a bridge team.
7. Ted and (I, me) are learning to operate a small business.
8. After the bank has trained you and (I, me) to be managers, we can afford new cars.
9. The neighbors asked (he and she, him and her) about it.
10. According to Brenda and (she, her), the examination was easy.

EXERCISE II: PRONOUN CASE

Write sentences using the following combinations correctly. Remember to read your sentences with each pronoun by itself to be sure they are correct.

Example: her and me

They gave cornet lessons to her and me.

1. you and I

2. Robert and me

3. she and her brother

_____

4. we undergraduates

_____

5. we and they

_____

6. him and her

_____

7. us Americans

_____

8. you and him

_____

9. he and she

_____

10. us and them

_____

EXERCISE III: PRONOUN CASE

Circle the correct forms in parentheses.

For most of (we, us) young Americans nowadays, Michael Jackson has become a source of entertainment and amazement. (He, Him) and his brothers formed the Jackson Five in the 1960s, when (he, him) and (they, them) were still children. Michael is close to his family; like (them, they) he is a Jehovah's Witness. He lives with his mother and is close to both (she, her) and his father, who has supervised the Jackson Five. He has provided for (we, us) viewers and listeners some of the best record albums, live concerts, and rock video clips. Michael has a phenomenal rapport with his fans. He and (they, them) remind us of the Beatlemania of the 1960s. As much as any entertainer in modern times, he has also been able to cross over racial lines. To you and (me, I) and people of many ethnic groups and levels of education, he has enormous appeal.

Pronouns and Antecedents

Since pronouns are words that take the place of nouns, they always have nouns called antecedents, usually in the same sentence or one just before it, to which they refer. Pronouns must agree with their antecedents in number, person, and gender.

1. Pronouns and antecedents agree in number:

> The *book* lost *its* cover. (*Book* and *its* are both singular.)
>
> Most *people* enjoy *their* birthdays. (*People* and *their* are both plural.)

2. Pronouns and antecedents agree in person:

> The *company* changed *its* name. (*company* and *its* are both in the third person.)
>
> *You* must wear *your* tuxedo. (*You* and *your* are both in the second person.)

3. Pronouns and antecedents agree in gender:

> *Inez* wore *her* red sweater. (*Inez* and *her* are both feminine.)
>
> *James* found *his* motorcycle. (*James* and *his* are both masculine.)

Most mistakes made in agreement of pronouns and antecedents have to do with number. Do not shift from a singular noun to a plural pronoun, or vice versa.

> Awkward shifts:

> The *company* announced *their* profits for the year. (*Company* is singular; *their* is plural.)
>
> People who try water *sports* find *it* exciting. (*Sports* is plural; *it* is singular.)

Remember that indefinite pronouns like *everyone, anybody, someone,* and *nobody* are singular. Use singular forms like *he, his, she, her,* or *his or her* to agree with them:

> *Everybody* should submit *his or her* term paper on Friday.

EXERCISE I: PRONOUNS AND ANTECEDENTS

Circle the correct pronoun in each sentence.

1. Every woman in the audience knows this is true for (them, her, she).
2. All of the people who voted in the last election expressed (his, her, their) preferences.
3. A law that is not enforced loses (their, his, its) validity.
4. Steps are being taken to prevent looting because (they, it) causes enormous damage.
5. The standard of living has risen slightly, but (they, he, it) may rise faster in the next year.
6. Mothers and fathers have recently pooled (her, his, their) knowledge in writing this book.
7. A firefighter who stays on the force for twenty years receives (his, her, his or her, their) retirement benefits.
8. Students of astronomy find that (he, she, they) need mathematics.
9. A father of small children often finds (their, his, its) time taken up with domestic responsibilities.
10. Songs are often presented to the public in video clips that express (its, his, their) feeling visually.

EXERCISE II: PRONOUNS AND ANTECEDENTS

Rewrite the first five sentences by changing the pronouns and antecedents from singular to plural. In the last five, change them from plural to singular. Be sure that all verbs agree with their subjects.

Example: An ambitious entertainer usually has an agent to look after his or her interests.

Plural: Ambitious entertainers usually have agents to look after their interests.

1. Singular: An undergraduate who hopes to pursue a graduate degree has to earn high grades in his or her major subject.
   Plural: Undergraduates who _____

   _____

2. Singular: The last job at which I worked offered too few rewards for its difficulties.
   Plural: The last jobs _____

   _____

3. Singular: A child who writes poetry often develops his or her imagination and language skills at the same time.
   Plural: Children who _____

   _____

4. Singular: A man who wants to become a professional chef can pursue his career at a college of culinary arts.
   Plural: Men who _____

   _____

5. Singular: A company that uses computers effectively can increase its efficiency and maximize its profits.
   Plural: Companies that _____

   _____

6. Plural: Women who run for public office often make their way against opposition from their peers.
   Singular: A woman who _____

   _____

7. Plural: Pedestrians who refuse to obey the lights are risking their lives.
   Singular: A pedestrian who _____

   _____

8. Plural: Men who attend colleges that were once for women only sometimes find themselves in a minority group.
   Singular: A man who _____

   _____

9. Plural: Newspapers that sensationalize the news they print and use simple language are called tabloids.
   Singular: A newspaper that _____

   _____

10. Plural: Children who skip grades in school have to adjust to finding themselves in more mature social groups.
    Singular: A child who _____

    _____

REVIEW EXERCISE: PRONOUNS

Underline any incorrect pronouns and write the correct forms in the margin. Change the verb forms if necessary to agree with the pronouns.

Ray Albert Kroc was a rare example of the ordinary person like you and I who became a multimillionaire. The son of a relatively poor Czechoslovakian immigrant, Kroc became the founder of the McDonald's Corporation, with their 7500 restaurants in 31 countries. He followed the pattern of many self-made tycoons of the past. Like they, he did not have much formal education, dropping out of high school in Oak Park, Illinois, and joining the ambulance corps in World War I. Later he held various jobs but was not satisfied with it; eventually he joined the Lily Tulip Cup Company for seventeen years and became their Midwestern sales manager.

In 1941 he decided to set out by hisself and began selling a machine that made five milkshakes at once. In 1954 he heard about the McDonald brothers in San Bernardino, California, who were becoming known in the area for his fast-food operation. On visiting them, Kroc came up with an idea that us Americans are all familiar with today—the McDonald's hamburger chain. The McDonald brothers soon became a minor part of the scheme. A deal between he and they allowed him to build a chain of restaurants using there methods. His first restaurant appeared in a Chicago suburb in 1955; the next two opened in California. McDonald's outlets were so successful that it was soon familiar in all parts of the country. In the 1960s and 1970s the chain grew into the largest food service organization in the country, with their own "Hamburger University" for training new managers.

Kroc met his wife Joan in 1956 when him and her were both married to other spouses. They married each other in 1968. In 1976, Kroc and her created Operation Cork (Kroc spelled backwards), a national program to aid families of alcoholics. In 1974 Kroc also purchased the San Diego Padres baseball team. However, it was so unsuccessful that he gave up control of them five years later. He thought he could make bigger contributions through hamburgers than through baseball, which he thought was losing their original spirit and meaning. Some of his methods were, in fact, important contributions. His hiring of teenage employees and his choice of effective managers with company loyalty were the source of much publicity. It also provoked occasional controversy. For instance, Senator Harrison Williams of New Jersey once charged he and his company with trying to bribe the Nixon administration to change laws concerning teenage workers. Despite such setbacks, Kroc's personality and career are facts of modern life. It will be remembered for a long time by both his admirers and his detractors.*

SHIFTS OF PERSON

When you write a paragraph or essay, you may choose to write it in the first, second, or third person.

---

*From "Ray A. Kroc Dies at 81, Built McDonald's Chain" by Eric Pace, *The New York Times*, January 15, 1984. Copyright © 1984 by The New York Times Company. Reprinted by permission.

First Person.   The *first person* refers to the writer or speaker (I) or to the group including the writer or speaker (we). Stories and essays are often written in the first person, meaning that the writer or narrator (an imaginary speaker) refers throughout the story to himself or herself by using *I*, *me*, *my*, and *mine*. Editorials in newspapers and company reports sometimes use the first person plural, the "editorial we." Such editorials and reports sound as if they are expressing the opinions of a whole group.

Second Person.   The *second person* means the reader or listener (you). Whole essays are seldom written entirely in the second person. Procedural writing, which contains a series of instructions to the reader often is. Personal letters usually contain many statements in the second person because the writer is addressing a specific reader whom he or she knows.

Third Person.   The *third person* means any person or thing written about. Most college writing is in the third person because most of it is about topics studied in college courses, not about the personal life of the writer or reader. A statement that someone does something ("James writes country music") is in the third person. It may be singular (she, he, it) or plural (they).

Shifts of Person.   Do not shift awkwardly from one person to another in your writing. Watch especially for the temptation to slip *you* into an essay that is supposed to be in the third person:

> A *person* who wants to learn how to sing well has to think about several elements at once. *He* or *she* has to learn to open and relax the throat. *You* also have to use the diaphragm to support *your* breathing.

This sort of shift from *he* or *she* to *you* is awkward and confusing. Either write the whole set of instructions in the second person, using *you* throughout, or keep it in the third person, using either he (or she) or *one*. (Note: You may shift between *one* and *he* or *she*, since you are remaining in the third person.)

Writers also sometimes make the mistake of shifting into the first person (I) when it is not appropriate:

> Before *you* go out to run or participate in a vigorous sport, *you* should warm up with some stretching exercises. Before jogging, *I* always do leg stretching exercises and touch *my* toes several times.

This whole passage should remain in the second person, *you should* instead of *I*. Remember that when you give commands or instructions, the word *you* is often understood and does not have to be repeated frequently: "Always do leg stretching exercises" is shorter than "You should always do leg stretching exercises."

EXERCISE I: SHIFTS OF PERSON

Underline the word or phrase containing a shift of person and write the correct phrase above it.

Example:

                        you   *turn*

When you follow this recipe, <u>one</u> always <u>turns</u> out a delicious pie.

1. Everyone who wants to register this morning should have your bursar's receipt ready.

2. If one belongs to a credit union, you can borrow money easily.

3. However I study for an examination, it usually turns out to be harder than you expected.

4. You can never tell what unexpected world events will intervene in one's life.

5. We always used to look for mushrooms in the woods, but you had to be sure you didn't eat any poisonous ones.

6. One has to struggle to achieve what I want in life.

7. Anyone who does not watch foreign films does not know what you're missing.

8. Waiting for our grades to be posted, you could really become impatient.

9. Someone should bring raspberries if you don't find them too expensive.

10. Your sums are likely to be incorrect if one doesn't use a calculator.

EXERCISE II: SHIFTS OF PERSON

Complete each sentence using a form of the pronoun that is used at the beginning. If the sentence has a noun rather than a pronoun, use a third person pronoun (one, he, she, or they) to complete the sentence. Do not shift persons in completing the sentence.

Example: If you want to become a doctor, _____*you should*_____

_____*excel in your science courses*_____

1. If anyone wants to become a model, _____

_____

2. When we find out who stole our car, _____

    _____

3. After you have read the instructions, _____

    _____

4. While I am shopping for a used car, _____

    _____

5. If we see a restaurant at the next exit, _____

    _____

6. Whenever one drinks too much bourbon, _____

    _____

7. If a mother leaves her children with a babysitter, _____

    _____

8. Although a man may earn a large salary, _____

    _____

9. As your knowledge of psychology increases, _____

    _____

10. When people go to shopping malls, _____

    _____

EXERCISE III: SHIFTS OF PERSON

The following paragraph should be in the third person throughout. Underline all pronouns that are not in the third person and write the correct forms in the margin. Change the verb forms if necessary to agree with the pronouns.

To write an effective essay, a student has to consider at least three things: content, organization, and correctness. You have to have a clear main idea and develop it. Content includes a main thought as well as specific material to support it. The writer should have plenty of examples to illustrate the idea; sometimes it helps to jot down more examples than I would ever use. Organization is important too. A writer should not just state facts in any order without thought to arrangement. Your first example should be a powerful one; your last one should be the most important of all. And we should not forget to make transitions between examples. Finally, I should always proofread my essay to find mistakes in grammar or phrasing. A good writer never assumes that the first draft needs no corrections or revisions. You should always be ready to make as many small corrections and improvements as the essay needs. As the last step, the writer should give the essay an effective title. Good titles often come to me when I am composing an essay. The title should suggest the topic but not necessarily announce it. You should use your title to arouse interest. Often the conclusion of one's essay will contain a word or phrase used in the title.

PARALLELISM

Sentences with two parts joined by *and* or three or more parts in a series should have parallel construction. Parallelism in writing means that parts fit together—nouns with nouns, adjectives with adjectives, modifying phrases with similar phrases, and so on. Here are some examples.

              noun   *noun*   *noun*   *noun*
We found an hourglass, a telescope, an anchor, and a harpoon in the old lighthouse.

                  prep. phrase   *prep. phrase*
The marathon went along the avenue, over the suspension bridge,
     prep. phrase   *prep. phrase*
past the courthouse, and into the park.
           adj.   *adj.*   *adj.*   *adj.*
The party was crowded, noisy, wild, and hilarious.

In the following sentences an element is not parallel. Can you identify it?

1. We discovered a battery, a radio, a generator, and looked for a hubcap.
2. Both girls were attractive, worked in publishing houses, ambitious, and talented.

In sentence 1 there are three nouns in a row, followed by "looked for a hubcap"—a phrase that is not parallel with the rest. In sentence 2 there is a series of adjectives. "Worked in publishing houses" does not fit; it is a descriptive phrase with a verb. Compare these examples:

Nonparallel	*Parallel*
She is tall, pretty, and has skill.	She is tall, pretty, and skillful.
They wanted to advance in their jobs, earn a lot of money, as well as enjoying their work.	They wanted to advance in their jobs, earn a lot of money, and enjoy their work.
The journey left her contented, better informed, and an optimist.	The journey left her contented, better informed, and optimistic.

Jason studied before school, after work, and he read assignments during lunch break.
From too little sleep and because I was anxious about the examination, I got a headache.

Jason studied before school, after work, and during the lunch break.
I got a headache from too little sleep and anxiety over the examination.

EXERCISE I: PARALLELISM

It helps to think of parallel elements as lists. When you number the parts, you can see more easily which one may not fit. In the following lists, circle the part that does not fit. Then rewrite it in the blank in a form that is parallel with the others.

Example:

1. well-coordinated
2. quick
3. (has a lot of accuracy)   *accurate*
4. strong

1. knows several languages
2. sings country music
3. acquainted with foreign countries
4. understands computers

1. famous
2. wealthy
3. unusually talented
4. good voice

1. over the bridge
2. the highway
3. under the viaduct
4. around the museum

1. knee bends
2. doing pushups
3. lifting weights
4. jumping rope

1. willingly
2. rapidly
3. efficiency
4. calmly

1. who lived many years
2. working for the post office
3. who belonged to a union
4. who founded a political party

1. to participate in sports
2. to build electronic gadgets
3. how to draw blueprints
4. to develop photographs   _____

1. afternoon
2. in the evening
3. before lunch
4. at bedtime   _____

EXERCISE II: PARALLELISM

Circle the nonparallel part in each sentence and rewrite the sentence so that all parts are parallel.

Example:

She was tall, attractive, and (had a lot of talent.)

She was tall, attractive, and talented.
_____

1. He is stocky, athletic, and has a lot of poise.

_____

_____

2. We searched in the restaurant, in the parking lot, and even tried to find it under the car.

_____

_____

3. Shirley knows how to make films, choreograph musicals, and can even play the clarinet.

_____

_____

4. When you are shopping for a home computer, be sure to compare prices, talk with friends who own computers, read company brochures, and asking advice of people who work with computers.

_____

_____

5. As a child, Belinda was adventurous, had a sense of humor, and imaginative.

_____

_____

6. The camera stopped, was starting again, and suddenly raced forward.

_____

_____

7. Gracefully, easily, and moving with rapidity, he slipped through the defensive line.

_____

_____

8. Paul enjoys current fiction, science fiction films, and he likes to watch television programs like *60 Minutes.*

_____

_____

9. Some schools are troubled by drug abuse, they have problems with student discipline, and absenteeism.

_____

_____

10. The training program includes sales techniques, how to manage a retail store, and leadership skills.

_____

_____

EXERCISE III: PARALLELISM

The following paragraph contains four sentences whose content is not parallel. Rewrite the sentences in the blanks, making them parallel and smooth.

> El Salvador, which used to be a little-known country, is now familiar to Americans, to the Soviet people, and it is known to people in almost all countries. Although a small country geographically, it is densely populated and politically important. It is a productive country agriculturally, its chief income coming from coffee, cotton, and cattle are also raised there. Its current political unrest is nothing new. Since it gained independence from Spain in 1821, it has been plagued by interference from dictators of neighboring countries, internal struggles, and there were economic problems. The tensions now come from the pressure from leftists for economic reform and the efforts of the wealthy to hold onto their power. El Salvador will probably remain troubled, unpredictable, and have a lot of tension for years to come.

Rewrites:

1. _____

2. _____

3. _____

4. _____

MIXED SENTENCES

Some writers have problems putting the words of their sentences together. They may leave out necessary words, phrase ideas awkwardly, put words in the wrong order, or use words in the wrong form—as nouns instead of adjectives, for example. Such problems either make the sentences hard to understand or make them read awkwardly. What is wrong with these sentences?

1. In trying to swim with her clothes on was difficult.
2. I wondered was she the right girl for me.
3. Tim was a quarterback belonged on a professional team.
4. Our society is too militarism.

Each of these sentences contains a familiar kind of mistake.
   Sentence 1 contains a phrase that does not match the rest of the sentence: "In trying to swim" cannot be the subject of "was difficult." The sentence should read:

Trying to swim with her clothes on was difficult.

Or

In trying to swim with her clothes on, she had difficulty.

Sentence 2 contains words in the wrong order. The sentence begins as a statement, then switches to a question. The sentence should read:

I wondered if she was the right girl for me.

Or

Was she the right girl for me?

Sentence 3 has a word missing. The sentence should read:

Tim was a quarterback *who* belonged on a professional team.

Sentence 4 contains a word used in the wrong form. *Militarism* is a noun when the word needed is an adjective. The sentence should read:

Our society is too *militaristic*.

EXERCISE 1: MIXED SENTENCES

Each of the following sentences contains a phrase that does not fit. Rewrite the sentence so that all parts fit together.

1. By giving in to her demands was a sure way to make her bossier.

_____

_____

2. In repeating the answers to himself helped him do well on the test.

_____

_____

3. While driving with the brake on caused a burning smell.

_____

_____

4. After living in a big city was why she liked excitement.

_____

_____

5. By wearing their seat belts saved them from serious injuries.

_____

_____

Each of these sentences contains mixed-up word order. Rewrite the sentence with the phrasing straightened out.

6. She wondered, should she join her sister at the video arcade.

_____

_____

7. I asked my father was there any unemployment compensation in his day.

_____

_____

8. Tina asked did they have any watches for sale.

_____

_____

9. The police officer questioned had he been drinking.

_____

_____

10. A student wanted to know did psychologists agree about homo-sexuality.

_____

_____

EXERCISE II: MIXED SENTENCES

Each of the following sentences has a word or set of words missing. Indicate where the word is missing with a caret (∧) and write the missing word or words above the line.

Example:

She was a worker␣*who*␣never shunned a difficult task.

1. The Rolls-Royce is a car never loses its value.

2. After the downpour was too muddy to have the class outdoors.

3. Because of inflation isn't any way for many families to finance a college education.

4. A heavy cocaine user needs a lot of money may resort to crime.

5. There too many players who care more about money than basketball.

6. When the sun is setting is difficult to drive on Route 30.

7. While it was raining in Philadelphia, was snowing in Cleveland.

8. A student in California wants to transfer to an Eastern college can expect to pay higher tuition.

9. They found the records been scratched.

10. Jessica be in Houston next month when you visit.

EXERCISE III: MIXED SENTENCES

In the following sentences, a word appears in the wrong form. Cross out the word and write the correct form above it.

Example:

The lyrics were not very ~~interested~~ *interesting*.

1. Some people insist that America is still a sexism society.

2. Larry found it hard to be interesting in the slides.

3. How you dress for a job interview is very importance.

4. The assailant was not presence when the police arrived.

5. The traffic on the Beltway was worst today than it was yesterday.

6. Working with the handicapped takes a lot of patients.

7. A religion belief sometimes gives hope to terminal patients.

8. In his day there were few education opportunities.

9. Pluralistic is one of the most important features of our society.

10. His absent made the vote invalid.

REVIEW EXERCISE: MIXED SENTENCES

Rewrite each sentence, eliminating any mixed phrases, adding missing words, correcting words in the wrong form, or putting words into correct order.

1. They questioned should there be a traffic light on the corner.

   _____

2. One problem in the Soviet Union is too much authoritarian.

   _____

3. While studying with the television set on is hard to concentrate.

   _____

4. A museum does not include a section on technology is out of date.

   _____

5. Janet asked her mother's helper could she be there on Friday.

   _____

6. *Sophie's Choice* was a very interested novel.

   _____

7. By using too much water made the dough sticky.

   _____

8. When the award is announced, is likely to be some objections.

   _____

9. Driving a truck all night is very tired.

_____

10. The interviewer asked the students were they planning to get married right after graduation.

_____

PUNCTUATION

The major elements of punctuation are commas, apostrophes, end of sentence marks, semicolons, and colons.

Commas

Know the rules for commas, and use commas only according to the rules. Putting in too many commas does more harm than leaving some out.
Use commas:

1. in dates and place names
2. in a series and between several adjectives in a row
3. after introductory phrases and clauses
4. before and after interrupters
5. before and after nonrestrictive *who* and *which* clauses
6. before and after appositives
7. before short conjunctions in compound sentences
8. before and after persons spoken to
9. before and after contrasting parts
10. before and after direct quotations
11. in correspondence
12. to prevent confusion

Commas in Dates and Place Names.   Put commas between the day of the week, the date, and the year. Most writers use a comma after the year as well:

> He was born on Wednesday, January 6, 1910, and grew up in Ohio.

Many writers do not put a comma between the month and year:

> The Chicago fire occurred in October 1871.

Separate a street address from the city and the city from the state or country, but do not put a comma before the zip code:

> He worked at 199 Chambers Street, New York, New York 10007.

EXERCISE: COMMAS IN DATES AND PLACE NAMES

Insert commas where they are needed.

1. Jackie Robinson was born in Cairo Georgia on January 31 1919.
2. President Kennedy was assassinated on November 22 1963 in Dallas Texas.
3. Richard Nixon left the White House on August 8 1974.
4. Astronauts landed on the moon in July 1969.
5. The address is 1600 Broadway New York New York 10019.
6. She was born on Wednesday October 10 1968.
7. On May 6 1974 they were married in Cincinnati Ohio.

Commas in a Series and Between Several Adjectives in a Row.   Place a comma after each element in a series except the last one; the comma before *and* is optional:

> They ate sandwiches, potato salad, and pie for lunch.

or

> They ate sandwiches, potato salad and pie for lunch.

A series can contain any kind of words or phrases:

Nouns:	Books, records, and magazines lay on the table.
Verbs:	We ate, drank, sang, and danced at the party.
Pronouns:	I think that you, we, and they all look alike.
Adjectives:	The letters were terse, hard-hitting, and factual.
Adverbs:	The Jets played aggressively, efficiently, and shrewdly.
Prepositions:	The detective looked in, around, over, and under the safe.
Phrases:	The company preferred sales managers who were cordial with employees, knew the business, and demonstrated loyalty to the organization.

EXERCISE I: COMMAS IN SERIES

Put commas where they belong in these series. One sentence does not need commas.

1. We toured China Japan and the Philippines.
2. The invitations were sent the presents were bought and the house was decorated for the party.
3. The child ran and ran and finally caught up with the dog.

4. Slowly delicately thoughtfully and thoroughly she explained the problem.
5. Separation from home from parents from a spouse or from friends produces anxiety.
6. Pay attention to the rhythm the notes and the dynamics at the same time.
7. Make your essays concise fluent and cohesive.
8. Roosevelt Truman Eisenhower and Kennedy had distinct personalities.

EXERCISE II: COMMAS IN SERIES

Write four sentences using commas to separate items in a series.

1. _____

2. _____

3. _____

4. _____

Commas Separating Coordinate Adjectives. Several adjectives in a row modifying the same noun are called **coordinate adjectives**. They should be separated by commas if you can put the word *and* between them. Do not put a comma between the last adjective and the noun.

> an intimidating, overpowering defense
> an enchanting, imaginative, subtle performance
> a squat, talkative official
> a large, hairy, playful sheepdog

In these examples you could put *and* between the adjectives: a large and hairy and playful sheepdog. When you cannot put *and* between the adjectives, do not use commas:

> a fine old chair (not a fine *and* old chair)
> a navy blue beach towel (not a navy *and* blue *and* beach towel)

EXERCISE I: COMMAS BETWEEN COORDINATE ADJECTIVES

Put commas where they are needed. Remember to test each series of adjectives by putting *and* between them.

1. She always wrote prompt courteous lively notes.
2. An ambitious young woman joined the faculty.

3. The counselor was prepared for a quarrelsome rebellious student.
4. A well-polished 1980 Corvette was parked next to a tired-looking over-loaded Ford pickup.
5. Talkative entertaining vital people attended the meeting.

EXERCISE II: COMMAS BETWEEN COORDINATE ADJECTIVES

Write four sentences using commas correctly between coordinate adjectives.

1. _____

2. _____

3. _____

4. _____

Commas After Introductory Phrases and Clauses. Put commas after most introductory words, phrases, and clauses:

> Well, you can never be sure.
> No, that is not a good idea.
> Otherwise, the plan will work.
> A few hours later, she began to cry.
> When you have finished reading the article, may I borrow the magazine?

Interjections (single words at the beginning like *well, yes, oh,* and *ah*) are followed by commas. Interrupting words like *however, otherwise, meanwhile, first, nevertheless,* and *consequently,* when they begin a sentence, should be followed by a comma. Interrupting phrases (also called parenthetical phrases) like *of course, by the way, after all,* and *in a sense* normally take commas as well when they begin a sentence. Short descriptive phrases like *in a minute, after the game, next to the produce, along the railing,* and *during the performance* are usually followed by commas. Sometimes, however, they fit smoothly into the sentence and do not need them. Compare these two examples:

> After a thirty-minute wait, she saw the doctor.
> In the fifth problem there was a typographical error.

In the first sentence, the introductory phrase has a pause after it and should be followed by a comma. In the second sentence, the introductory phrase is necessary to the statement and reads better without a comma after it.

Whole clauses (word groups containing subject-verb combinations) normally are followed by commas when they begin sentences:

Although the pay was good, the job was unsatisfactory.
When he thought about the past year, he felt pleased.
Since you joined the faculty, the students have been ecstatic.
Because the message was translated, we could understand it.

EXERCISE I: COMMAS AFTER INTRODUCTORY PARTS

Put commas where they are needed after introductory parts in these sentences. Do not use unnecessary commas.

1. Yes this episode of *The Young and the Restless* is absorbing.
2. When an unusual phone call from Jessica makes Cricket suspicious she goes to the hospital early.
3. Finding her mother outside the building hailing a cab Cricket is shocked and can't believe her mother wants to run away again.
4. Forcing Jessica into a showdown Cricket finally discovers that her mother has AIDS.
5. Having made her mother promise never to leave again Cricket takes Jessica home with her.
6. When John comes to the hospital later he finds out that Jessica has gone home with her daughter.
7. Not sensing anything is wrong John waits until Cricket arrives at his home.
8. Devastated by the news Cricket gives him John roams Genoa City, trying to figure out the situation.
9. Eventually he goes to Cricket's apartment to see Jessica.
10. Sadly and despairingly Jessica tells John he must forget her and try to get on with his life.*

EXERCISE II: COMMAS AFTER INTRODUCTORY PARTS

Compose sentences using commas after the introductory parts suggested.

1. Write a sentence beginning with a one-word interjection like *yes*, *no*, *oh*, or *well*.

_____

*Adaptation of *The Young and the Restless* from *Soap Opera Digest*, August 23, 1988, p. 64. Reprinted by permission of Network Publishing Corporation.

2. Write a sentence that begins with an interrupting word like *otherwise, meanwhile, consequently, however,* or *nevertheless.*

_____

3. Write a sentence that begins with a dependent clause in which the first word is *although, because, since, if,* or *when.*

_____

4. Write a sentence beginning with a prepositional phrase like *after a few minutes, during the semester,* or *in the beginning.*

_____

Commas Before and After Interrupters.   Sentence interrupters, or parenthetical expressions (think of *parentheses* before and after a phrase), are separated from the rest of the sentence by commas. When they appear in the middle of a sentence, put commas *before* and *after* them. Of course, when they come at the beginning, you can't put a comma before them; when they come at the end, you put a period after them.

Here are some of the common interrupters:

however	of course	as a matter of fact
consequently	by the way	for example
nevertheless	in a sense	in fact
to be sure	in my opinion	in the first place

These interrupters are usually set off by *pairs* of commas:

She knew, *by the way,* that the television set didn't work.
The subway, *in my opinion,* is too noisy.
The check, *however,* will not be honored at this bank.

Descriptive phrases containing past participles and present participles (-ing verb forms) after a noun often serve as interrupters as well:

The captain, *puzzled by the strange blips on the radar screen,* cut the speed of the craft.
An immigrant stonemason, *hoping for steady work,* appeared in the office.

Adjective phrases that come after nouns are also set off by pairs of commas.

The instructions, *dense and hard to read,* gave them little aid.
Two fathers, *anxious about their sons' grades,* called the principal.

EXERCISE I: COMMAS AROUND INTERRUPTERS

Put commas *before* and *after* the interrupting phrases in these sentences.

1. The income tax laws complicated and confusing take up volumes.
2. The causes of alcoholism in my opinion are both psychological and physiological.
3. Students without courses in chemistry will however have to fulfill their science requirements later.
4. Professional sports according to many fans have changed from a religion to show business.
5. Some people as a matter of fact still believe in exorcism.
6. Investors cautious about the latest changes in the prime rate did little trading on Thursday.
7. Some new cars for example have too much fiberglass.
8. A group of news reporters hoping for a break in the talks gathered outside the negotiating chamber.
9. Close relatives nervous and impatient waited for a word from the operating room.
10. American foreign policy apparently self-contradictory at times has been a mixture of principles and self-interest.

EXERCISE II: COMMAS AROUND INTERRUPTERS

Write sentences modeled after the ones following, using commas before and after interrupters.

1. Write a sentence using a one-word interrupter like *consequently* or *however.*
   Model sentence: The money, *however,* had all been spent for groceries.

   Your sentence: _____

   _____

2. Write a sentence using an interrupting phrase like *in my opinion, by the way,* or *as a matter of fact.*
   Model sentence: This book, *by the way,* belongs to the library.

   Your sentence: _____

   _____

3. Write a sentence using a participial phrase after the subject.
Model sentence: The commercial, *designed to heighten public interest in health foods*, ran for two months.

Your sentence: _____

_____

4. Write a sentence using an adjective phrase after a noun.
Model sentence: The lion, *hungry and weary from the pursuit*, charged at the hunters.

Your sentence: _____

_____

Commas Before and After Relative Clauses.   Descriptive clauses beginning with *who, which*, or *that* are called **relative clauses**. Relative clauses beginning with *who* or *which* are sometimes set off by commas.
Here are the rules:

> **Do not** set off restrictive clauses with commas.
> **Do** set off nonrestrictive clauses with commas.

What are restrictive clauses? Restrictive clauses contain information necessary to the meaning of the sentence and therefore should not be separated from the rest of the sentence by any marks of punctuation.
Example 1:

> Students who receive A grades may skip the second course.

The clause *who receive A grades* should not be separated by commas because without it the sentence "Students ... may skip the second course" means something completely different.
Example 2:

> The essay that won the prize was about illiteracy.

The clause *that won the prize* is restrictive; without it, the sentence does not specify which essay was about illiteracy.
Example 3:

> The town in which the research took place was in California.

The clause *in which the research took place* is restrictive because the sentence has no specific meaning without it.

What are nonrestrictive clauses? Nonrestrictive clauses are relative clauses beginning with *who* or *which* (only restrictive clauses begin with *that*) that add extra details to the sentence but are not crucial to the meaning.

Example 1:

> Fax machines, which send messages and graphics instantaneously, are beginning to replace the postal service.

The clause *which send messages and graphics instantaneously* is nonrestrictive because it merely adds information but is not crucial to the meaning of the sentence.

Example 2:

> Philip Johnson, who designed some of America's most interesting buildings, failed the New York State licensing examination.

The clause *who designed some of America's most interesting buildings* is nonrestrictive because it adds information but is not necessary to identify the subject, Philip Johnson, whose name is already given.

EXERCISE I: COMMAS WITH RELATIVE CLAUSES

Put commas before and after the relative clauses in these sentences if the clauses add descriptions of subjects that are already specific. Do not add commas if the subjects are vague and need the clause to identify them.

(Note: A relative clause at the end of a sentence, of course, ends with a period.)

1. Dorothy Day who was a famous journalist and creative writer supported the cause of American socialism.
2. A person who lives in luxury may have a misunderstanding of poverty and unemployment.
3. Acronyms which are short words formed by the initials of other words have become widely used.
4. CREEP which stood for Committee to Reelect the President was an acronym used during the Nixon administration.
5. An acronym that is familiar to most people is SNAFU, a combination that stands for "situation normal; all fouled up."
6. CINCUS is an acronym that had to be abandoned after Pearl Harbor; it means Commander in Chief, U.S. Fleet.
7. A person who specializes in pediatrics needs patience and humor.
8. Alfred Kinsey who was a pioneer in sex research was known in high school as the boy who never had a girlfriend.

9. Elvis Presley who was to become the most famous popular singer in his era failed his first audition for the Arthur Godfrey show.

10. The population of the world which is now more than 4.5 billion is increasing rapidly.

EXERCISE II: COMMAS WITH RELATIVE CLAUSES

Write sentences using *who*, *which*, and *that* clauses as follows:

1. Write a sentence using a *which* clause that contains extra information; use commas to set off the clause.
Model sentence: My Ford Mustang, which has stayed in the garage for six months, needs a new battery.

Your sentence: _____

_____

2. Write a sentence with a *that* clause that identifies the subject and is not set off by commas.
Model sentence: A car that has been left unattended may be stolen.

Your sentence: _____

_____

3. Write a *who* clause that contains extra information; use commas to set off the clause.
Model sentence: My brother Edward, who attends the University of Illinois, is an economics major.

Your sentence: _____

_____

4. Write a *who* clause that identifies the subject and is not set off by commas.
Model sentence: A student who majors in economics must also take courses in statistics and sociology.

Your sentence: _____

_____

Commas Before and After Appositives.   Appositives are phrases that come after nouns or pronouns and describe or identify them. They are usually set off by pairs of commas:

> Peter Arno, *the great cartoonist*, was voted America's best-dressed man in 1941.
>
> Neil Armstrong, *the first man to step on the moon*, earned his pilot's license when he was 16.

Some very short appositives are not separated by commas:

> The Emperor Nero was a psychopath.
> My sister Karen will join us.

EXERCISE: COMMAS WITH APPOSITIVES

Put commas before and after the appositives in these sentences unless they are very short and read without a pause.

1. Samuel Taylor Coleridge the romantic poet of the nineteenth century was a heavy user of opium.
2. My uncle Ted used to be an opera singer.
3. Sandra the youngest member of the board voted for the proposal.
4. Dr. Benjamin Spock the author of the famous book on baby care joined the peace movement in the 1960s.
5. Malcolm X the Black Muslim political leader studied languages and history in prison.
6. Jason the smartest student in his biology class explained how to dissect a frog.
7. A. Philip Randolph the great labor leader organized a union of Pullman car workers.
8. My sister Carol teaches elementary school in California.
9. Richard the vice president of the class spoke to the dean about a new student lounge.
10. The model chosen for the cover a tall, willowy girl with dark brown hair stepped forward.

Commas Before Short Conjunctions in Compound Sentences.   Use a comma plus a short conjunction to link independent clauses in compound sentences. The short conjunctions are *and, but, or, for, nor,* and *so.* Remember to put commas *before* them but not *after.*

Independent clause	*Independent clause*

1. The location was desirable, *and* the price was reasonable.
2. Efforts were made by the police, *but* no suspects were found.

Independent clause   *Independent clause*

3. You may pay by check today, *or* you may have the store bill you later.
4. The first group stayed in the city, *for* they came from urban environments themselves.
5. The passengers were not injured, *nor* was the boat seriously damaged.
6. Sally had visited Puerto Rico before, *so* she knew where to eat in San Juan.

Remember that these short connectives are used in other ways and often do not have commas before them when they connect shorter parts such as words or phrases:

Ted *and* Mary took a walk along the shore. (*And* joins two subjects.)

The prizes went to Sam *and* Alice, *and* the awards for leadership went to Beverly. (One *and* connects two nouns; the other joins two independent clauses.)

The engine *but* not the suspension system was rebuilt. (*But* joins two subjects.)

I suggest the veal *or* the shrimp. (*Or* joins two nouns.)

Neither the acting *nor* the script was exceptional. (*Nor* joins two subjects.)

The beach was *so* beautiful that they went swimming as soon as they arrived. (*So* used with *that* is an adverb—no comma.)

EXERCISE I: COMMAS BEFORE CONJUNCTIONS

Put commas before short conjunctions that join independent clauses in these sentences. Do not put commas before them if they join shorter elements.

1. I like to study with the radio on but this music makes me nervous.
2. Buying lottery tickets gives me a sense of adventure and I always expect to win a million dollars next time.
3. You can turn left at the next light or you can follow the main highway for three blocks.
4. The history of World War II and the theory of communism are both special interests of Professor Jones.
5. My cat is ill so I plan to take her to the veterinarian.
6. The college has room for 900 freshmen but 1500 high school seniors have applied for admission.
7. The view was so breathtaking that they stared at it for hours.
8. The committee will meet twice next week for it has some new business to discuss.

9. Looking for an apartment is easier if you have connections so you should call your friends in the city before you arrive.

10. Some players use lightweight bats for line drives and placement and others prefer heavy bats for height and distance.

EXERCISE 11: COMMAS BEFORE CONJUNCTIONS

Compose your own compound sentences using the following short connectives. Put commas before the connectives.

1. and

_____

2. but

_____

3. or

_____

4. for

_____

5. so

_____

6. nor

_____

Commas Before and After Persons Spoken to (Direct Address). When you speak directly to a person, using his or her name in a sentence, separate the name from the rest of the sentence. Use commas in *pairs* unless the name comes at the beginning or end of the sentence:

> I remember, *Martha*, how you looked in high school.
> *Martha*, I remember how you looked in high school.
> I remember how you looked in high school, *Martha*.

Many writers omit these commas and ignore the difference in meaning: "I remember Martha" is not the same as "I remember, Martha."

EXERCISE I: COMMAS WITH DIRECT ADDRESS

Put commas in these sentences to separate the names of persons spoken to from the rest of the sentence.

1. You know Steve that the rest of us agree with you.
2. Barbara will you please give me some advice.
3. These are the photos that you took in Arizona Richard.
4. You may find Gladys that you like the other therapist better.
5. Herman can we send you a brochure about life insurance?
6. Here is good news cardholders for those of you planning to travel.
7. Tony please describe the area.

EXERCISE II: COMMAS WITH DIRECT ADDRESS

Write three sentences of your own using commas to separate the name of a person spoken to from the rest of the sentence.

1. Sentence with the name at the beginning:

   _____

2. Sentence with the name in the middle (two commas):

   _____

3. Sentence with the name at the end:

   _____

Commas Before and After Contrasting Parts.   Use commas before and after contrasting phrases beginning with *not*:

> The Yankees, not the Dodgers, won that series.
> The weather was cooler, not warmer, than predicted.
> The capital of Pennsylvania is Harrisburg, not Philadelphia.

EXERCISE I: COMMAS WITH CONTRASTING ELEMENTS

Put commas in these sentences to separate contrasting elements.

1. The women not the men supported the action.
2. Arkansas not Tennessee was the first state to open a branch.
3. Lessons are available in karate not kung fu.
4. The clocks should be set forward not back.

5. Drive through the intersection not onto the service road.
6. Ham and cheese not liverwurst is what I ordered.
7. These sweaters come in blue not green.

EXERCISE II: COMMAS WITH CONTRASTING ELEMENTS

Write three sentences of your own using contrasting elements—one with the contrasting parts at the beginning, one with them in the middle, and one with them at the end.
Your sentences:

1. _____

2. _____

3. _____

Commas Before and After Direct Quotations.   Before quoting a whole statement, put a comma after the introductory word *said, stated, asked,* and so on:

> He said, "This is the road to Seattle."
> She asked, "Will this book explain how to sell real estate?"
> The catalog stated, "This course includes intermediate algebra."

Put commas after quotations when the quotations come at the beginning of sentences. Commas belong inside quotation marks:

> "After dinner, let's play Scrabble," Sue suggested.
> "Don't leave any questions blank," the instructor said.

Short quoted phrases often fit smoothly into the sentence and should not be set off by commas:

> Trevor called his brother a "universal genius."
> Joanne was often called the "Bo Derek look-alike."
> Shakespeare called music the "food of love."

EXERCISE I: COMMAS WITH QUOTATIONS

Use commas to separate the following quotations. Do not use commas when a short quoted phrase fits smoothly into the sentence.

1. Sheila said "You have the same opinion I do."
2. "Let's meet in the cafeteria for lunch" Harry suggested.
3. They termed the procedure "a computerized approach to gambling on sports."

4. "I admire your determination" the manager said. "However, there are some errors in the reports."
5. The author stated "Few crime statistics reveal the source of the problem."
6. "The first day may be difficult" she explained.
7. Sandra asked "Why should we wait for them to call us?"

EXERCISE II: COMMAS WITH QUOTATIONS

Write three sentences of your own. In the first, put the *he* or *she said* before the quotation; in the second, put the quotation first. In the third, fit a short quoted phrase into your sentence without a comma.
Your sentences:

1. _____

2. _____

3. _____

Commas in Correspondence.   In business letters and personal letters, the closing is always followed by a comma:

Business Letters	Personal Letters and Notes
Sincerely yours,	Yours truly,
Yours very truly,	Yours,
Yours truly,	As always,
Cordially yours,	Best wishes,
	Love,

In personal letters, put commas after the greeting:

Dear Janet,	Dear Mom,
Dear Tom,	Dear Grandpa,

Commas to Prevent Confusion.   Occasionally, you may need a comma to separate words that might appear to belong together when the meaning requires that they be separated. Watch especially for prepositions (in, around, over, through, etc.) that appear to go with the words after them when they do not:

Inside, the room looked bright and airy. (*Inside the room* is not a phrase to be read together.)

Not long after, the candidates gave speeches. (*After the candidates gave speeches* is not a clause.)

All around, the landscape looked lush and mysterious. (*Around the landscape* should not be read as a phrase.)

EXERCISE: COMMAS TO PREVENT CONFUSION

Put commas in these sentences to prevent confusion.

1. Far and near the house and the whole property were snowbound.
2. I knew that when he thought it over the top figure would not seem very high.
3. The board decided that if the company ever went under the margin of profit among the competitors would increase.
4. It appeared that when the auditors were through the office would be more relaxed.
5. People who can usually buy cars on credit.
6. Those who should always win early promotions.
7. Joe thought that since he had enough to get by the funds that remained in the trust were not necessary to him.

Apostrophes

Apostrophes are used for two purposes:

Uses of Apostrophes

1. Use apostrophes in contractions, where letters have been left out:

   do not = don't
   should not = shouldn't

2. Use apostrophes to indicate possession:

   's for singular possessives: Karen's dress
   s' for plural possessives: four students' grades

Exception: plurals that do not take *s*, such as *men* or *children*, take 's in the possessive:

   men's hats
   children's games

Some common mistakes:

- Carelessly leaving apostrophes out of contractions: dont, instead of don't; shes, instead of she's; wouldnt, instead of wouldn't
- Writing possessives without apostrophes: Karens dress, instead of Karen's dress; womens opinions, instead of women's opinions

- Putting apostrophes in the wrong place: my mothers' attitudes, instead of my mother's attitudes; its' cold, instead of it's cold
- Using apostrophes with personal pronouns: write hers, not her's; yours, not your's (Impersonal pronouns do take apostrophes: everyone's opinions; somebody's car.)

EXERCISE I: APOSTROPHES

Circle the correct form in parentheses.

1. The English language (doesn't, dosen't, doesnt) go back as far in history as Latin and Greek.
2. According to most (experts, expert's, experts') opinions, Old English, or Anglo-Saxon, (didnt, did'nt, didn't) exist in the time of the ancient Greeks.
3. Old English, in any case, (couldn't, could'nt, couldnt) really be called English as we speak it.
4. Many influences altered the way English was spoken over the centuries, but English (hasnt, has'nt, hasn't) lost its basic structure.
5. After the Norman Conquest in A.D. 1066, the biggest change in English came from the French (aristocrats', aristocrat's, aristocrats) speech.
6. Consequently, most languages (cant, can't, cann't) compete with English for richness of vocabulary.
7. Still, people in (Shakespeare, Shakespeares', Shakespeare's) time (would'nt, wouldnt, wouldn't) have guessed how widespread their language would become.
8. (Englands, England's, Englands') growth during the eighteenth and nineteenth centuries brought the language into use all over the world.
9. Although (people's, peoples, peoples') accents differ when they speak English all over the world, their vocabulary is similar.
10. (Theres, There's, Theres') no world language yet, but English is the nearest to becoming one.

EXERCISE II: APOSTROPHES

Write the correct contractions or possessives for each of the phrases given.
Examples:

have not _____*haven't*_____ the coat belonging to Sam _____*Sam's coat*_____

1. the car belonging to Lucy _____

2. are not _____

3. the opinions of students _____

4. will not _____

5. was not _____

6. the staff of the mayor _____

7. they are _____

8. stories for children _____

9. were not _____

10. rights of citizens _____

11. the rules of the company _____

12. there is _____

13. does not _____

14. we will _____

15. the ears of the dog _____

End Punctuation: Periods, Question Marks, and Exclamation Points

Use periods to end statements and indirect questions:

Statement: The store had a sale on January 2.
Indirect question: Sam asked whether the store was having a sale.

Use question marks after direct questions:

Is this book overdue?
When will you be back?
Why, if no one objects to the proposal, are we waiting until March to begin?

Don't forget to put the question mark at the end of long, complicated questions like the last one. Use periods, not question marks, after requests:

Would you please send me an application form.
Would you please let me know if you are interested.

Use exclamation points after sentences that express excitement or strong feeling:

> Get out of my sight!
> Watch out for that elephant!
> That was a fabulous performance!

Use exclamation points after single words or phrases that express astonishment or strong emotion:

> Help!
> Stop!
> No more war!

EXERCISE: END PUNCTUATION

Put the correct end punctuation after these sentences.

1. The instructor asked whether the class had read the assignment
2. If you want help, why don't you ask one of us for it
3. Get out of that van It's going to explode
4. Would you please send me travel literature and maps of Florida
5. Will you be spending your vacation in Greece
6. Ask for the color and size that you want
7. If the restaurant is open, shall I make a reservation

Semicolons

Use semicolons to separate independent clauses in compound sentences when there are no short connectives.

> Children of illegal aliens often attend public schools; some states have asked the federal government to pay for the cost of their education.
>
> Buying on credit has disadvantages; one may overestimate one's ability to pay.

Semicolons, not commas, should also be used to separate independent clauses when there is a long connective word (a conjunctive adverb) like *however, therefore, meanwhile, nevertheless, consequently,* or *moreover* between the clauses. Use a comma *after* the connecting word:

> Separate conference rooms are available for the two meetings; *however,* you may convene together afterward if you like.
>
> We have already sent you a brochure; *meanwhile,* we are awaiting your request.

Use semicolons to separate independent clauses with the word *then* between them. *Then* is not a short connecting word like *and*; do not put a comma before it:

> Not: We always swim at four o'clock, *then* we do aerobics.
> But: We always swim at four o'clock; *then* we do aerobics.

EXERCISE I: SEMICOLONS

Put semicolons or commas between the independent clauses in these sentences—commas before short connectives (*and, but, or, for, nor, yet, so*) and semicolons in all other sentences.

1. A few years ago, two teenagers tried computer hacking once too often and they suffered the consequences.
2. They dialed into Arpanet, a computer network maintained by the Pentagon their intrusion resembled what happened in the film *War Games*.
3. Computer experts were already alarmed about the growing problem of hacking therefore they were particularly on the lookout for such computer banditry.
4. The two students had gained access to a computer network on the UCLA campus they used it to explore secret work being done by computer scientists.
5. They were remarkably clever however they were finally caught.
6. During July and August 1983, computer experts at UCLA began tracking them down by September 21 they had been identified.
7. There was disagreement over how serious their crime was nevertheless they were arrested by the FBI on September 22, 1983.
8. Officials doubted that they had a malicious intent or did serious harm still they set a dangerous example that could not be tolerated.
9. People using only home computers may be able to break into large networks for fun but serious criminal abuse of such networks is a real possibility.
10. Such examples have warned many large institutional users to tighten their security they especially have had to use passwords that are difficult to guess.*

EXERCISE II: SEMICOLONS

Put a C next to the correctly punctuated sentence in each pair.

_____ 1. The road was bumpy; it caused many blowouts and accidents.
_____   The road was bumpy, it caused many blowouts and accidents.

*From Rian Malan, "The Game Is Up," *California*, January 1984, pp. 46ff.

_____   2. A medical checkup every few years may not seem necessary, however, it could save your life.

_____   A medical checkup every few years may not seem necessary; however, it could save your life.

_____   3. Exploring other planets strikes some people as a waste of money; but we never know what benefits may come from it.

_____   Exploring other planets strikes some people as a waste of money, but we never know what benefits may come from it.

_____   4. We used to go surfing on Saturday afternoons, then we would bake clams on the beach.

_____   We used to go surfing on Saturday afternoons; then we would bake clams on the beach.

_____   5. The police had not enforced the law against selling marijuana; therefore, the two men were surprised to be arrested.

_____   The police had not enforced the law against selling marijuana, therefore the two men were surprised to be arrested.

_____   6. There used to be an oversupply of teachers; now, however, we are beginning to face shortages in some areas.

_____   There used to be an oversupply of teachers, now however, we are beginning to face shortages in some areas.

_____   7. July 14th is called Bastille Day in France, it is the day on which in 1789 the French Revolution began.

_____   July 14th is called Bastille Day in France; it is the day on which, in 1789, the French Revolution began.

_____   8. Manuel never used his turn signals; consequently, he occasionally received warnings and traffic tickets.

_____   Manuel never used his turn signals, consequently he occasionally received warnings and traffic tickets.

_____   9. Studying for the nursing examination requires concentration; furthermore, it creates anxiety in many students.

_____   Studying for the nursing examination requires concentration furthermore, it creates anxiety in many students.

_____   10. The procedures for adopting a child are complicated in most states prospective adoptive parents should expect delays.

_____   The procedures for adopting a child are complicated in most states; prospective adoptive parents should expect delays.

EXERCISE III: SEMICOLONS

Write sentences of your own using semicolons.

1. Write a sentence using a semicolon with no connecting word.
Model sentence: The course is too easy; you should take a more advanced one.

Your sentence: _____

_____

2. Write a sentence using a semicolon before *however.*
Model sentence: We appreciate your concern; however, the bill cannot be reduced.

Your sentence: _____

_____

3. Write a sentence using a semicolon before *meanwhile.*
Model sentence: The student government will vote on the issue next Monday; meanwhile, students are signing a petition.

Your sentence: _____

_____

4. Write a sentence using a semicolon before *then.*
Model sentence: Lay the wooden pieces on the diagram; then glue them together at the corners.

Your sentence: _____

_____

Colons

The colon (:) is used to introduce something. Use colons after *as follows* or *the following* to introduce lists:

She called out the following names: Roberta, Carl, Tracy, Janice, and Lamont.

Open the bottle as follows: press down on the lid, align the arrows, and turn lid to the left.

Use colons when you introduce a list formally with a whole statement:

> The events happened like this: a hurricane, followed by heavy rains, and finally a flood.
>
> We like the school except for a few problems: a lack of athletic facilities, a boring neighborhood, and overcrowded classes.

Do not use colons before lists that are not formally introduced:

> The order included three hamburgers, two Cokes, and a Pepsi.

Do not use a colon or semicolon after *such as*:

> We encountered strange people, such as a self-taught French chef, a one-armed prizefighter, and a professional gambler.

Use colons to separate independent clauses when the second clause explains the first:

> Joan approached the interview with only one thought in mind: she had to show them that she understood the job.

EXERCISE I: COLONS

Put colons in any of the following sentences where they belong.

1. Many simple organisms reproduce by asexual reproduction or cloning; this has advantages such as simplicity, rapidity, and total inheritance of characteristics.
2. Therefore scientists puzzle over the following question why did sexual reproduction develop and continue?
3. There have been three theories explaining this phenomenon the best man theory, the red queen theory, and the tangled bank theory.
4. The best man theory argues as follows sexual reproduction proved better than cloning because it produced more varied individuals that could survive changes in environment.
5. The red queen theory (named after the character in *Through the Looking Glass*) has a slightly different argument it says that sexual reproduction produces varied species that can fight off or escape from their enemies.
6. The tangled bank theory goes as follows the varied individuals produced by sexual reproduction survive well because their environments contain slightly varied conditions.
7. All of these theories try to explain one simple fact sexual reproduction of many species has continued for millions of years.
8. It exists in many examples such as mammals, reptiles, and complex plant life.

9. So far, scientists have come to this conclusion no theory has proven once and for all why sex exists.

10. The answer could increase our understanding of the following human development, evolution of species, and the interaction of humans and their environment.*

EXERCISE II: COLONS

Write sentences using colons.

1. Write a sentence using *as follows* to introduce a list.

Model sentence: Do the procedure as follows: remove the lid, loosen the blue and green wires from their terminals, and attach them to the terminals on the left side.

Your sentence: _____

_____

2. Write a sentence using *the following* to introduce a list.

Model sentence: The course included the following topics: geriatric nursing, nursing the handicapped, and surgical nursing.

Your sentence: _____

_____

3. Write a sentence introducing a list with a formal statement.

Model sentence: The new model possesses these features: a tinted windshield, a cassette tapedeck, rear speakers, and a rear window defroster.

Your sentence: _____

_____

4. Write a sentence in which the second independent clause explains or completes the first.

Model sentence: Sam knew exactly what he would do next: he would forget Susan and ask Pauline for a date.

Your sentence: _____

_____

*Facts from "Why Sex," by Gina Maranto and Shannon Brownlee © 1984 Discover Publications, Inc.

5. Write a sentence using *such as* to introduce a list; do *not* use a colon. Model sentence: There are many forms of entertainment in a big city, such as discos, theater, night clubs, opera, and trade fairs.

Your sentence: _____

_____

Capital Letters

Learn the rules for using capital letters.

Rules for Using Capital Letters

Capitalize:

- The first word of every sentence and the first word of every quoted sentence: He said, "The tape is missing."
- The word I and the proper name of every person: John Smith, Sally Fields, Mr. Jones, Jimmy Swaggart
- The name of every city, state, country, and other specific place name: San Juan, Puerto Rico; Yankee Stadium; Golden Gate Park
- The name of every day of the week, month, and holiday: Monday, October, Thanksgiving Day (but *not* spring, summer, fall, and winter)
- The title of every book, play, magazine, short story, film, song, or television show: *The Oprah Winfrey Show, Time Magazine, A Raisin in the Sun, Gone with the Wind*. Note: Little words like *of, the,* and *a* are not capitalized unless they begin the title.
- The name of a company, organization, religion, school, or college: the Ford Motor Company, Livingston High School, Carleton College, St. Luke's Church. Note: Do not capitalize words like *church, high school, company,* or *college* if they are not part of a specific name.
- The name of a specific product: Coca Cola, Wheaties, Rolls-Royce. Note: Do not capitalize the word for the category of product: a Mack truck, Smirnoff vodka, English toffee.
- A person's nationality: a French woman, a Japanese student, a Canadian hockey player, an American Indian.
- The title of a specific course: Sociology 101, Mathematics 104, American History 110. Note: Do not capitalize subjects like sociology or mathematics when not used to name specific courses.

EXERCISE I: CAPITAL LETTERS

Proofread the following passage and circle the *ten* errors in capitalization.

Timothy's Least Favorite Courses

Although Timothy likes most of his courses, he took some in high school and College that he did not enjoy. In high school he took a course in History that bored him to death because the teacher, Mr. postlethwaite, demanded that the students learn one-hundred dates from the discovery of America to the War in vietnam. then in college Timothy took a course called statistics 110, which was taught by a Professor from Harvard university. This course was so hard he withdrew after the first week and decided to take General Math 101 in the Spring. Next he took a course in russian and barely passed it. In his second year he decided to become a psychology major. He declared, "at last I've found the right subject for my talents."

EXERCISE II: CAPITAL LETTERS

Write the following, using correct capitalization:

1. The name of your college   _____

2. The title of a book you have read _____

3. The name of a product you use   _____

4. A sentence with a direct quotation _____

5. The title of a course you are taking _____

6. The city and state in which you were born _____

7. Today's date (including day of the week) _____

8. The name of a store where you shop _____

9. A television show you watch   _____

10. The name of a public official (with title) _____

SPELLING

To become a better speller, attack the problem from several directions at once. And don't expect to improve rapidly without really concentrating and memorizing. Only a few rare people can spell correctly without effort; the rest of us need a many-sided strategy, along with old-fashioned study and repetition.

What should you do to improve your spelling?

- Learn the patterns and rules. Although English spelling is irregular, with most rules having exceptions, you will do well to learn the rules.
- Master the look-alikes/sound-alikes. A large percentage of misspellings come from words being confused with others that look or sound almost like them.
- Drill on frequently misspelled words. Study tricky words, or spelling "demons," especially those in your area of work or study. A corporate employee should never misspell *business* or a nurse misspell *medicine*.
- Take personal responsibility for your spelling. Don't expect any book, course, or teacher to work magic for you. It's up to you; make lists of your own most often misspelled words—and study them.

Spelling Rules

The first step toward spelling competence is to learn the few main patterns— even though they may have exceptions.

Rule 1.   You probably have heard, and may know, the old rule:

> *i* before *e*
> except after *c*
> or when sounded like *a*
> as in *neighbor* or *weigh*.

Learn the jingle if you do not already know it. But be prepared to run into many exceptions. Study the patterns.

1. *i* before *e*: Bel*ie*ve. Most words with an *e* sound do follow the rule when there is no *c* before the combination:

> ach*ie*ve (ch, but not c)
> fr*ie*nd (even though pronounced *eh*)
> f*ie*nd
> gr*ie*ve
> l*ie*n
> n*ie*ce (the c comes *after* ie)
> p*ie*ce
> p*ie*rce
> pr*ie*st
> rel*ie*ve
> repr*ie*ve
> retr*ie*ve
> shr*ie*k
> th*ie*f

2. Except after *c*: Receive. Despite exceptions, this pattern usually holds true, too:

> ceiling
> conceited
> conceive
> deceive
> perceive
> receipt

3. Or when sounded like *a*: Weigh. Combinations that are sounded like *a* or *i* are usually *ei*:

> eight
> freight
> height
> neighbor
> vein
> weight

4. Some exceptions to the rule: A few words take *ie* even though it comes after *c*:

> financier
> society
> species

A few *ei* words with the *e* sound and no *c* before them can fool you, too:

> either
> leisure
> neither
> seize
> weird

Rule 2. Keeping or Dropping the Final *e*. When adding an ending to a word with a final *e*, keep the *e* if the ending starts with a consonant:

> arrange + ment = arrangement
> hope + ful = hopeful
> nine + ty = ninety
> sincere + ly = sincerely
> face + less = faceless
> manage + ment = management

Drop the *e* if the ending starts with a vowel:

> give + ing = giving
> have + ing = having

erase + ure = erasure
locate + ion = location
guide + ance = guidance

Exceptions: To keep a *g* or *c* soft before a vowel, we sometimes keep the *e*:

manage + able = manageable
service + able = serviceable

The word *judgment* does not keep the *e* except in British spelling. *Dyeing* keeps the *e* to prevent confusion with *dying*.

Rule 3.   Doubling Final Consonants. This rule is somewhat complicated, but it does not have many exceptions and it includes many common words. Learn the pattern.

The rule applies to words like *begin*, *control*, and *occur*. When you add an *ed*, *ing*, or *er* ending to these words, do you double the final consonant? Yes: beginning, controlled, and occurred.

What do these words have in common? The rule says that they *end with a single consonant* (not *ck* as in shock, or *st* as in post) *preceded by a single vowel* (not a double vowel, as in br*ea*k or m*ee*t). And the accent must be on the last syllable (not earlier, as in *travel*, where the *l* does not have to be doubled, or *pivot*, where the *t* is not doubled).

To sum up: These words contain

- A single final consonant: begi*n*
- A single vowel preceding the final consonant: beg*i*n
- An accent on the last syllable: be**gin**

Many common words follow this pattern. When you become familiar with it, the rule is extremely useful. Here are only some of the examples:

begi*nn*ing	forge*tt*ing	refe*rr*ed
commi*tt*ed	occu*rr*ing	sto*pp*ed
contro*ll*ing	omi*tt*ed	thro*bb*ing
exce*ll*ing	prefe*rr*ing	

(The rule applies to one-syllable words as well.)

EXERCISE I: SPELLING RULES

Some of the following words are correct, and some are misspelled. Write *C* next to the correct ones, and spell the others correctly in the blanks. Review the rules first; try not to guess.

1. belief _____
2. occurance _____
3. placing _____
4. arrangment _____
5. weight _____
6. percieve _____
7. writeing _____
8. definitly _____
9. achieve _____
10. commited _____

11. stately _____
12. noticeable _____
13. hopful _____
14. movement _____
15. chief _____
16. refering _____
17. replacment _____
18. removing _____
19. permiting _____
20. strokeing _____

Notice any words you did not spell correctly in the first set. Review the rules to see why the misspellings occurred; then do these twenty the same way.

1. neighbor _____
2. loseing _____
3. sincerly _____
4. ninty _____
5. feirce _____
6. deterring _____
7. combating _____
8. spiteful _____
9. leaveing _____
10. conceited _____

11. niece _____
12. advisment _____
13. controlled _____
14. blameless _____
15. exciteing _____
16. shamful _____
17. forgeting _____
18. height _____
19. deceive _____
20. begining _____

EXERCISE II: SPELLING RULES

Review the rules one more time, and do this exercise perfectly. Circle the correctly spelled word in each pair.

1. soceity   society
2. chaseing   chasing
3. friend   freind
4. movement   movment
5. patroling   patrolling
6. believing   beleiving
7. saving   saveing
8. changless   changeless
9. lovely   lovly
10. ceiling   cieling
11. encouragment   encouragement
12. thief   theif
13. priceless   pricless
14. peacful   peaceful
15. alloting   allotting
16. reprieve   repreive
17. bereavment   bereavement
18. practicing   practiceing
19. species   speceis
20. committed   commited

Spelling: Common Mix-ups

The following words are often misspelled because they contain combinations that are easily confused with those in similar words. Study the groups carefully, looking for the trouble spots.

1. ability   (The last two do *not* contain *ability*.)
   responsibility
   possibility

2. accumulate
accommodate
recommend
(Study the *c*'s and *m*'s in these common words.)

3. across
address
(Both are often misspelled; notice the single *c* and double *d*.)

4. alone
along
(Two simple words but often carelessly mixed up)

5. amount
among
(Be careful not to write amo*u*ng, even though it rhymes with yo*u*ng.)

6. arithmetic
athletics
mathematics
(Not ath*e*letics or ath*e*lete, and don't forget the *e* in mathematics.)

7. believe
receive
(These two most common *ie/ei* words do follow the rule.)

8. committee
committing
commitment
(Note the single *t* in commitment.)

9. definitely
immediately
(Don't confuse *-itely* with *-ately* words.)

10. develop
developed
envelope
(There is no such word as *develope*.)

11. divide
decide
(Not d*e*vide)

12. familiar
similar
(The extra *i* in *familiar* gives it an extra syllable.)

13. fulfill
foretell
(Don't spell it *for*fill or *fore*fill.)

14. necessary
occasionally
professional
(Only one *c* in necessary, one *s* in occasionally, and one *f* in professional)

15. pastime
part-time
(Don't double that *t* in pastime.)

16. accidentally
publicly
(Not public*a*lly)

17. relevant
prevalent
(Two difficult words; notice the *e*'s and *a*'s and the *l*'s and *v*'s.

18. separate
desperate
(*Not* sep*e*rate)

19. surprise
suppose
(Do not write s*u*prise or su*r*pose.)

20. strictly
stick
quickly
(Not strick or strick*l*y)

21. till
until
(Not unti*ll*)

EXERCISE I: SPELLING MIX-UPS

The following paragraph contains fifteen misspelled words. Underline them and write the correct spellings in the margin.

> Writing well is definately a marketable skill that you should develope. In business, law, and medicine, effective writing is neccessary. Students who do not beleive this is true are often supprised to discover too late that they lack this important proffesional requirement. Not untill they learn the hard way—by recieving criticism of their work—do many employees realize how prevelant the demand for good writing is. Amoung executives it is understood that the committment to writing goes alone with the strickly technical aspects of a job. Colleges accross the country are publically declaring their dedication to effective career writing.

EXERCISE II: SPELLING MIX-UPS

Each of the following groups contains one misspelled word. Circle it and write the word correctly in the blank.

1. accumulate
   athletics _____
   seperate
2. relavent
   suppose _____
   part-time
3. decide
   similiar _____
   strictly
4. adress
   necessary _____
   till
5. accomodate
   publicly _____
   fulfill
6. prevalent
   receive _____
   surpose
7. desperate
   pastime _____
   devide
8. occassionally
   familiar _____
   across
9. responsability
   professional _____
   recommend

10. definitely
    possibility _____
    amoung

EXERCISE III: SPELLING MIX-UPS

Write these misspelled words correctly.

1. accidently _____

2. immediatly _____

3. past-time _____

4. comittment _____

5. develope _____

6. athelete _____

7. beleive _____

8. reccomend _____

9. occassionally _____

10. seperate _____

Spelling: Pronoun Mix-ups

Forms of the common pronouns—I, you, he, she, they, and we—are often confused with other words. Study the groups below; these are simple words you should know perfectly.

1. He, his, he's

   His means belonging to him; *he's* is short for *he is*. *He's* looking for *his* wallet.

2. Its, it's, its'

   Its shows possession; *it's* is short for *it is* or *it has*. The jury made *its* decision. *It's* a cool day for July. *It's* (it has) been an entertaining evening. There is no such word as *its'*.

3. Mine, mind, mines

   Don't confuse *mine* (belonging to me) with *mind* (a smart mind). Although *mines* is widely spoken in dialect, there is no such pronoun in standard written English. (That pen is *mine*, not *mines*.)

4. Our, are, or

Our is possessive—belonging to us: *our* schedules. Don't confuse it with the verb *are*: Sally and Timothy *are* married. *Or* is a connective word: Either Tom *or* Randy will wait for you.

5. They, their, they're, there, there's, theirs

The word *they* is used as a subject, referring to a number of people or things: *They* belong to the gang.

Their means belonging to them: *Their* ideas are right.

They're is short for *they are*: *They're* going to be rich.

There means at that place, or it may be just a structure word: *There* is a new hair style this year.

There's is short for *there is* or *there has*: *There's* a noisy party upstairs.

Theirs means belonging to them: *Theirs* is the best pizza in town.

6. We're, were, where, wear, ware

We're is short for *we are*: *We're* the first people here.

Were is a verb: *Were* those books expensive?

Where asks about the place something happens: *Where* did you go last night? Don't mix up *where* and *were*. They look similar but don't sound alike.

Wear, as a verb, means to clothe: *Wear* your designer jeans. The noun *wear* also refers to clothing: Men's *wear* is sold here.

Ware refers to equipment and utensils: hardware, software, silverware. Don't confuse this with formal *wear* or evening *wear*, the noun, referring to clothing.

7. Who's, whose

Who's is short for *who is* or *who has*: *Who's* the manager of the store? *Who's* been making long distance calls?

Whose asks about ownership: *Whose* book is this?

8. You're, your, yours, yours'

You're is short for *you are*: *You're* never home when I call.

Your shows possession: *Your* contract is in the mail.

Use *yours*, not *yours'*: That idea was *yours*.

EXERCISE I: PRONOUN MIX-UPS

The following paragraph contains fifteen misspellings. Underline them and write the correctly spelled pronouns in the margin.

If your having trouble remembering names and facts, its very likely that you can benefit from using memory tricks called mnemonic devices. Their the little gimmicks, like rhymes, that help people remember names, words, numbers, and spellings. Theirs a familiar device for recalling names, for instance, that is often used at parties. Each person tries to remember all the names of the people their by joining there names with crazy adjectives—Ferocious Fran, Studious Stu, and so on. Most of us find that are memories work better when we associate new names or facts this way with familiar words or traits. Suppose you meet a new acquaintance who's name is Richard, and suppose that his expensively dressed. You're easiest way to remember his name is to think of him as "rich." Its also easier to remember spelling words by using tricks. Notice were the problem letters are, and exaggerate the pronunciation: say Feb *roo* ary, for instance. Unless you're memory is sharper than mines, your going to need such mnemonic devices now and then.

EXERCISE II: PRONOUN MIX-UPS

In each pair of sentences, one sentence is correct (write *C* in the blank) and the other contains a misspelled word. Write the corrected word in the blank.

1. They're going to join the society next week.   _____
   The teacher is reading there scores.   _____

2. Its been a wonderful visit.   _____
   The tree lost all of its bark.   _____

3. Theirs a riot going on in the suburbs.   _____
   There's a new way to solve those equations.   _____

4. We rented are house to a young couple.   _____
   Our vacation this year was exciting.   _____

5. Whose been making those crank calls?   _____
   Do you know whose sneakers these are?   _____

6. Where have all the customers gone?   _____
   Some of them where at the parade.   _____

7. Would you mind giving me a hand?   _____
   That idea was mind, not yours.   _____

8. I think his not as smart as he looks.   _____
   Let him have his way.   _____

9. Don't wear boring clothes to the party.   _____
   This is the place wear it happened.   _____

10. Their is a beautiful beach on the sound.   _____
    The neighbors took their dog with them.   _____

EXERCISE III: PRONOUN MIX-UPS

Circle the correct words in these sentences.

1. A player (who's, whose) planning to retire usually looks for a college (were, where) a coaching job is available.
2. The trouble with (you're, your) handwriting is that I can't read it when (you're, your) writing rapidly.
3. (Are, our, or) town has cable television, and (were, where, we're) planning to make it available to rural customers.
4. (They, there, their) are seven fast food outlets between here and (there, their, they're).
5. (It, it's) been delightful meeting (your, you're) family.
6. Campers along the shore (were, where, we're) alarmed because they had been swimming (where, were, we're) the undertow was strongest.
7. The Nets won first place in (their, there, they're) division by concentrating on (their, there, they're) defense.
8. The actress (whose, who's) agent called yesterday thinks that (your, you're) planning to use her for the commercial.
9. (Its, it's) turning cold again, and the company is having (it's, its) heating plant repaired.
10. We (were, where, we're) listed in the yellow pages, but not many customers saw our advertisement (there, their, they're).

Spelling: Look-alikes/Sound-alikes

This list contains words that are often confused with each other because they look or sound alike. Say each word aloud in its example in order to hear the differences. Since these are common words, you should master all of them.

1. a, an, and, any

Use *a* before consonants, *an* before vowels: *a* computer, but *an* old computer. Use *an* before words beginning with silent *h*: *an* honest worker. Use *a* before *u* words that start with a *y* sound: *a* union leader. Use *a* before *one* because of the *w* sound: *a* one-cylinder motor. The rule is to use *a* before consonant *sounds* and *an* before vowel *sounds*. *And* is the connective word: Sam *and* his wife. *Any* refers to an amount or unit: We do not have *any* new employees.

2. advice, advise

Pronounce them correctly and you will spell them correctly: *Advice* contains the word *ice*: You give *advice* (a noun). *Advise* rhymes with *wise* and is a verb: You *advise* someone.

3. affect, effect

Affect is the verb: This *affects* all of us. *Effect* is the noun: What is the *effect* of crime? (Exception: *effect* can sometimes be a verb, which means to bring about or create: Let's *effect* an improvement in communications.)

4. a lot, alot

Always write this as two words: We need *a lot* of financial backing. There is no such word as *alot*.

5. already, all ready

Already means now; *all ready* means prepared: It is *already* two o'clock; we are *all ready* to leave.

6. always, away

These do not sound alike, but because they look similar, many writers mistakenly write *alway*. Don't drop the *s*.

7. bought, brought

Be sure to write these as they sound: *bought* is the past tense of *buy*: We *bought* a surfboard. *Brought* is the past tense of *bring*: I *brought* it to the beach.

8. breath, breathe

Pronounce them: *Breath* is the noun, rhyming with *death*: I took a deep *breath*. *Breathe* is the verb, rhyming with seethe: Try to *breathe* through your nose.

9. buy, by

To *buy* is to purchase: We *buy* merchandise. *By* is usually a preposition: We pass *by* the museum.

10. choose, chose

The present form is *choose*—rhymes with *news*: I *choose* a different program each week. *Chose* is the past tense—rhymes with *rose*: Last month we *chose* the spot for our vacation.

11. conscience, conscious

Your *conscience* (pronounce it: kon shuntz) is your sense of right and wrong: Let your *conscience* be your guide. To be *conscious* (kon shuss) is to be aware: She was *conscious* of someone approaching.

12. convenience, convince

Listen to the sound: *convenience* (kun veen yuntz). I'll do it at your *convenience*. I'll *convince* (kun vintz) you to buy it.

13. does, dose

Notice the spelling and the sound: *does* sounds like *duzz*: She *does* everything. *Dose* rhymes with *close*: a *dose* of medicine. Notice the spelling of *doesn't* (*not* dosen't).

14. fine, find, fined

Fine means excellent: She was a *fine* dancer. To *find* means to locate: *Find* a date for your cousin. *Fined* (pronounced the same as *find*) means to be ordered to pay a fine: She was *fined* for double parking.

15. have, of

Don't write, I would *of* enjoyed that. It should be, I would *have* enjoyed that. Watch all those combinations—should have, might have, must have, could have. *Have* sounds like *of* in some phrases: She should've been here—short for *should have*.

16. know, no, now

Know and *no* sound alike and are often confused. Remember the word *knowledge*—that which you *know*. Don't write, I *no* how to swim. *Now* (rhymes with *cow*) means at present: We are *now* in the fourth act.

17. lead, led

Lead (or *leads*)—rhymes with *need*—is present tense: I usually *lead* the trumpet section. *Led* is the past tense: She *led* (rhymes with *red*) the parade last year. However, the metal *lead*, as in a *lead* pipe, is pronounced the same as *led*.

18. loose, lose, loss, lost

Pronunciation is the key again. *Loose*, meaning not tight, rhymes with *moose*: The nails had come *loose*. *Lose* is the verb, rhyming with *fuse*: Don't *lose* your temper. *Loss* is a noun: One *loss* won't affect your league standings. (*Loss* rhymes with *boss*.) *Lost* (rhymes with *cost*) means gone: They were *lost* in the forest.

19. pass, passed, past

The verb is *pass* (present tense) and *passed* (past tense): I *pass* the store every day; I *passed* all my courses last semester. Use *past* as the noun or the preposition: She lives in the *past*; we drove *past* her house.

20. principal, principle

Remember that *principle* (it has *le* like ru*le*) means a rule or law: the *principle* of gravity. *Principal* means important: the *principal* of the school, the *principal* part in a play.

21. personal, personnel

Personal means private: a *personal* letter. *Personnel* (accent on the last syllable, rhymes with *shell*—and notice the double *n*) means employees: a *personnel* manager.

22. quiet, quit, quite

Notice the extra syllable in *quiet*, meaning silent: the room was *quiet*. (*Quiet* rhymes with *diet*.) To *quit* (rhymes with *hit*) means to stop: He *quit* his job. *Quite* (rhymes with *white*) means very: She is *quite* talented.

23. rise, raise

Both are verbs, but only *raise* takes an object: the sun will *rise* by itself, but you *raise* the blinds. Past tense: the sun *rose*; you *raised* the blinds.

24. since, sense

Since is the connecting word: It has been lonely *since* you left. *Sense* means understanding: She has good business *sense*.

25. sit, set

Sit means to take a seat: She always *sits* in the front row. Past tense: She always *sat* there. *Set* means to place something: He *sets* the cans on the shelf. Past tense: He *set* the cans there.

26. sort, sought

Sort can be a noun or a verb: A *sort* of all-around athlete; They *sort* the pastries in rows. *Sought* is the past tense of *seek*: They *sought* everywhere for an apartment. Don't write, "It was *sought* of cold today."

27. than, then

Use *than* for comparisons—funnier *than* Eddie Murphy. Use *then* for time: *Then* we started dancing.

28. taught, thorough, though, thought, threw, through, throughout, tough

Master this difficult group by pronouncing each word carefully.

Taught (rhymes with *fought*) is the past tense of *teach*: She *taught* calculus.

Thorough (rhymes with *borough*) means complete: a *thorough* investigation.

Though (rhymes with *go*) is a connective word: *Though* he was nervous, he performed well.

Thought (rhymes with *bought*) is the past tense of *think*: We *thought* it was a good restaurant.

Threw (rhymes with *new*) is the past tense of *throw*: We *threw* a big party. Don't mix up *threw* and *through*; they sound the same.

Through (sounds the same as *threw*) means finished (when they were *through* eating) or inside (*through* the tunnel).

Throughout (pronounced throo owt) means everywhere within an area: *throughout* the whole state of Ohio.

Tough (rhymes with *puff*) as in "rough and *tough*"—means hard or difficult.

29. to, too, two

Two, the number, is usually spelled right: There were *two* cars in the garage. The trick is to know when to use *too*. Remember that *too*, with *more than one o*, means *more than enough*: There is *too* much noise here. It also means in addition: You come *too*. All the other meanings take *to*: travel *to* Cuba; *to* win at poker.

30. worse, worst

Both are forms of *bad*: bad, worse, worst. Use *worse* to compare two things, persons, or situations: Her illness became *worse*. This film is *worse* than the other one. *Worst* is the superlative form; it describes one thing that stands out from the rest: the *worst* dinner I ever ate; the *worst* car in the lot.

EXERCISE I: LOOK-ALIKES/SOUND-ALIKES

Choose the correct word in each sentence.

1. Many people give (advice, advise) without being asked.
2. The (principles, principals) of economics are complex.
3. Do you (no, know) how to check a patient's vital signs?
4. This proposal has too many (loose, lose) ends.
5. Students who have (past, passed) the test will take English 2.
6. Have you ever (taught, thought, though) about buying a condominium?
7. Banks nowadays have (too, to, two) many kinds of checking accounts.
8. Cholesterol has an (affect, effect) on the circulation.
9. All hospital (personnel, personal) were warned about a case of cerebrospinal meningitis.
10. See if you can (find, fine) an advertisement for a used motorcycle.

EXERCISE II: LOOK-ALIKES/ SOUND-ALIKES

Underline the incorrect word in each sentence and write it correctly in the blank.

1. Marie considered musical comedies a sought of lowbrow form of entertainment.

_____

2. Changes in society have not effected the popularity of marriage: there are more weddings every year. _____

3. The filmmakers should of studied teenage vigilante groups like the Guardian Angels before shooting the film. _____

4. From her shy and quite appearance, no one would guess that Eleanor had been an Air Force officer. _____

5. Tournaments that include to many basketball teams are likely to lose public interest. _____

6. Motorcycle racing in the desert demands more stamina and expertise then driving a racing car. _____

7. After Edward had past the test for a chauffeur's license, he leased a limousine. _____

8. The student union is one of the worse buildings on campus. _____

9. The new model dose not have power brakes or air conditioning. _____

10. Even after ten years we have not paid off much of the principle on the mortgage. _____

EXERCISE III: LOOK-ALIKES/SOUND-ALIKES

Circle the correct phrase in each group.

1. alot of money
   a lot of money

2. alway prepared
   away prepared
   always prepared

3. a loss treasure
   a lost treasure
   a lose treasure

4. hotter then the Sahara
   hotter than the Sahara

5. quit intelligent
   quite intelligent
   quiet intelligent

6. the personnel office
   the personal office

7. two much attention
   to much attention
   too much attention

8. worse than a tornado
   worst then a tornado

9. an original taught
   an original thought
   an original though

10. the total effect
    the total affect

11. sensible advice
    sensible advise

12. an hour later
    a hour later
    and hour later

13. should of remembered
    should have remembered

14. brought at Macy's
    bought at Macy's

15. She past the test
    She pass the test
    She passed the test

16. sit the table
    set the table

17. plenty of common sense
    plenty of common since

18. raise the flag
    rise the flag

19. a find performance
    a fine performance

20. a clear conscious
    a clear conscience

INDEX